# Cultural Interpretation

# Cultural Interpretation

## Reorienting New Testamen Criticism

**Brian K. Blount**

**Fortress Press**
**Minneapolis**

CULTURAL INTERPRETATION
Reorienting New Testament Interpretation

Cover design: Marti Naughton
Author photo: Krystin Granberg

Library of Congress Cataloging-in-Publication Data

Blount, Brian K., 1955–
    Cultural interpretation : reorienting New Testa-
ment criticism / Brian K. Blount.
        p.   cm.
    Includes bibliographical references and indexes.
    ISBN 0-8006-2859-4 (alk. paper)
    1. Bible   N.T.—Criticism, interpretation, etc.—
History—20th century.   2. Bible.   N.T.—Hermeneutics.   3. Bible.   N.T.—Social scientific criticism   4. Sociolinguistics.   5. Christianity and culture.   6. Bible.   N.T.   Mark XIV, 53–65—
Criticism, interpretation, etc.   7. Jesus Christ—
Trial.   I. Title.
BS2361.2.B56   1995
225.6'09'04—dc20                           95-25436
                                                CIP

Manufactured in the U.S.A.                    AF 1-2859
                        4   5   6   7   8   9   10   11

# Contents

For
Sharon,
Joshua,
and Kaylin Rose

# Preface

IT IS NOW COMMONPLACE TO HEAR BIBLICAL
scholars admit that textual inquiry is influenced by the contextual presuppositions of
the researcher. What is not so evident is the
process by which this influence takes place,
recognition of its dramatically powerful influence, and acceptance of its implications.
This book is intended to further the discussion on each of these accounts.

The method of sociolinguistics provides the
clearest way to probe these questions. Its basic
tenet is that context shapes the creation and use
of language. Therefore, the meaning derived
from language is also shaped by context. The
sociolinguistic theory of M. A. K. Halliday is
particularly helpful to this endeavor because he
designates three principal functions of language and describes their relationship to its
context. Indeed, one of these language functions is primarily concerned with how meaning is established through the interaction of
text grammar and concepts with the situation
of the language user. Halliday calls this function
the interpersonal. By evaluating this interpersonal language function and examining how it
interacts with the other two, we will be able to
see precisely *how* the process of cultural interpretation takes place. We will see precisely *why*
context is so important to text interpretation.

This appeal to a sociolinguistic methodology will also demonstrate the radical significance of an interpreter's cultural context. Cultural position is not a variable which can be isolated and then treated. One cannot account for it in such a way that, once identified, it can be sifted out of the interpretative process. It is like a virus that, though recognized and treated, still courses unabated through the evaluative process. A researcher cannot determine that he or she interprets out of a particular context, acknowledge the probable influence of that context on the interpretative process, and then methodologically set it aside as if he or she can work independently of it to draw an unaffected meaning from the text. Historical and more lately literary criticism have maintained that scientific principles of critical historical investigation or literary analysis could either eliminate or at least stifle such influence. Sociolinguistic analysis demonstrates that they cannot. This work illustrates just how radically *all* interpreters are influenced by the cultural context out of which they write. The meaning they derive from historical-critical and/or literary investigations, or some mixture of the two, therefore, says as much about them as it does about the biblical material they analyze.

Texts do not have "meaning." Instead, they have "meaning potential." Interpreters access this potential interpersonally, that is, contextually. The context of the interpreter directs him/her towards particular slices of that meaning potential. Other interpreters who see another "meaning" in the text need not, therefore, necessarily be in error regarding their conclusions. It may well be that they too see clearly into the text, but because of a different contextual point of entry, conclude with a different piece of the "meaning potential."

The implications of this kind of discussion are dramatic. We are not only arguing that context discovers "meaning"; we are also proposing that contextual interpretation is beneficial to the program of biblical inquiry. If, indeed, there is not "meaning," but "meaning potential," and if interpreters access only portions of that potential as it relates to their particular contextual situations, then a more comprehensive discovery of a text's "meaning potential" can only come about as interpreters from a vast array of interpretative backgrounds are invited into and accepted within the investigative process.

The book will pursue its sociolinguistic evaluation by beginning with a study of M. A. K. Halliday's functional approach to language. Halliday's program gives us a model for understanding how language and culture interact to establish meaning. But it is insufficient for our purposes because it does not deal with the power issues that come from such contextual recognition. Enrique Dussel recognizes that some contexts are "preferred" over others. We will therefore turn to some of his work for an understanding of these

power dynamics and a proposal that suggests a strategy that allows interpreters of different contexts to hear, interact with, and learn from the various slices of "meaning potential" that each brings to the investigative endeavor.

Part One of the book takes a look at the process of cultural interpretation.
Using sociolinguistics we demonstrate precisely how context shapes the
interpretative process by assessing the ways several selected communities
and thinkers draw conclusions about the meaning of biblical language and
text. In a limited study we cannot investigate every community. There are,
for instance, feminist and womanist studies, Hispanic studies, Asian studies,
and many others, of biblical language and text that could be incorporated into a study like this one should the space be available. Indeed, in the
Cultural Hermeneutics course I teach at Princeton Seminary I apply the
sociolinguistic model in evaluating each of these kinds of cultural interpretations.

In Part Two we will appeal to a particular text, the trial scenes in the
Gospel of Mark. We will begin by establishing the vast potential of meaning
in the text. We will then undertake a sociolinguistic analysis of various authors who have investigated the text to demonstrate how in each case context shaped the interpretative process. Each interpreter draws out of the
meaning potential an interpretative slice that relates specifically to the cultural circumstances out of which he/she operates. The investigation demonstrates that investigators understand Jesus to have been condemned for reasons that clearly relate as much to their contextual perspective on the text as
from the language in the text itself. In other words, it would appear that the
Jesus who rises out of the trial scenes is a Jesus of substantially different character depending on the cultural perspective from which an interpreter evaluates the language of those trials. The trial scenes, it appears, compose a vast
meaning potential. That potential is accessed interpersonally.

There are many colleagues to whom I am indebted for assistance during the work on this project. Most especially, Hendrikus Boers, my disserta-
tion adviser who shepherded me through the process, introduced me to
linguistics, and was a wonderful friend and model adviser as I worked
throughout my four years at Emory University. I am also indebted to the
NT faculty as a whole at Emory. Carl Holladay, Fred Craddock, Vernon
Robbins, Gail O'Day, Arthur Wainwright, and David Moessner (Columbia
Theological Seminary) offered helpful guidance in course work and disserta-
tion writing that provided the opportunity for the successful completion
of this inquiry. Many thanks, finally, to Peter J. Paris, Cain Hope Felder,
and Geddes Hanson, whose mentoring has been instrumental and much
appreciated.

The goal and scope in this work have been descriptive and, therefore, limited. Still ahead lies the task of engaging in the actual interpretation of designated texts by taking into consideration the principles proposed by this investigation.

*Brian K. Blount*
*Princeton, New Jersey*

# 1

# A Contextual Approach to New Testament Interpretation

> And he said to his disciples, "Therefore I tell you, do not be anxious about your life, what you shall eat, nor about your body, what you shall put on. For life is more than food, and the body more than clothing. Consider the ravens: they neither sow nor reap, they have neither storehouse nor barn, and yet God feeds them. Of how much more value are you than the birds! And which of you by being anxious can add a cubit to his span of life? If then you are not able to do as small a thing as that, why are you anxious about the rest? Consider the lilies, how they grow; they neither toil nor spin; yet I tell you, even Solomon in all his glory was not arrayed like one of these. But if God so clothes the grass which is alive in the field today and tomorrow is thrown into the oven, how much more will he clothe you, O men of little faith! And do not seek what you are to eat and what you are to drink, nor be of anxious mind. For all the nations of the world seek these things; and your Father knows that you need them. Instead, seek his kingdom, and these things shall be yours as well."
>
> (Luke 12:22-31)

THIS PASSAGE HAS ALWAYS MEANT A GREAT deal to me. The academic goals that have structured and guided my life have demanded a disciplined existence of delayed gratification. Even as a student in a master of divinity program I realized that if I were to achieve my intellectual and spiritual aims, my desires

1

for monetary accumulation and the physical accoutrements it could afford must be suppressed. During the course of my work this biblical text was a source of inspiration and a cause for faith. The words that Luke attributes to Jesus indicate that those who eliminated their anxiety over the physical necessities of life and compensated by increasing their dedication to spiritual demands would be rewarded immeasurably. Not only would they ultimately have access to the reign of God, but to the physical requirements of life as well.

With such a perspective in mind I used this text as the point of departure for a youth group meeting. I was, at the time, a second-year master of divinity candidate at Princeton Theological Seminary. The youth group, which I served as part of a seminary field education requirement, was composed of inner-city teenagers and preteens from Trenton, New Jersey. We were concerned with the topic of career and life goals; Luke 12:22-31 was to be our pivotal text. I explained how the physical and the spiritual were contrasted in the text. I explained the ethic of delayed gratification. I presented a textual perspective suggesting that if a person aggressively sought the spiritual demands of the reign of God, he or she would be so energized by faith that material goals that previously had seemed unattainable might fall incredibly within reach.

Based on that text and my interpretation of it, I asked for a response. The first reply indicated that my meaning had not been conveyed. A twelve-year-old replied, "I can't be nothing. When I grow up I can't be nothing." When I asked if she had properly understood the message of the text, she nodded. Indeed, it was my interpretation that helped channel the despair she already felt into such a negative verbal conclusion. If the text meant that one were to seek the spiritual reign while trusting that God would provide for physical reality, it must be ultimately meaningless for this child. My spiritual interpretation was unacceptable because it implied that no concerted human effort need take place to change her reality of constant physical deprivation; such was apparently God's work. Spiritual uplift thereby became a hindrance rather than an avenue toward necessary social and material change. It was not a change in herself that this girl desperately sought, but a change in the societal structure of her environment that denied her the opportunities I took for granted. To suggest therefore that she surrender a pursuit of physical needs in favor of spiritual ones was to imply not the delay of gratification, but its ultimate obliteration.

"Instead, seek his kingdom, and these things shall be yours as well." The interpretation that had energized me had paralyzed her. In the world of the middle class this passage, so interpreted, is a challenge; in the world of the inner-city poor it becomes a threat, an opiate. Therefore, if the text is to speak meaningfully beyond the boundaries of those who can afford a life of delayed gratification, there must be room for an alternate interpretation. The text—indeed, all of the New Testament text—must have a meaning that is not confined to the reality of a single interpretative ideology.

That is not to say, however, that a text should be interpreted arbitrarily according to the needs of whatever populace is studying it at any particular moment. It is to suggest instead that texts are already interpreted arbitrarily, not according to individual constituent expectations, but according to a perspective of standard white Eurocentric values. Groups living outside that value system are expected to appropriate the interpretative norms that the system has established, and subsequently adapt their individual circumstances to those norms. In accordance with such expectations, I was dutifully attempting to convey a Eurocentric interpretation of the text in a form that was adaptable to the inner-city youth group under my charge. I was trying to draw them into the sociological and linguistic framework of Eurocentric biblical interpretation and make them fit there, just as I had found for myself an adequate fit.

The problem with such a scenario is that this Eurocentric perspective is a restrictive rather than an inclusive concept. Already firmly established as the normative method of biblical interpretation because of its foundation in historical-critical and literary models, it also represents itself as the only accurate measure of biblical interpretation. Thus if one is to interpret text academically for scholarship, or to interpret text correctly and faithfully for a congregation, one must use this Eurocentric perspective. And if the sociological and linguistic perspective of the people to whom one writes or speaks does not match, *their* perspectives must be altered appropriately. Since the perspective of present analysis is "scientifically" correct, it must remain static.

We are now coming to realize, however, that the perspective of science need not be neutral, that it can be sociologically and linguistically restrictive and, therefore, ideological. It will be my argument in this study that this is indeed the case where New Testament text interpretation is concerned. By using the methodological approach of sociolinguistics, I intend to demonstrate that the perspectives of the marginal members of society are excluded from the present methodologies of New Testament interpretation, and that when those perspectives are included, biblical interpretation can have new meaning and impact in both the academic and ecclesiastical arenas.

It will be the intention of this study to contest the requirement that marginal members of society adapt their understanding of the text to Eurocentric values and norms already in place. I will argue instead that if one is to achieve a nonideological method of biblical interpretation, the interpretative perspectives of the societal marginals must be included. The result will not be a reform of the traditional perspective, but a reorientation of it.

Unfortunately, the historical-critical approach to the New Testament has narrowed the use of language to the extent that the perspectives of society's marginal members are excluded. People on the margins interpret the text differently; for them the social and political ramifications are as critical as the religious.

To make a marginal-political approach exclusive, however, is as ideological as the Eurocentric approach about which we are concerned. We will seek instead an approach that is inclusive of both the marginal and mainstream perspectives. Only at such a point of inclusion can what has been ideological become more appropriately scientific as a result of the dynamics of encounter between social contexts.

At the heart of the issue is the language by means of which we approach a text. It is not the case that everyone uses the same language but nonetheless arrives at different conclusions. Language is the framework in which we live; it is the structure that gives meaning to our existence. People in different sociological environments operate with different linguistic forms. The interaction between their sociolinguistic perspective and the language of a text results in a unique understanding about the power and meaning of that text. One therefore should not expect that persons in one sociolinguistic framework will interpret a text in the same way as people living in a different one. If the marginal members and insiders of a society were to come together to discuss a text, there would be no guarantee that one side would hear the concerns of the other. Each side uses a different language, approaches the text from a different linguistic perspective. If one side is to understand the other, it cannot simply listen to what the other says in terms of its own use of language; it must see the text from the other's sociolinguistic perspective. In other words, it must grasp the other's use of language.

We can see the process already at work in the New Testament. Consider, for instance, Matthew 5:3: "Blessed are the poor in spirit, for theirs is the kingdom of heaven," and Luke 6:20b: "Blessed are you poor, for yours is the kingdom of God." The key concern here is not which version of the saying is the oldest. We are concerned instead with the fact that the different sociolinguistic environments of the two evangelists caused them to render the same saying differently. While Matthew moralizes the "poor," Luke, ever cognizant of the socioeconomic dichotomy between the rich and the poor, identifies a social rather than a moral reality. It is not a matter of one interpretation being right and another wrong. Sociolinguistically, each is legitimate in a particular sociolinguistic setting. Therefore both must be considered when a complete interpretation of this text is attempted.

The annunciation story in Luke 1:26-38 is another case. In its present form the story has two key components: the announcement that Mary's child will be the messiah, verses 26-38, and that the conception will take place through the power of the Holy Spirit, verses 34-35. Verses 36-37 are editorial. Luke uses them to connect the annunciation with Mary's visit to Elizabeth. Hendrikus Boers notes that the announcement depends heavily on Scripture. At verse 31 Luke quotes Isaiah 7:14 almost exactly, and the sonship material that follows in verses 32-33 is clearly reminiscent of 2 Samuel 7:12-14, where God makes a similar announcement to David through the prophet Nathan. The Lukan context shifts the meaning so that a prophecy that originally referred to Solomon now refers to the messiah. The transference succeeds because it was expected that the messiah, too, would be the adopted son of God. Indeed, the Targum on Psalm 7 gives a similar interpretation of the divine sonship of the Davidic messiah. Since "each of these sayings could be understood within the framework of Jewish messianic expectations," Boers appears justified in his conclusion that, "For Jewish thought, nothing unsettling appears in Luke's story of the annunciation up to verse 33."[1]

The community to which Luke was writing, however, was composed of people from a sociolinguistic background different from that of the original Jewish setting of the story. This original story, which made sense in its Jewish environment, would have little impact in a Gentile community. "For such Gentile ears the original emphasis on the Davidic messiahship of the child was of little significance because a Davidic Messiah had little meaning in a non-Jewish environment."[2]

Therefore Luke (or the Lukan tradition), writing from the perspective of a Gentile Christian community, interprets the Jewish Christian source in such a way that its language can have a dramatic impact. The result is the addition of verses 34 and 35, which depict the Holy Spirit as the divine initiator of Jesus' birth. Gentiles, Boers advises, when told this version of the Jewish Christian annunciation story, would have assumed that the conception must have been divinely generated. Hellenistic antiquity is filled with similar birth stories about heroic figures. This element of the story, Holy Spirit as progenitor, certifies for Hellenistic Gentile readers that Jesus' origin and mandate were divine. The Lukan addition is thus less an interpretation than a making explicit of what would already have been heard through Gentile ears. Luke, then, formulated the Jewish Christian story (verses 26-33, 38) in a manner that made sense to people from a Gentile sociolinguistic background.[3]

Generations of Western scholarship have maintained that the thematic structure and content of the New Testament materials discourage social and political interpretation. The focus instead has been on the soteriological and the christological. The believer's individual, spiritual relationship with Jesus, the central figure of the cult, has been considered the key textual theme. The emphasis has been primarily on religious salvation, not on social inequity.

The careful reader will correctly point out that certain New Testament materials raise explicit social concerns. For example, in Matthew 25 Jesus graphically illustrates how social concern is a vital and obligatory component of discipleship. The apocalyptic framework of the passage heightens its intensity. At the last judgment severe punishment is meted out to those who ignored their social obligations. Luke-Acts especially provides a powerful mandate to consider the poor and helpless in society: the Magnificat (1:46-56), Jesus' interpretation of his calling (4:16-21), the parable about Lazarus and the rich man (16:19-31), the concerns for community members in need that resulted in a form of primitive social service (Acts 4:32-37), and the concern for widows and orphans (Acts 6:1-7) are concrete examples of social concern. The Epistle to James also comes to mind. Its social concern demonstrates both a sophisticated awareness of community problems and an intense demand for Christian action. Explicit social concerns are present in the New Testament.

Our argument does not debate the existence of texts with social concerns, nor do we claim that scholars have failed to interpret them with an appropriate social and political awareness. We recognize that such passages, and others like them, have been discussed socially and politically. What we are concerned to demonstrate is that even passages that are primarily soteriological and christological are not understood completely unless one takes into account the social dimensions that also contribute to their meanings. Inversely, one must recognize the presence of soteriological and christological features in the overtly social passages. For example, Matthew 7:21 states explicitly, "Not every one who says to me 'Lord, Lord,' shall enter the kingdom of heaven," revealing that Matthew's social concern is understood within the framework of his soteriology and Christology. We believe that the integration of the sociopolitical and soteriological/christological dimensions applies to other passages as well, and would always be recognized in interpretations that take into consideration marginal as well as mainstream Eurocentric sociolinguistic perspectives.

Sociological considerations are by definition integral to our study because the term *marginal* is, as we understand it, a sociological concept. Our concerns, however, are not limited to sociology. In the New Testament we are dealing not with sociological models or identifiable social communities that correspond with communities in the present, but with texts. We are concerned with language and with how people in different sociological categories use language to interpret texts. It is our contention that in the time of the New Testament, and in the present as well, different people experience language functioning differently. Therefore, if our interpretation of a text is to escape the charge of being mere ideology, it must consider the text sociolinguistically: it must recognize that the language in the text can legitimately have different meanings for persons from distinct sociological and linguistic backgrounds.

Unfortunately, the New Testament has been more often a minefield than a gold mine for scholars, students, and believers interested in themes of liberation and empowerment of the disenfranchised. Two problems are evident. First, traditional Eurocentric scholarship maintains that New Testament texts must be interpreted historical-critically, not interpersonally. That is to say, meaning is to be derived exclusively from a comprehensive consideration of grammatical-textual and conceptual-ideational issues resident in the material. Any consideration of the interpersonal interaction between the text and the sociopolitical circumstance of the reader, it is charged, prejudices the interpretative process. The interpreter is said to be reading information *into* the text rather than mining information *from* it. Therefore any interpretation that consciously takes into account the sociolinguistic perspective of the text reader is marginalized and thereby devalued.

Second, some liberation theologians show a tendency to prioritize the interpersonal interaction between the text and the circumstance of the interpreter so highly that they pay too little attention to grammatical-textual and conceptual-ideational issues. Where historical-critical and literary issues are not accorded proper consideration, the text becomes a mirror that reflects the interpreter's own sociopolitical concerns rather than a source from which meaning may be mined.

Rather than emphasizing either of these two extremes, it is our intention to seek an accommodation in which both sides can benefit by taking note of what the other is doing. We propose neither an apology for sociolinguistic interpretation nor a naive acceptance of historical-critical procedure. Instead we are concerned about a comprehensive use of language that includes the grammatical-textual and conceptual-ideational as well as the social-interpersonal functions of language. Only when all such implications have been considered can it be said that a text has been interpreted fully.

## Our Proposal

Enrique Dussel provides a sociological model capable of defining the different interpretative strategies of the marginal members and the "insiders" of society. Sociology, however, is a reality external to the texts. We are interested not only in the different social categories, but more especially in how people from those different categories use language. We will therefore amplify Dussel's model with M. A. K. Halliday's linguistics, which includes a sociolinguistic component. To establish a full overview of sociolinguistics, we will also provide documentation and research findings from other scholars. Because we are not creating a work on sociolinguistics, however, but on New Testament studies, we will not attempt a complete study of sociolinguistics. Halliday's work will act as a center around which our linguistic investigation will be focused.

Halliday's model utilizes three categories of text-linguistic inquiry: textual, ideational, and interpersonal. Although each of these components will be clarified fully below, a brief description provides a useful introduction. The textual category considers language as its functions grammatically. Here the investigator is concerned with the way the components of language—words, phrases, sentences—are structured syntactically so as to establish meaning. The ideational category considers the conceptual implications that lie behind the lexical terms and phrases. Meaning is more than the placement of terms and phrases, it is also the conceptual reference or references signified by those terms and phrases.

In both textual and ideational categories, meaning is understood to reside within the formal boundaries of a particular text's language. To create or apprehend meaning, the language user manipulates the textual and ideational evidence and draws the proper conclusions. In the third, interpersonal category, however, sociolinguistic factors play a determinative role. Language is understood to function interactively so that its meaning cannot be comprehended by considering textual and ideational features alone. The sociocultural environment of the language user functions as a primary variable in the determination of language's meaning.

It is our contention that present methods of New Testament inquiry focus primarily on the more formal textual and ideational categories. As a result, the ways in which a text is allowed to speak have been limited because the interpersonal category has gone unobserved. According to Halliday's model, the full potentiality of the meaning of language can be grasped only when all three linguistic categories have been applied fully. The interpreter who wishes to secure a more complete picture of a text's meaning must therefore operate beyond the boundaries of formal linguistic criteria.

## M. A. K. Halliday's Functional Approach to Language

Halliday's approach to language as a system of communication focuses simultaneously on both the language of the text and the communicative relationships in which that language functions. The basic premise of this functional approach is that language is oriented toward, and structured according to its use in, an act of communication. Theoretical discussion about the internal makeup of a language is no longer considered sufficient; meaning is associated as much with the use of language as with the infrastructure of language. Theoretical and practical considerations are merged.

This functional approach has two major implications. In Halliday's words, "A functional approach to language means, first of all, investigating how language is used: trying to find out what are the purposes that language serves for us, and how we are able to achieve those purposes through speaking and listening, reading and writing."[4] Language has a distinct instrumental component that must be comprehended. Second, the approach implies a certain correspondence between the internal makeup of a language and its functional directives. Language systems are determined in accordance with the functions they have evolved to serve.[5]

Halliday illustrates his method by appealing to the pattern of language acquisition in children. With children, he contends, there is a direct relationship between the internal structure of a language and that language's use. "What the child does with language tends to determine its structure."[6]

At the earliest stage language serves a purely instrumental function. The child's singular intention is to act upon the environment, or, in Halliday's words, "to get things done." The child finds that language is a highly appropriate mechanism for achieving this end. Language therefore quickly evolves into an "I want" kind of infrastructure. It is simple, easily adapted to unique situations, and efficient. Most important, it works; the child finds that the environment is responsive.

As the child recognizes that some needs exceed the "I want" stage, the child's linguistic horizons become enlarged. New infrastructures are needed to accommodate new functional requirements. Halliday describes the second developmental stage of language use as the instrument of control. The child realizes how the language of others exerts pressure on the child just as the child's language exerts pressure on others. Halliday colloquially calls this regulatory model of language the "do as I tell you" function.

Closely related to this regulatory function is the social interactional function of language, which Halliday terms "me and you." This function, along with the personal model that follows it, is important for our study because it approximates the interpersonal function found in adult language. Halliday recognizes how the child's language is responsible for the orientation of the child's social environment. "Even the closest of the child's personal relationships, that with his mother, is partly and, in time, largely mediated through language; his interaction with other people, adults and children, is very obviously maintained linguistically."[7]

The personal model, which Halliday calls the "here I am" function, furthers the linguistic structuring of the child's environment. Instead of focusing on the child's perception of his or her relationship with others, however, in this case language establishes the child's sense of personal individuality. "We are not talking here merely of 'expressive' language—language used for the direct expression of feelings and attitudes—but also of the personal element in the interactional function of language, since the shaping of the self through interaction with others is very much a language-mediated process."[8]

The fifth, "tell me why," function, comprises the heuristic model. Here the child uses language to explore the environment. In the sixth, "let's pretend," function, the imaginative model provides for the child's ability to manufacture a "linguistically created environment."[9] Finally, the representational model comprises the "I've got something to tell you" function. Since the most important linguistic concern for adults is the competent transference of information, Halliday contends that this model, which concentrates on communicating information, is the only one many adults have. It is, however, the least developed model in the child's functional inventory. The child depends on all of the prior six models, using each as the situation requires, combining them when necessary. Only in adulthood does the representational model become the dominant—in most cases, exclusive—means of communicating with others. Significantly, it is this model that approximates the ideational and textual functions of adult language use.

Immersed in Halliday's model, we can see why adult language usage is often linguistically deficient. An interactive-interpersonal component adds richness to a child's language. This component is unexplored by most adults.

This deficiency in adult language can become an acute problem for the child in an educational environment because the authority figures who establish the rules of language—the teachers—operate from such a different linguistic perspective. Halliday notes that many children fail in school, not because they lack language skills, but because the functional language skills most critical for their particular social community may be different from the representational model demanded by teachers. The child is evaluated not according to the child's own standards of language use, but those of the teachers. Failure therefore often results because the requirements are not linguistically relevant for the child.

We are learning, in other words, that a child's linguistic environment plays a critical role in the child's comprehension of reality. If we are to understand that child, we must not operate from an uniquely adult representational model and expect the child to adapt to it. We must rather attempt to ascertain which linguistic perspective is most critical for the child. To understand the world as the child understands it, we must comprehend the world from the child's linguistic perspective. Linguistic meaning has a critical contextual component.

Halliday's functional model sums up the key differences between the child's and the adult's use of language in terms of grammar. Because function is directly equivalent to use for the child, there is no need for an intervening grammar. With adults, however, the situation is radically different:

> With the very young child, "function" equals "use"; and there is no grammar, no intermediate level of internal organization in language, only a content and

> an expression. With the adult, there are indefinitely many uses, but only three or four functions, or "macro-functions" as we are calling them; and these macro-functions appear at a new level in the linguistic system—they take the form of grammar.[10]

Three macro-functions are the basis of the adult grammatical system. They are the textual; the ideational, which Halliday sometimes divides into logical and experiential; and the interpersonal.[11] A key consideration is Halliday's assertion that every speech event entertains all three of these macro-functions. This being the case, no analysis of a speech event can be functionally complete unless all three semantic categories have been properly considered.

The most obvious of the three macro-functions is the textual. It comprises the grammatical component that enables the speaker to organize his or her material effectively so that it can perform its function as message. In order to achieve that function the material must make "operational" sense in its immediate context.

Second is the ideational macro-function, the most representative of the adult mode of communication. In both its experiential and logical modes it accomplishes the function of relaying information efficiently and expressing experiences. The specific function of this category of language is the encoding of our experience in the form of ideational content.[12]

The third and, from our perspective, critical macro-function is instrumental in establishing one's relationship with others in the social environment (the interpersonal) and thereby in establishing one's sense of self as part of and yet distinctive from others in that environment (the personal). The language we use conditions our perception of both our selves and the social structure in which we live and act: "But the interpersonal element in language extends beyond what we might think of as its rhetorical functions. In the wider context, language is required to serve in the establishment and maintenance of all human relationships; it is the means whereby social groups are integrated and the individual is identified and reinforced."[13]

The interpersonal category alerts us to the fact that language is social. Therefore, meaning in language must be determined as much from its social context as from its internal structure. This realization is the key to an understanding of Halliday's systemic approach.

Language occurs in what Halliday calls a "context of situation." This context of situation relates specifically to the linguistic context in which a speech event takes place. Language does not occur in isolation, but comes to life only when functioning in some particular environment. The context critically influences the meaning. Halliday lists three types of linguistic situations: first, what is actually taking place—the field of discourse; second, who is taking part—the tenor or style of discourse; and third, what part the language is playing—the mode of discourse.[14] These situational categories match the three semantic macro-functions. According to Halliday's program, the field of discourse connects with the ideational function, the tenor of discourse with the interpersonal function, and the mode of discourse with the textual function. When all these variables are taken together they will determine the range, or register, within which meanings will be selected. Halliday maintains that given the linguistic situation or context of a speaker, one can predict the kind of language that speaker is likely to use.[15]

This recognition assists in our interpersonal effort to interpret biblical texts more completely because it directs us to analyze the tenor or role relationships in the text. "The selection of interpersonal options, those in the systems of mood, modality, person, key, intensity, evaluation and comment and the like, tends to be determined by the role relationships in the situation."[16]

Halliday also recognizes a second kind of language context, that of culture, a broader concept that specifies the global social environment of the speech event. "It is the social context that defines the limits of the options available; the behavioural alternatives are to this extent context-specific. But the total range of meanings that is embodied in and realized through the language system is determined by this context of culture—in other words by the social structure."[17]

Dell Hymes agrees that one of the most critical and comprehensive contexts that may affect how the potential of meaning is actualized is the cultural background of the interpreter. "Even the ethnographies that we have, though almost never focused on speaking, show us that communities differ significantly in ways of speaking, in patterns of repertoire and switching, in the roles and meanings of speech."[18]

Norman Fairclough's observations give practical support to Halliday's more theoretical propositions. Fairclough attends specifically to concerns of text production and interpretation in a social environment. He argues that language is conditioned by nonlinguistic elements in society through the process of socialization. "People internalize what is socially produced and made available to them, and use this internalized MR (members' resources) to engage in their social practice, including discourse."[19] These internalized forces thereby gain an important foothold in the psyche of an individual in society and influence from within (linguistically) how texts are both produced and interpreted. In other words, social conditions shape the members' resources, which in turn shape the way in which texts are prepared and understood:

> So, in seeing language as discourse and as social practice, one is committing one's effort not just to analyzing texts, nor just to analyzing processes of pro-

duction and interpretation, but to analyzing the relationship between texts, processes, and their social conditions, both the immediate conditions of the situational context and the more remote conditions of institutional and social structures.[20]

This situational understanding of language as behavior suggests that a sociolinguistic method will most appropriately allow for the full consideration of the interpersonal function of language in the biblical text. Halliday states the case explicitly:

> So in putting language into the context of "language and social man," we are taking up one of the options that are open for the relating of language study to other fields of inquiry. This, broadly, is the socio-linguistic option; and the new subject of socio-linguistics that has come into prominence lately is a recognition of the fact that language and society—or, as we prefer to think of it, language and social man—is a unified conception, and needs to be understood and investigated as a whole. Neither of these exists without the other: there can be no social man without language, and no language without social man.[21]

Sociolinguistics, the study of language in relation to society, maintains first that the social structure in which we live as individuals is realized through language. That is to say, we perceive the world through language; the world's sense of reality is linguistically based. Halliday recognizes that this process beings at an early age when the child learns to fashion its social reality according to linguistic prerogatives: "Language is used to define and consolidate the group, to include and to exclude, showing who is 'one of us' and who is not; to impose status, and to contest status that is imposed; and humor, ridicule, deception, persuasion, all the forensic and theatrical arts of language are brought into play."[22] This process continues, but becomes more complex in adulthood. Language is used to transmit values, define social roles, and sanction or reject patterns of social behavior. Language, in other words, is the mechanism of socialization. It is the tool through which the values and belief systems of one's particular culture are adopted and internalized. One, in turn, relates to that culture by means of language, internally in one's thought processes, and externally through various means of interpersonal communication.[23] Language, then, both establishes our view of the world and conditions the way in which we interpret events taking place in that world. "A possible consequence of this would be that speakers of different languages could stand side by side and experience precisely the same event and yet understand it in profoundly different ways. . . . Furthermore, each would find it difficult or impossible to understand the event from the other's perspective."[24]

"Different languages" here should not be limited to major languages like English, German, and French, but should include linguistic variations within those languages—for example, city/urban, rural and coastal, or in the United States, eastern, southern, midwestern, and western. "Moreover, there is an even more important reason for focusing on the individual in sociolinguistics. . . . We can be sure that *no two speakers have the same language, because no two speakers have the same experiences of language*." [25] In other words, this sociological dimension of cultural context is not limited to peoples separated by vast spaces of geography. Citizens of the same country, who use the same language, may be subculturally distinct and may, by virtue of their distinct use of speech patterns, therefore belong to different speech communities. Ralph Fasold notes that even in the United States, where a common language spreads across a vast geographical space, not all citizens have the same speech patterns. He points, for example, to the contrast between white Americans and Native Americans. The contrast between black and white Americans is just as illuminating. "A black student probably uses speech in ways when talking to other black people that white students would not be able to understand or appreciate." [26] Even within a particular subcultural group, distinct differences in language use can exist. Not all blacks, for example, belong to the same social class, even if they are part of the same racial subculture. Regional distinctions play a powerful role as well. In the United States, great differences in speech pattern and linguistic perspective exist between whites in the East, West, North, and South. In fact, it is probable that regional linguistic differences override racial distinctions. For example, in some respects whites and blacks from one particular region may agree linguistically with each other more than with whites and blacks from a different geographical perspective.

R. A. Hudson agrees that we all construct models of the communities in which we live on the basis of sociolinguistic data. Since the particular model that each individual constructs will reflect his or her personal experience, people with different sociolinguistic backgrounds will be led to construct correspondingly different models that are relevant to their specific language and society. "Rather the individual *filters* his experience of new situations through his existing model, and two people could both hear the same person talking, but be affected by his speech in different ways." [27]

Sociolinguistics also maintains that one's sense of personality is realized through language. Halliday argues that it is the linguistic interchange with the group that determines the status of the individual and shapes him or her as a person. In other words, language is the medium through which one's sense of person is established. In Halliday's own formulation, "the individual is a derivation from and extension of his participation in the group." [28] The same language that is responsible for one's view of society is also responsible for one's sense of personality.

## Considerations for Biblical Interpretation

The functional model of speech analysis presented by M. A. K. Halliday concerns the operational program of the producer of a text. We intend, however, to utilize his methodological considerations of textual, ideational, and interpersonal phases of speech from the vantage point of the reader. More is involved here than a mere reversal of the process; the contextual perspective of the reader adds a new situational element to the interpersonal phase. This element can be integrated successfully into the program because contextual perspective is an accepted and vital part of Halliday's program. To consider the interpreter's viewpoint is not to add a foreign element to Halliday's program, but to reorient a key ingredient—contextual perspective—to text reader as well as to text producer.

Halliday's functional approach allows for unlimited possibilities of text interpretation that correspond to ever-changing sociolinguistic contexts. A text, as written speech event, thus does not have a single, closed meaning, but a "meaning potential," or more appropriately in a functional framework, "behavior potential." The text, from this point of view, is a range of possibilities, an open-ended set of options in behavior that are available to the individual interpreter.[29] This potential allows for variable interpretations of texts according to the interpreter's sociolinguistic framework.

Based on this premise it is possible for a single sentence, operating through the different sociolinguistic perspectives of distinct individuals, to have different meanings. This is what Halliday refers to as part of the creativity of language:

> But in any case, as Ruqaiya Hasan has pointed out, creativeness does not consist in producing new sentences. The newness of a sentence is a quite unimportant—and unascertainable—property, and "creativity" in language lies in the speaker's ability to create new meanings: to realize the potentiality of language for the indefinite extension of its resources to new contexts of situation. It is only in this light that we can understand the otherwise unintelligible observation made by Katz and Fodor, that "almost every sentence uttered is uttered for the first time."[30]

In our consideration of language as social behavior this means that we treat language as a form of behavior potential. Language is what the speaker "can mean." What the speaker can mean is related through the use of sentences, words, and phrases to what the speaker "can do." The intermediate step between these two ends is what the speaker "can say." "The potential of language is meaning potential. This meaning potential is the linguistic realization of the behaviour potential; 'can mean' is 'can do' when translated into language. The meaning potential is in turn realized in the language system as lexico-grammatical potential, which is what the speaker 'can say.'"[31] Each text—indeed, each linguistic form—has a variety of possible meanings. Sociolinguistics therefore suggests that the social context of the reader determines which potential meaning is most appropriate. Therefore it should not be overly surprising that people from different sociolinguistic backgrounds might interpret the same texts in radically different ways.[32]

## A Sociopolitical Caution

A significant problem arises with sociolinguistics as we have discussed it here. As Fairclough notes, it can be a highly positivistic method.[33] By this he means that while sociolinguistics accurately describes what happens in the interpretative process, it often does not go far enough into the analysis of consequences. Even though sociolinguistics recognizes that people of different cultures interpret texts and social events differently, it does not deal with the fact that the dominant culture too often presents only its interpretations as "correct" or "scientific." When rules are fashioned, or, in our case, when commentaries are made, it is along the lines of the dominant culture's interpretative perspective. What sociolinguistics typically leaves out, then, is the issue of power, the power of one community's sociolinguistic perspective to dominate and devalue the sociolinguistic perspectives of other communities:

> Sociolinguistics is strong on "what?" questions (what are the facts of variation?) but weak on "why?" and "how?" questions (why are the facts as they are?; how—in terms of the development of social relationships of power—was the existing sociolinguistic order brought into being?; how is it sustained?; and how might it be changed to the advantage of those who are dominated by it?).[34]

At this critical juncture the work of Enrique Dussel can be of significant assistance.

## Enrique Dussel's Sociological Model

Enrique Dussel's philosophy of liberation provides an important foundation on which our sociolinguistic premise will operate. His sociological method maintains that an interpreter's "spatial, worldly setting" is a primary and reliable indicator of the perspective that structures and gives focus to the interpreter's work. "I am trying, then, to take space, geopolitical space, seriously. To be born at the North Pole or in Chiapas is not the same thing as to be born in New York City."[35]

Whether we are considering something as significant as a community's evaluation of a momentous event in world history or something as isolated as a private individual's reading of a newspaper editorial, Dussel would propose that one's spatial and political location in life determines what one sees, or at least how one sees. An identical event or circumstance is bound to be subject to a multiplicity of interpretations. Dussel recognizes that all perspectives are not considered equal when a determinative interpretation is being formulated. Instead, a collective perspective that has been embraced by those who maintain political and numerical superiority becomes the "official" one. Minority opinions may be entertained, but they are seldom included as resources for any programmatic standardization of rules and regulations. In other words, they lack political legitimation and, therefore, power. This is Halliday's interpersonal hypothesis sharpened to a sociopolitical edge.

This process is as real in the scientific and scholarly arenas as it is in politics and society. In fact, the problem is even more acute in the scientific and scholarly arenas because thought that originates from outside the boundaries of accepted, "official" interpretation is considered unscientific and therefore unacceptable. Acceptance is bought only at the high price of assimilation with the centrist, "official" view. In this manner, the "official" interpretation becomes the only "scientifically correct" interpretation. "Thought that takes refuge in the center ends by thinking it to be the only reality. Outside its frontiers is nonbeing, nothing, barbarity, non-sense."[36]

In the language of sociolinguistics we are, then, suggesting that each text has a vast potential of meaning or behavior. How access is made to that potential determines how a reader or interpreter creates meaning from that text. Sociolinguistics indicates that this access is established interpersonally. The background of the reader or interpreter determines which elements of the potential are utilized and transcribed as meaningful. Dussel's work suggests, however, that power dynamics are at play. Even though different contexts will yield different meanings, only the dominant centrist context allows itself the privilege of "correct" or "meaningful" interpretation. Therefore, in our case of biblical inquiry, meaning that is derived from beyond the boundaries of the historical-critical/literary arena of inquiry, where the conversation consciously invites interpersonal rather than allegedly exclusive textual and ideological concerns, is considered suspect. The center as Dussel describes it has in this way become an ideology.

Dussel maintains that a nonideological position will recognize the validity of all points of view, entertaining the totality of the "center" and the "other" on equal theoretical terms:

> The philosophy that knows how to ponder the reality, the de facto world reality, not from the perspective of the center of political, economic, or military power but from beyond the frontiers of that world, from the periphery— this philosophy will not be ideological. Its reality is the whole earth; for it the "wretched of the earth" (who are not nonbeing) are also real.[37]

This discussion is of particular importance in our analysis of language use. We have noted how texts and the linguistic signs of which they are composed are themselves events that are open to interpretation. Dussel recognizes that "scientific" interpretations of linguistic signs are often ideological interpretations that have been validated by the interpretative perspectives of the center. Even persons on the peripheries of society can be induced to read linguistic signs in a way that validates, not their experiences and sociopolitical backgrounds, but the backgrounds and experiences of those who are in control of society. Text interpretation that purports to be neutral and scientific will thereby be ideological instead. "Ideologies are closely linked to language, because using language is the commonest form of social behaviour, and the form of social behaviour where we rely most on 'commonsense' assumptions."[38]

Ideology thus connects with power. The interpretation of language determines not only understanding, but political and scientific control. The culture that determines the interpretative norms also determines the kind of life that those norms ideologically mandate:

> The sign (it can be idea, word, form, image, sound, aroma) has as horizon of meaning only the oligarchical neocolonial or imperialist culture. Popular culture is silenced; its expression is repressed, its exposition violated. . . . The prevalent contemporary ideological mentality is one that is founded on a dominative semiotic totality. A people, as an alienated mass, can have a naive ideological mentality that passively accepts the domination it undergoes. In this case the sign does not disclose the reality of oppression; it conceals oppression; it is false.[39]

Just as a philosophy of liberation would operate by demanding the inclusion of perspectives from the periphery as valid interpretations for establishing societal and scientific direction, a semiotics of liberation would demand a linguistic system of analysis that fully appreciates the sign interpretation of the societal "other." Dussel notes how this process occurs historically when an old system of signs gives way to a new order. Thus, he documents the coming into being of the Romance languages from Latin as a result of the invasion of "exterior and oppressed Germanic peoples during the time of the Roman Empire." He argues that in the history of languages the fruit of such language invasion is the passage to new linguistic systems that recognize elements that had heretofore been considered as alien. "In the same manner, the peripheral exteriority of Latin American, Arabic, black African, Indian, Southeast Asian, or Chinese semiotics will promote through their irruption into history (if a process of political liberation takes place) a new global and future semiotics." Dussel labels the result semiotic-liberation. "The praxis of semiotic-liberation creates new words because it renews the sense of the

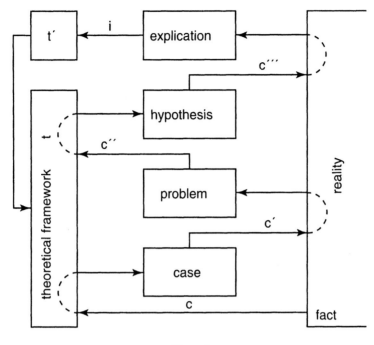

**Figure 1**

world; it creates new cultural and historical codes."[40] This process occurs within a scientific model, which is outlined in Figure 1.[41]

The point of departure for this model, as it is for all of science, is the fact. In our case we might refer to the fact as a linguistic sign, or perhaps an entire biblical text. "A fact is the real constitutive note of a thing by which it is actualized or appears in the world."[42] According to Dussel, the scientific process starts from the fact as a phenomenon. Science is not concerned with the fact as fact, but rather with its explication. It is the *why* of the fact that his scientific model illustrates.

Following the arrows, which originate with the fact, we see that the fact is confronted (*c*) with an *a priori* theoretical framework or body of existent theories (*t*). The fact is first interpreted in its everyday sense, as a representative of similar facts, as a case to be studied. It is then again confronted (*c'*) with reality in order that it may be interpreted precisely, scientifically. It is at this point that one does or does not discover a problem. If a problem exists, it is defined clearly in an appropriate scientific code. That problem is then confronted (*c''*) with a theory, from which a hypothesis for scientific investigation is worked out. The hypothesis is then confronted (*c'''*) with reality.

From this full experimental method a conclusive explication must follow. If the hypothesis is verified in this manner, it is integrated (*i*) into the theory, which is thereby modified (*t'*), either because it has been corroborated and thus has more force, or because it has been complemented, or because it has been negated. The modified theory (*t'*) gives feedback to the theoretical framework and thus becomes a new theoretical framework for the next scientific investigation.[43] In this way a new sign is effected.

The problem with this scientific—or, as Dussel terms it, ontic—scenario is that it is completely ideological; the adjustments are made within a totalistic framework that co-opts rather than accepts input from the periphery. This can occur, not because the process is itself inappropriate, but because the model refuses to recognize that the process operates within a centrist totality that is positioned against an exterior totality, or alterity. For example, while an African American interpretative perspective of a linguistic sign or sign system may be acknowledged, it is added to the system only as a minority view. As such, it may provide an alternative exposition within the semiotic system, but it may not actually provoke a change in that system. In this way society can recognize that a distinctive use of language occurs in a poverty-stricken inner-city black environment, but will not allow that recognition to influence language expectations on such critical evaluative tools as scholastic achievement tests.

Figure 2 (p. 21) shows a model that more appropriately represents the interpretative perspectives of both the centrist and exterior segments of a society.[44] If we ignore the lines *y* and *x* at the bottom of the model and consider only the full circle, "totality," and the partial circle, "exteriority," we can achieve a fuller appreciation of Dussel's competing options for interpretation. We see the ontic process in complete form in the center of the circle labeled "totality." Now, however, because we recognize that a mere consideration of facts is not an end in itself but part of a larger practical process, we move from the scientific to what Dussel calls the dialectical arena: "The scientific process begins with theory and explains its results; it is explicative. The dialectical process, with regard to sciences, begins with theories or with science as a totality and raises itself to their historical, social, or economic presuppositions. It raises itself from the abstract (science) to the concrete (practical or poietic totalities)."[45] The dialectical movement is a negative one that recognizes another totality exterior to itself, but meets that other in confrontation rather than acceptance. In this manner it is a necessary but insufficient mechanism in Dussel's model. Without the dialectic there is no recognition of a real and potent reality outside of the centrist totality. The dialectic process, however, is unable to promote an effective interchange between the two realities.

## TOTALITY

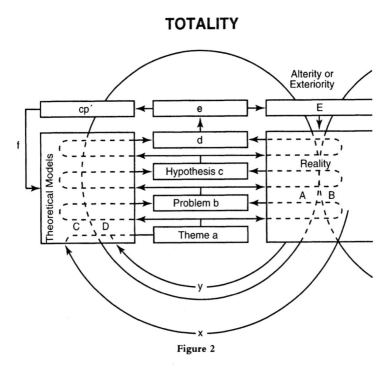

**Figure 2**

The arrows *x* and *y* represent the effective interchange between totalities that Dussel calls the analectical moment. The analectical begins by recognizing the exterior, but goes further and analyzes reality from that marginal perspective. "The point of departure for its methodological discourse (a method that is more than scientific or dialectic) is the exteriority of the other. Its principle is not that of identity but of separation, distinction." Such analysis establishes an affirmation of exteriority and thereby poses a threat to any system that maintains a singular affirmation of the centrist totality of the current social system. It is more than a negative dialectical recognition of opposites—it is the positive recognition that those opposites may work together to create a new, vibrant, and more inclusive whole. "To affirm exteriority is to realize what is impossible for the system (there being no potency for it); it is to realize the *new,* what has not been foreseen by the totality, that which arises from freedom that is unconditioned, revolutionary, innovative." [46]

We are now ready to give final consideration to the analytical model in figure 2 as discussed by Ely César. We recognize immediately that the totality of centrist society includes both reality (*A*) and theoretical aspects (*D*). While

*A* indicates reality as it is interpreted from the center, *D* "represents the accepted theoretical models which operate within the official social system and are effective for disclosing only the reality which is manifested by the perspective of the center." César correctly defines *D* to include everything from the values we use to organize the family to the sciences taught in the schools, in order to prepare professionals who will perform for reality *A*.[47]

*B* represents the reality of those on the periphery of society, the marginal members, "the oppressed, cut off from the controlling system." "Here is the person who, from the standpoint of the center, is the one who is not, who does not count, who is the negation of being and whose history is denied."[48] While César and Dussel were particularly concerned with the perspective of Latin Americans, we are most concerned with the perspective of African Americans who also reside in this partial circle of alterity. Because their reality, *B*, is denied, the theoretical perspective, *C*, from which that reality is analyzed is considered highly suspect.

In this analectical model, these two realities (*AB*) and theoretical perspectives (*CD*) are coordinated in such a way that an inclusive interpretation of social and political realities is allowed. The internal program operates in much the same way as in the ontic process discussed above. This case, however, includes a notable difference: it is recognized that the procedure takes place within a totality that interacts with an exteriority. The theme thus springs up as much out of *B* as *A* (lines *x* and *y*). Just as importantly, when the process concludes, not only do the "projective criteria" influence a reorientation of the theoretical model, but the new input *E* significantly affects the makeup of reality, so that as the analectical process continues, reality is more and more defined from a perspective that is inclusive of both centrist and exterior perspectives.

Based on this analectical model, Dussel appears well grounded in his assertion that liberation theology is not a mere chapter of doing theology: "It is a way of doing *all* theology."[49] Only in this manner can the perspectives of all groups in society be considered appropriately. Just as important, Dussel recognizes that the task of establishing such an analectical model must be placed in the hands of the marginal members in society. People who live in the totality cannot create change because they are caught up in the ideology that surrounds and suffocates them. Even those on the exterior who have been co-opted by that ideology will be impotent; they, too, are immersed in only one apparent reality. Dussel uses the appropriate image of revelation. A people caught up and blinded by sin cannot effect an escape from it. Salvation must come from without, from a reality exterior to the all-encompassing totality of sin. It must come from God.[50] In the case of the analectical model, it must come from the marginalized in society.

This model is as appropriate for a study of language as it is for an analysis of ethical and political societal norms. The analectical model of linguistic interpretation of biblical texts will be promoted in this study. Linguistic symbols and systems can, like scientific and social facts, be studied narrowly within ideological parameters that negate the sociolinguistic perspectives of those on the peripheries of society. This is especially critical for New Testament study because analysis of biblical language is not only used to establish the correct interpretation of texts, but text interpretation is often used in turn as a model for creating norms of ethical behavior in a Judeo-Christian societal context.

Our challenge, then, according to Dussel's analectical model, is to read Scripture not in light of societal totality, as an ideology, but from the perspective of the exterior, to see with the marginal members of society the full revelation of God. This is, of course, a sociological mandate. For Dussel, the starting point of theology is one's historical praxis. Sociolinguistically, this would be true for biblical interpretation also. The starting point is where one is sociologically, in the totality or in the exteriority. For those who start from the totality, from the center of societal values, the peripheral will not be a part of their theology. This is what takes place typically today in the interpretation of biblical texts: Interpretation is done from the centrist viewpoint. Peripheral issues and mandates do not surface.

Dussel's model is thus of extreme significance in hermeneutics. But because it is oriented to the exterior, to sociological factors, it has no specific program for handling the biblical material textually, as a directive for exegesis. His philosophy of liberation is social-external. It looks at the world from the position of the oppressed, but only in their external sociological sense. Having established how these external parameters must be approached from a nonideological perspective, we also want to make an internal study, to look at society from within, from the way in which oppressed peoples and marginalized peoples use language. At this point we turn to a concern for language as it operates in an analectical sense. Language operates differently, we believe, according to whether one is located sociolinguistically on the periphery or in the center of societal existence. If one's linguistic perspective is that of the social center, the linguistic perspective of those on the social periphery will be a foreign and unacceptable reality, if indeed it is even visible. Our interpersonal task will be to present the sociolinguistic perspective from the exterior and bring it into contact with the perspective of the center. In this way, as Dussel's model demonstrates, we will not only present something new, but this new reality will in turn force a change in the old. The entire program of ideological biblical interpretation will be challenged.

# PART ONE  Cultural Contexts and Biblical Interpretation

# 2

# Existential
# Interpretation

COMMUNICATIVE CONTEXT DOES INFLUENCE
the reading of biblical materials, and in these
four chapters we will see how. In the existentialist work of Rudolf Bultmann, the *Gospel
in Solentiname*, Negro spirituals, and black
church sermons we will present concrete historical examples of the interpersonal factor at
work from the standpoint of the text inter-
preter/reader. In this way we will demonstrate that the process can work in the direction we propose, and at the same time we will
present examples that establish the theoretical
process in practical application. These case
studies demonstrate the validity of a portion
of our thesis, that sociolinguistic context can
and does affect the manner in which texts are
interpreted. These case studies will demonstrate clearly how sociolinguistic factors correspond directly to the kinds of interpretations rendered. Unique factors allow and
determine unique kinds of interpretative
moves and conclusions.

It is not our intent, however, to show only
that sociolinguistic context influences interpretation of a text. We want to demonstrate
exactly how this is done. We intend to reveal
how interpersonal factors interact with textual
and ideational components in the written material so that access to the text's potential for

meaning or behavior is gained in a way that is meaningful for the community or interpreter in question and at the same time appropriate to textual and ideational factors.

We are suggesting, then, that the text language has a potential of meaning whose boundaries are limited by textual and ideational data. A text cannot be made to mean anything a community desires. Meaningful conclusions must respect established textual and ideational parameters. This still allows for a vast potentiality of meaning, but it is a limited potentiality. Within that range of potentiality the interpersonal dynamics have free play. Thus, when conclusions are reached that fit within this textual-ideational boundary and simultaneously interact beyond this boundary with the interpersonal context of the reader, the result is a conclusion that is both linguistically accurate and contextually appropriate. This process allows for distinct and yet accurate conclusions regarding the meaning of a particular text or set of texts. It is this process that we will observe and evaluate in four case studies.

## The Existential Context

Rudolf Bultmann argues that language cannot be applied effectively if its symbols and terminology are foreign; it must first be interpreted, translated into an understandable idiom. According to Bultmann, biblical language about God is mythical and thus is inappropriate to the mentality of modern, scientific society. It must therefore be translated. Bultmann attempts to process this translation existentially.

Bultmann argues that an existentialist approach to biblical interpretation is appropriate because the Bible's mythical language is concerned with understanding human existence. The purpose of myth is to describe transcendent control over the world and the humans who populate it, but the mythical terms impede this descriptive ability for modern readers, for whom such terms are foreign. While accurately explaining that humans are not in control of the world, myths unscientifically objectify the power that does control it.[1]

The significance of New Testament mythology, then, lies not in its terminology or imagery of the world, but in its understanding of human existence in relationship to the divine, and thereby to itself. The real concern is not whether its imagery is accurate or appropriate, but whether its understanding of existence is accurate and appropriate. "Faith claims that it is, and faith ought not to be tied down to the imagery of New Testament mythology."[2] The modern reader is therefore directed, through existentialist interpretation, to the kerygmatic understanding of existence contained in the myth rather than to the myth itself.

Bultmann thus claims that a process of demythologization through existentialist interpretation is the single scientific method of New Testament interpretation. For him, correct text interpretation is a hermeneutical enterprise in which an individual's understanding of the written material can result in conclusions that have objective, universal validity.[3]

According to Bultmann, the difference between his approach and that of traditional historical exegesis is demonstrated in the concern that lies behind two critical questions of text inquiry: "What is said?" and "What is meant?" Although Bultmann is aware that in order for any text study to be historically controlled, the former question must be accurately answered, it is his progression toward a full consideration of the latter question that uniquely marks his methodology. "Since this question is concerned not with explaining nature but with understanding history, to which we ourselves belong, it implies: What does it mean for me and how am I to understand it on its objective ground?"[4]

The objective ground of which Bultmann speaks is the general conception of modern humanity that forms the universal lens through which all individual human inquiry and interpretation are perceived. Bultmann argues that a writer who speaks through a particular text does not exhaust his or her meaning in a "fixable, relative moment," but allows for a potential of meaning that lies beneath the surface and can be mined only when the investigator reflects on his or her own existential possibility as it relates to the text. The text then is no longer simply a material entity that we view as though it were a mere object; rather we confront it, just as we confront other persons with whom we establish meaning and existence only in the crucible of encounter and relationship.

This concern for human existence adds a contextual element to Bultmann's interpretative inquiry and thus brings us into the functional arena M. A. K. Halliday calls the interpersonal. Bultmann came to realize that the universal human condition of every reader affects how the text is read. This is why demythologization is necessary. Myth is no longer intelligible to the modern reader; it must therefore be interpreted according to the new existential context, that of modern humanity.

In other words, we are talking about a language of interpretation that is existentially—that is to say, contextually—conditioned. The meaning of a text is no longer considered an immobile, static possession that is passed through time intact and inviolate. Instead, the meaning results from the encounter between the text and the interpreter's relationship to his or her own life existence that is expressed in the text. This does not have to result in subjective interpretations that recognize no interpretative controls. On the contrary, Bultmann's method exhibits two powerful investigative restraints. The first is the consideration of what the text said originally, which is ascertained through a meticulous observance of historical-critical principles. The second is the grounding of the interpretation in the universal human experience of the modern era through which the individual interpreter refracts his or her particular meaning. It is a contextual method, but the contextual element is existentially, not individualistically, operative.

Consider, for example, the introduction to Bultmann's *Jesus and the Word*. He argues—against the traditional understanding—that one cannot gather the essence of history by attempting to "view" it as one might view one's natural environment. Human beings are separate from nature and can therefore observe nature objectively, as something distinct from ourselves. We are, however, a part of history, so that when we say something about history, we are in effect saying something about ourselves.[5] Our encounter with history therefore must take place in dialogue. History makes a demand on us and speaks to us only when we bring to it questions about our own existence. "Thus I would lead the reader not to any *view* of history, but to a highly personal *encounter* with history."[6]

This dialogical relationship with history is of immense importance for someone encountering the history of Jesus. Because we cannot *view* history, we do not pursue facts about Jesus' biography or psychological makeup; we instead attempt to encounter Jesus. We do not talk about Jesus the great man, the genius, or the hero; we do not pontificate about the eternal value of his message. Nor do we lose ourselves in the question of whether he knew himself to be the messiah. Instead, we focus on his work, for in his work we find ourselves in contact with him. "Attention is entirely limited to what he *purposed,* and hence to what in his purpose as a part of history makes a present demand on us."[7]

In this manner we interact with Jesus' history not as neutral observers, but as persons motivated by the question of how we, standing in the same current of history as Jesus, can comprehend our own existence and gain insight into the contingencies and necessities of our own life purpose.[8] Jesus' purpose is contained in his teachings. We, then, interact with those teachings existentially. "When we encounter the words of Jesus in history, *we* do not judge *them* by a philosophical system with reference to their rational validity; *they* meet *us* with the question of how we are to interpret our own existence." In fact, unless we approach a historical observation of the text in such a dialectical manner, our entire investigation is flawed. "That we be ourselves deeply disturbed by the problem of our own life is therefore the indispensable condition of our inquiry."[9]

At this point Bultmann sees context specifically affecting one's interpretation of the language of the text. He distinguishes between the "correct" and the "true" reading of a text. The correct reading is a static possession that is supposedly scientifically loyal to the textual and ideational language of a text. The true reading is fluid because it is achieved interpersonally, through a dialectical engagement between the existential situation of the reader and the language of the text.

Historical understanding in Bultmann's interpretative framework therefore expects that an interpreter will approach a text with dialectical presuppositions in mind. Whether this process is conscious or unconscious, it is constant.[10] This does not mean that an interpreter should have presuppositions with respect to results, so that the outcome of an inquiry is settled before the investigation begins. An interpreter, however, necessarily carries certain presuppositions with respect to method. "This means that I cannot understand a given text without asking certain questions of it."[11] The existential variables that govern this textual inquiry will influence how the text's language is ultimately understood. Bultmann labels these variables *preunderstanding* and *life-relation*.

Preunderstanding involves the interpersonal dialectic between interpreter and history. An interpreter cannot comprehend history, or, for that matter, a historical text, unless he or she acknowledges that part of himself/herself stands in history and is responsible for it. "We speak of this encounter with history that grows out of one's own historicity as the *existentiell* encounter. The historian participates in it with his whole existence."[12] This encounter becomes for Bultmann a fundamental presupposition for understanding history, or, in our case, historical text. And because the outcome of this dialectical encounter must be unique for every interpreter, every text interpretation must be existentially conditioned.[13]

The accompanying interpersonal variable is what Bultmann calls the life-relation. "You obtain the conceptions from your own psychical life. The resulting or corresponding presupposition of exegesis is that you do have a relation to the subject-matter (*Sache*)—in this case to the psychical life—about which you interrogate a given text. I call this relation the 'life-relation.'"[14] In other words, historical understanding for Bultmann presupposes a relationship of the interpreter to the subject matter expressed in a given text. This relationship gives the interpreter a unique perspective and consequent understanding of the matter discussed in the text. From such an understanding come the conceptions of exegesis. Bultmann claims that only with such a life-relation and the preunderstanding that works with it can one possibly expect to comprehend and interpret a text. "This is, then, the basic presupposition for every form of exegesis: that your own relation to the subject matter prompts the questions you bring to the text and elicits the answer you obtain from the text."[15] There can be no clearer assertion that interpretation of New Testament language is contingent on the existential context of the text interpreter. The process is intensely interpersonal.

The key sociolinguistic factors in Bultmann's program are thus preunderstanding and life-relation. These two elements are the identifiable variables that make text interpretation existentially—that is to say, contextually—contingent. These factors reach their logical interpretive conclusion in Bultmann's understanding that no text is fully understood until it has compelled personal response. In Bultmann's dialectical program the historical language of the New Testament meets us as an address that mandates decision. This category of response serves to heighten the uniqueness of the interpretative circumstance. Existentialism asserts that human existence is only real in the act of existing, that is to say, in the act of personal responsibility, openness to the future and decision in the face of it. Because such decision is necessary to understanding a text, and because it is personal, existential circumstance again becomes a critical component in text interpretation. Hearing, understanding, comprehending, Bultmann concludes, "can take place only in personal decision." We therefore understand the text by a combination of hearing it, responding to it, and living it. One's existential relation to the text remains critical. Bultmann suggests that we consider what happens when a text reader comes upon the New Testament language of love. "The existentialist analysis can do nothing more than make it clear to me that I can understand love only by loving. No analysis can take the place of my duty to understand my love as an encounter in my own personal existence." [16]

We are now able to consider Bultmann's program of existentialist interpretation directly in light of Halliday's three functional categories: textual, ideational, and interpersonal. While Bultmann operates in all three, it is the interpersonal that is critical to his work.

The textual category is the simplest to identify. Here we consider specifically the grammatical and syntactical components of a text. Bultmann's interpretative approach considers firm, critical textual inquiry a vital part of the investigative process. Indeed, his *History of the Synoptic Tradition* is a fine example of his primary concern for the textual function in the Synoptic materials. At this point he is not concerned about the incomprehensibility of myth to modern consciousness, but simply engages the language of the text in terms of its own grammatical setting. Syntactical considerations are primary here. Bultmann realizes that syntactic restraints limit the range of the text's meaning. Any interpretative conclusion, if it is to be scientifically accurate, must demonstrate recognition of those constraints. "It belongs to the historical method, of course, that a text is interpreted in accordance with the rules of grammar." [17]

The ideational category is more complicated. Here we contend that Bultmann must be considered on two levels. The first level identifies time-bound concepts—that is, meanings—in their original mythological setting. The second level seeks to establish the timeless concepts integral to the Christian kerygma that lie behind the mythical concepts. On the first ideational level, Bultmann recognizes that the cultural context of the producer of the text is mythological, and he seeks to understand how the producer uses and understands language mythologically.

On another level, he searches for the Christian kerygma that lies behind these mythological concepts. In this way he attempts to rescue the permanent conceptual truth of the gospel from a conceptual language that is tied to an obsolete worldview. To use Bultmann's own language, the critical distinction lies between the *Sache,* the subject matter, and the mythical concepts or ideas that are used to bring the *Sache* to expression. It is the *Sache* that transcends the limitations of historical time frames and can therefore be as meaningful to the modern reader as to the earliest readers of the New Testament. The words and ideas in which that *Sache* is encased are temporally limited.

While the second ideational level, which deals conceptually with Christian kerygma, the *Sache,* points us beyond myth, it is in the interpersonal phase that Bultmann's program comes to a climax. The three functions are connected for Bultmann. Indeed, one cannot fully understand what the text says today unless one first understands what it said in its own historical context.[18] But Bultmann wants the interpreter to note that understanding what the text said, even with regard to the kerygma, is only the beginning of the interpretative enterprise. To fully interpret a text, one must know what it says, and because it "says"—that is, speaks existentially—one's interpretation of a text is contextually conditioned. The interaction between an interpreter and his or her own existential communicative context, described as preunderstanding and life-relation, becomes the key factor in the interpretative conclusions reached. In fact, it is Bultmann's work on the second level of the ideational phase, that of the subject matter or *Sache,* that makes the interpersonal operational. "To hear the scriptures as the Word of God means to hear them as a word which is addressed to me, as *kerygma,* as a proclamation."[19] In this way, even though the words and ideas are conditioned historically, the Word, the kerygma, the subject matter that is contained within can be timeless and can become appropriate to any historical context in which it meets each individual. Thus, the existential factor may influence what the text means for the modern interpreter.

An element of our modern language also operates on Bultmann's first ideational level: the conceptual linguistic forms that encase meaning for us are also time bound. They operate meaningfully only in our life context, our culture, which is different from that accepted in the New Testament world. Conversely, we derive meaning only when we function within the linguistic boundaries of our familiar conceptual world. We are led, as interpreters, to reject the mythological concepts and embrace our own; we see the text in a manner different from what was intended. Therefore the conceptual-interpretative language must change if the *Sache* is to remain meaningful, because our context and our forms of conceptualization have changed. Bultmann does not counsel a mere changing of words so that text vocabulary more neatly approximates our own, but a broader recognition that the conceptual forms, the New Testament ideas themselves, such as resurrection and heaven, must be renegotiated in terms of the scientific thought of modern humanity. For the *Sache,* the subject matter expressed in those ideas, to remain constant and viable, it must be conceptually reoriented according to the parameters of the modern era. In other words, we need a new language because we have a new context. The new language is de-mythologization by existential interpretation.

## A Contextual Critique of Existential Interpretation

Ironically, Bultmann's program of demythologization by existential interpre-tation has been accused of the same kind of charge that he levels against the mythological language of the New Testament. Many of his critics argue that his program of demythologization in actuality remythologizes the keryg-matic *Sache* into a linguistic frame that, instead of being objective and univer-sal, is limited to Bultmann's own historical era. Bultmann's method absolut-izes "modern humanity," which is in reality humanity in the perspective of the post–World War I period, and then makes that existential foundation the ground on which all critical interpretation should be based. Just as mythical terms and ideas impede the ability of myths to describe transcendent control over the world and the humans who populate it because those terms and ideas are foreign to modern readers, so also Bultmann's existential language, itself a product of its period in history, has become an impediment to under-standing in what is often referred to as the postmodern era. In that respect it is therefore incorrect to say that Bultmann "remythologized" the New Testament. It would be better to say that in his decoding of the mythological language of the New Testament he recoded it in existential language.

Bultmann is nevertheless to be credited for having raised the issue. He was correct in recognizing that terms and ideas that are meaningful in one sociolinguistic context will lose their communicative value when the context of human reasoning changes. His mistake was in not recognizing to what degree his own sociolinguistic setting codetermined the meaning encoun-tered in the text and in that way recoded that meaning. He claimed that the existential interaction with the text produced a meaning that was indepen-dent of any particular setting. That may be correct. What he did not recog-nize was that other meanings could be produced interactively (interperson-ally) in altered sociolinguistic settings. Such meanings do not have to contradict the existential meaning established by Bultmann, but they reveal that the meaning of the New Testament cannot be limited interpersonally to the existential dimension established by him; an altered sociolinguistic context, without necessarily contradicting Bultmann's existential meanings, can produce other meanings as well through the interpersonal function of the New Testament texts. That is what occurred in Ernst Käsemann's critique of Bultmann's existential interpretation.

A summary of Käsemann's critique is instructive; he recognized that Bultmann's solution was only partially valid. Because mythology is prevalent in the New Testament, and because its terms and images are indeed foreign in the sociolinguistic context of the twentieth century, Käsemann acknowledges that demythologization in an existential mode is necessary. He points out the error of scholars who argue against this position. All New Testament investigators, he contends, see the need for demythologization in Revelation, but then many claim, inconsistently, that the process is unnecessary elsewhere in the New Testament. To the contrary, Käsemann raises the images of the virgin birth, the ascension, the descent into hell, and the story of the creation; all are key New Testament images and all are mythological.[20] The interpretative process that is necessary for Revelation is necessary throughout the New Testament, just as Bultmann asserted. The existentialist key to the demythologization process, Käsemann continues, has its own unique benefits in a modern historical context that is sociologically and linguistically foreign to mythology.

Käsemann, however, moves beyond Bultmann with his recognition that existentialism, while an indispensable method of modern interpretation, cannot be considered the exclusive means of text exposition. "Its drawback is that, although it enables one to see the historicity of man, it does not give an adequate view of world history. It will not do for us to reduce world history, as a matter of course, to the historicity of human existence."[21] In other words, although it is an interpersonal approach, it is interpersonally deficient. Its devaluation of history, itself a part of the theologically interpretative trend that occurred after World War I, was viewed suspiciously by Käsemann and those who followed his lead in returning to a stronger appreciation of the historical. In the pre– and post–World War II world that was dominated by a concern for history and for God's work and control in the social and political moments of history, the sociolinguistic context changed so dramatically that the method Bultmann figured was universal was shown to be contextually determined and therefore limited in scope. "The world is more than a web of personal relationships, as the experience of the twentieth century is making clear to everyone."[22] Even Revelation, Käsemann notes, the most mythological of the New Testament books, is concerned not just with the problem of human existence, but with world history as well. Therefore, any program of demythologization, while benefiting from existentialism, must also be politically and socially aware. With his re-emphasis on history Käsemann introduces a new element of sociolinguistic concern; in addition to the existential context, the sociopolitical:

> Man is not simply the agent and the subject of history, for as he unquestionably belongs to nature, so he is also the object and scene of history as it is enacted. His life is determined, not merely by the individual who meets him, but equally so by all the anonymous powers that we have to include within the larger concept of "world." We can no longer be so apolitical that we find it possible to regard world history as an abstract or even a mythological cypher of the historicity of man.[23]

Bultmann's work was an exceptional advance precisely because he recognized that while an interpreter must recognize textual and ideational factors, he or she must also extend, interpersonally, beyond them. He subsequently locked his own expansive thought within a self-imposed boundary, however; he limited his interpersonal consideration to existential data. The result, as Käsemann so deftly pointed out, was an incomplete and therefore insufficient interpretative process.

## The Transition from Existentialist to Sociopolitical Interpretation

Dorothee Soelle agrees with Käsemann in her critique of Bultmann's existential program of demythologization, but she contends that it is, paradoxically, Bultmann's apolitical, individualistic work that prepares the way for the political theologies that have arisen in the second half of the twentieth century. She points to several crucial concerns shared by the two methodologies.

The first concern is the way in which the life of Jesus is explored. As with existential analysis, so in political theology, Jesus' work is not to be *viewed;* the interpreter is counseled to concentrate on what Jesus purposed rather than to pontificate about who Jesus was. As with Bultmann, so with political theology, identity becomes secondary to purpose:

> It is not a matter of compiling in a biblicistic sense materials pertaining to the political activity of Jesus and using them to establish whether or not he was a revolutionary. The main thing is not to describe his concrete behavior and imitate it, but rather to discern the intention or tendency of that behavior and to realize anew his goals in our world.[24]

A second concern is the decision-oriented exegetical process that is so much a part of existential analysis. According to Bultmann, the investigator not only interprets the text according to the existential situation, but that very relationship between text and existential life situation compels an existential response. One determines the meaning of a text not only by bringing to it one's questions and concerns, but also through the process of responding to it. Christopher Rowland and Mark Corner contend that a similar program is active in a politicized move in text interpretation, at least with regard to the first two features of their method: "Its emphasis is on the threefold method: *see* (starting where one is with one's experience, which for the majority in Latin America means an experience of poverty), *judge* (understanding the reasons for that kind of existence and relating them to the story of deliverance from oppression in the Bible) and *act*."[25]

Finally, political theology, like existential interpretation, is concerned with what the text means for the modern interpreter. Here political theology is distinguished from Bultmann's method because the complementary feature—what the text meant in its own historical setting—is not characteristic. This lack of textual and ideational control often opens political theological text interpretations to the charge of subjectivity. Both interpretative moves contend that the clarification of how and what the text *means* for the present reader is the ultimate goal of the hermeneutical process. The distinction between the two methods lies in political theology's unwillingness to limit its understanding of history to the historicity of human existence. "Its [political theology's] method of exegesis would claim to be adopting Bultmann's approach to interpretation while removing the 'individualist constriction' which it perceives in the particular tools that he advocated."[26] In other words, it pushes beyond Bultmann's existential/interpersonal boundaries.

Because of these parallels, Soelle concludes, "More and more it appears to me that the move from existentialist theology to political theology is itself a consequence of the Bultmannian position."[27] Such a recognition not only demonstrates the lasting value of Bultmann's work in raising the interpersonal feature in New Testament interpretation, but it also provides a basis for showing that political theology is not an aberrant form of exegesis. It traces both its identity and its contextual concern to a well-established and epochal form of New Testament interpretation.

Soelle makes the connection more explicit when she takes up one of Bultmann's key sociolinguistic factors, that of preunderstanding. The belief that an interpreter's preunderstanding will influence how that interpreter comprehends the language in the text is a fundamental principle for both political theology and existential interpretation. The critical difference between the two methodologies lies in how each perceives the content of this preunderstanding. Soelle contends that the *existentielle* preunderstanding that was appropriate for Bultmann was limited to his post–World War I world. A new preunderstanding has arisen in the latter half of the twentieth century. This difference explains why the two methods reach dissimilar interpretative conclusions. According to Soelle, while political theology recognizes that the question about individual existence must still be entertained, it also demands that the social context of the interpreter be considered. She argues that in the preunderstanding of Bultmann's historical generation, social evils were a fated given; one therefore dealt with concerns of individual rather than social transformation. But now the interpreter, owing to a change in the social worldview, employs a different preunderstanding that includes two key tenets. First, individual existence is inseparable from societal context. Second, the world need no longer tolerate social evil. The end result is the construction of a interpretative mechanism that recognizes that societal transformation is not only necessary but possible.

Ironically, then, a political theology that envisions redemption as transformation of the world is built on the same interpretative structure as Bultmann's. The difference lies in the fact that the sociolinguistic context—what Soelle refers to as the new preunderstanding—has changed. Bultmann's method is not only determined by sociolinguistic considerations, we now find that it is also transformed by them.

When Rowland and Corner conclude "Where one is determines to a large extent how a book is read,"[28] they are making an interpretative claim that is as valid for Bultmann as it is for the "liberating exegesis" they discuss. Liberating exegesis, however, is politicized because it takes the historical context of the reader seriously. Therefore, persons who are socially and economically oppressed find in a text different meanings than those argued by professional exegetes. Their interpretative conclusions are not unified, but differ according to the particular social circumstances of the various biblical interpreters or interpretative groups. Thus one witnesses today not *a* political theology, but political theologies, each of which actualizes a life-relation and preunderstanding appropriate to its specific sociological, historical, and existential context. As for Bultmann so also for the more recent political theologies, text interpretation is fundamentally a matter of sociolinguistics.

Because the methodological programs are so similar, the interpretative trap that snared Bultmann also threatens those who recognize the significance of sociohistorical contexts for language interpretation. Even after realizing how critical context is to interpretation, Bultmann still believed he could objectively interpret the biblical language through a universally understood direct speech. The temptation for the political theologies is similar. Recognition that context plays a role in the interpretation of the language of a text is no guarantee that an interpreter will recognize that an interpretation based on his or her specific sociolinguistic context cannot be considered universally normative. This is often the case when interpreters discuss textual matters without making the reader aware of sociolinguistic factors radically different from those operative in the work at hand. Such factors would not only imply, but virtually guarantee, different interpretative conclusions. The truths ascertained by feminist, black, Latin American, and other political theologies today are in this manner only partial manifestations of truth. In and of themselves they are sociolinguistically limited, as was Bultmann's work.

Each of these works, however, expands on the efforts of a strictly historical-critical or a literary method, which fall unrepentant into this same trap. Whereas Bultmann sought direct speech in existential language, the historical-critical and literary methods seek direct speech through their textual and ideational controls. Because one cannot control how a text *means* in the present, the interpreter is counseled to consider only what the text *meant* in the past or what it means within the constraints of literary, grammatical, and ideational boundaries. By limiting the meaning to the textual and ideational spheres, many historical-critical and literary practitioners assume that a single meaning in the text can be apprehended. This exclusive conclusion denies the validity of interpretative conclusions that value the interaction between text and sociolinguistic context in the attempt to understand what the text *means* in the present.

But even here, with all the sophisticated linguistic and historical controls available, sociolinguistic context skews the results. The interpreter's background still influences how the language of the text is understood. Bultmann, himself a skilled practitioner in the textual and ideational arenas of the historical-critical method, demonstrates the problem. One's sociohistorical context influences what one sees in the language. Every investigative exercise, historical-critical and literary included, has a powerful interpersonal component. Only when that component is acknowledged can one begin the process of controlling it, not through the establishment of a direct speech, but through an awareness that one's interpretative conclusions are sociolinguistically biased. Such an awareness induces an investigator to invite, and subsequently accept analectically, input from other sociolinguistic perspectives.

# 3 The Gospel in Solentiname

THE GOSPEL IN SOLENTINAME IS A COLLEC-
tion of discussions of Gospel texts by Nicaraguan peasants, *campesinos,* living in the small
Christian community of Solentiname on Lake
Nicaragua. Their ideas are expressed in discussions that were gathered by Ernesto Cardenal, under whose leadership the discussions
took place. Extracts have been put together
with paintings done in 1981 and 1982 by
peasants who returned there after the Sandinista revolution.[1] It is an excellent example of
a popular political interpretation of the Bible.
Viewed from the perspective of Nicaraguan
peasantry, the language of the biblical text
takes on powerful sociopolitical implications.
The pictures, which illustrate scenes from the
Gospels, do so in a way that identifies the
leading characters in the biblical events with
leading figures in the events that led up to the
1979 Sandinista revolution against Anastasio
Somoza Debayle. "For example, in a painting
illustrating the massacre of the innocents
(Matt. 2.16), we see soldiers in the uniform of
Somoza's National Guard. They carry auto-
matic weapons, not swords."[2] The peasant
community in Solentiname identified its own
experience of struggle with the experiences of
those who struggled in the biblical texts; they
interpret the texts in that light: "The argu-

ment is that a community with experience of persecution, exile and torture is justified in representing the biblical story in terms of its own environment precisely because of a historical correspondence between its own life and that of the Jesus movement in its early days." [3]

The emphasis here is on what the text *means*. The biblical text is important, not only because the meaning is indigenous to its own historical context, but because that historical meaning has relevance for their present political circumstances. Otherwise the text is a foreign entity, meaningless for their situation, impotent with regard to their sociopolitical predicament. "The people must see the possibility of their going to the Bible from within their own journey to receive it today as living Word of God." [4] The painting that depicts the shepherds of Bethlehem visiting the newborn Christ-child is illustrative. [5] The surroundings, a thatched-roof hut and lush vegetation, are those of Solentiname. The characters' dress mimics that of the Solentiname peasantry. The effect of this artistic recontextualization is that the Christ-child is born to, and has liberating meaning for, the people of Solentiname in the same manner that he had meaning for the poor of first-century Palestine. The poor receive the good news. The story lives not as a memorable moment in past history, but as an ongoing revelation in the life of these twentieth-century poor.

The peasants, even though they are unskilled in the theoretical discussion of Ernst Käsemann, would support Käsemann's contention that history should be taken seriously in an interpersonal, interpretative process. Their history of poverty and consequent oppression become the key lens through which their commentary on the text is focused. But Rudolf Bultmann's technique is likewise evident. The peasants realize that because they are involved in history, they cannot simply view it, but must see themselves in dialogue with it. Their dialogue with the biblical tradition produces a reading that is alive, a reading that engages the text with their own questions in such a way that the historical text sheds light on their present existence. Precisely because they take their historical context seriously, existential circumstances become for them a sociopolitical reality; they push themselves beyond Bultmann's limitations.

## Meaning Discovered or Imposed?

A potential problem with such an interpretative method is that the community may be tempted to create meaning based on its sociolinguistic reality and subsequently impose that meaning on the text. A consideration of the peasant's discussion of "The Alabaster Bottle" (Matt. 26:6-13) is illustrative. [6] The *campesinos* struggle when they try to interpret a passage that portrays the disciples' anger at a woman's waste of ointment when she uses it to anoint Jesus. "Why this waste?" the disciples ask, "This could have been sold for much money to help the poor."[7] It is not the disciples' reply that is a problem but Jesus' defense of the woman's action, namely his statement that the poor will always be around. The text is in disagreement with the peasants' belief that it is unacceptable behavior to present luxuries to individuals when the poor are suffering. To circumvent the obvious dilemma, one peasant envisions Jesus as a symbol of all poor even though there is no direct textual evidence to support such a conclusion: "when she offered it to Jesus, she was giving it, in his person, to all the poor."[8] The ointment was therefore not wasted, but became an illustrative example of giving one's finest material goods to help all who are in need. When a student from Managua challenges such an interpretation,[9] the *campesinos* continue to struggle with the issue. When another peasant suggests that the disciples will have all the time they need, later, to help the poor, but that now they must help Jesus, both he and his reference to Jesus' words that "you will always have the poor with you, but you will not always have me" are labeled "stupid" by another peasant. The peasants are understandably concerned about the conception that there will always be poor people. Such a statement fatalistically implies that a transformation based on societal justice, which their revolutionary text interpretation both suggests and encourages, will never come. In that way Jesus appears to be on the side of the modern-day oppressor. Cardenal notes in the discussion, "That's what the reactionaries say. That even though there may be a lot of progress in humanity there'll always be a difference between rich and poor."[10]

The peasants then try to mold their interpretation of the text to fit their revolutionary program. A student proclaims, "I've got it! He says 'among you.' He's referring to *them* [the disciples], but that doesn't mean there'll never fail to be poor; he's not talking to all of humanity." Finally, Cardenal must recognize that Jesus' statement is at odds with the Solentiname interpretative perspective. "And it seems to me that's not a good prophecy of Jesus, and that it contradicts his announcement of the Kingdom of heaven, saying that we'd always have beggars with us." He therefore returns to a variation of the first peasant's explanation of the statement, the one for which there is no direct textual evidence. Jesus becomes a representative of all the poor, and the woman's actions therefore become laudatory rather than problematic. "What the woman was doing with him, they'd have to do later with the poor, because he wasn't going to be there any longer, or rather, we were going to have his presence in the poor." The correct—or, we might say, forcefully corrected—interpretation of Jesus' remark is therefore, "there will always be poor people as long as Jesus isn't here. But when there's only equality and justice, and no needy, no beggars, Jesus will be with us again."[11] Here is a good example where the interpretative conclusions are forcibly molded to fit the sociolinguistic needs of the community. Textual and ideational controls have been overridden in favor of interpersonal demands. Instead of moving beyond the boundaries, the peasants in this case have destroyed them. The result is an inadequate and problematic interpretative conclusion.

## Frames of Reference

In most cases, however, Cardenal acts as a corrective to such tendencies, supplying the textual and ideational information that limits the peasants' interpersonal interpretative range. Cardenal demonstrates little concern for syntactic and grammatical complexities. He thus begins his work at the ideational level. He explains Greek and Hebrew terminology and discusses probable meaning of words for first-century readers. For example, in the discussion of the annunciation, Luke 1:26-36, he delivers a mini-commentary on the name *Jesus* that the angels gives to Mary. Appealing to the Hebrew, he notes that the name is usually translated "Savior" or "Salvation." He defines *Jeshua* as "Yahweh liberates" or "Yahweh is liberation."[12] In discussing John the Baptist's use of the term *repent*, Luke 3:1-20, he considers the Greek word μετάνοια and instructs that it signified conversion.[12] He is equally helpful with the term *baptism*, which the *campesinos* came upon in Luke 3:21-23, the text about Jesus' baptism. In order to set the parameters of discussion before the peasants begin to talk, he clarifies that the word meant "bath." He further comments that it was a purification rite used by the Jews and other peoples as a sign of ritual cleansing.[13] He opens the discussion of the wedding at Cana, John 2:1-12, by explaining that the enigmatic words Jesus uses in response to his mother's request to do something about the lack of wine—"Woman, why do you tell that to me?"—are strong words such as those that appear in lawsuits or when someone is being injured by another. He therefore translates them colloquially as "Stop bugging me."[15] He explains that the Eucharist receives its imagery from the Greek verb εὐχαριστέω (to give thanks).[16] And most helpfully he demonstrates the radicality in Jesus' speech about God when he gives the background to the use of the Aramaic *Abba*, which he translates as "papa," a designation used by a child for its father.[17]

Cardenal best demonstrates his prowess in ideational principles when he carefully instructs his hearers about biblical concepts as they were understood by first-century readers. To emphasize this feature he explains the historical context in which the ideas circulated, and he demonstrates how, through the Gospel writers' use of literary positioning, the meaning of a text must be understood in light of its immediate literary context. He is, for example, knowledgeable about Old Testament influence on the early Christian understanding of key religious concepts. While discussing the Johannine prologue, John 1:1-18, he explains the incarnational statement about the Word by appealing to the Old Testament imagery of God's tent pitched in the midst of the people. "And it recalls the time of the exodus when the Jews lived in tents. It means that with Christ God began to live in the midst of our camp."[18] His discussion of the annunciation provides further illustration. After explaining that the angel's greeting to Mary, "Hail Mary," is now thought by scholars to be a congratulatory statement, "I congratulate you, Mary," he goes on to explain how the prophets often congratulated "the daughter of Zion" (the people of Israel) because she would give birth to a messiah.[19] Jesus' humility is highlighted as Cardenal points out that Nazareth, the name of his home town and the basis for his nickname Nazarene, was considered of such little importance in the Old Testament that it was never mentioned there.[20] Jesus' sign of changing water into wine at the Cana wedding is given clearer focus when Cardenal explains the Old Testament prophecy that the messianic era would be like a wedding feast where wine would be the drink of choice.[21] In discussing the temple cleansing scene in Matthew 21:12-17, Cardenal explains that Jesus' statement that God's temple should be a house of prayer combined two quotations from prophets Jeremiah and Isaiah.[22]

Broader historical context and a clarifying frame of reference are just as important for Cardenal. Discussing the concept of idolatry, he considers it in the contextual terms of the Israelite people and the devotees of religions prominent during Jesus' time.[23] In order to explain more adequately the symbolism that surrounded Herod's massacre of children after Jesus' birth, he details the historical situation that surrounded Herod's Roman-sponsored reign, which was filled with paranoia.[24] The concept of the holy is clarified through its connection with the Jewish definition of "God's presence among us."[25] The temple cleansing is conceptually clarified by a discursus that explains the process of religious buying and selling that was common at the time.[26]

Cardenal is not alone in demonstrating a sensitivity for what the biblical concepts meant in their historical settings. At many points in the discussions the peasants show that they understand the conceptual background against which the Gospel writers were creating their kerygmatic portraits. It is certain that they understood the term *messiah* in light of its Old Testament context, where it signified for the Jewish populace of the time a political as well as a religious figure.[27] In discussing Jesus' stay in the temple when he was twelve, they demonstrate that they understand the concept of religious ritual that the Gospel writers portrayed so negatively. "He went to the temple to teach the teachers of the law, because these teachers knew the law by heart but they didn't put it into practice."[28]

In this way Cardenal and the *campesinos* demonstrate that they have a sense of the biblical concepts in the context in which they originally surfaced. Discussions on the incarnation, the Word, the messiah, justice, the Eucharist, faith, the reign of God, and resurrection are all conducted in relation to their original Old Testament and historical contexts before they are discussed in the light of the community's present situation. It is apparently Cardenal's belief that only when the concepts are understood in and of themselves can they be effectively translated into potent present images:

> There is no doubt that they all come to the text with a previous knowledge of the tradition, especially the tradition of a Messiah who brings a kingdom, a new time of love, justice, and human brotherhood. The theologian who is present will bring in, during the process, several selections from the Hebrew Scriptures that the community apparently does not know. Thus the tradition to which they turn is not an episodic anecdote, a story without a context. The *campesinos* of Solentiname and their theologian work with the tradition as history.[29]

## Interpersonal Dimensions

It is, however, in the interpersonal arena, both quantitatively and qualitatively, that *The Gospel in Solentiname* makes its interpretative case. The bulk of the conversations view the text from the present perspective of the *campesinos,* and it is during these discussions that the peasants and Cardenal exhibit the greatest creative proficiency. We begin our analysis by considering how Bultmann's categories of preunderstanding and life-relation serve as the interpretative foci for the Solentiname *campesinos.* We must keep in mind, however, the counsel of Ernst Käsemann and Dorothee Soelle, which suggests that in political theologies like the one that arises out of Solentiname, preunderstanding affirms the possibility of societal transformation, and life-relation acknowledges present historical context as seriously as it does the historicity of human experience. In Solentiname, biblical discussions are more practical than theoretical:

> It is unimaginable to see the community of Solentiname bent over the task of grasping the absolute, ahistorical truth about Christology, soteriology, theological anthropology: questions which with regularity assault the middle class in its Bible studies which lack a historical perspective. Because of the dominant character of the historical process which they live, the peasants of Solentiname have selective eyes and relevant objectives.[30]

It is this dominant character of their own unique historical process that serves as the sociological context critically influencing how they interpret the language of the biblical text. Their life-relation to the text is one of extreme poverty. They do not, however, accept their economic lot as a fate that can be overturned only in some future and otherworldly reign of God. It is their understanding that society can be transformed through political and revolutionary activism. Wealth is seen as an illegitimate possession that has been achieved at the expense of the poor and is used as a weapon against them. Thus capitalism, the socioeconomic reality of modern Western nations, which has been transplanted into Nicaragua via the Somoza regime, is condemned in favor of a Marxist communism that calls for an equitable distribution of all possessions among the citizenry. Throughout the four volumes of *The Gospel in Solentiname,* the *campesinos* speak of themselves as the poor of their society who must take it upon themselves, with others who share their economic lot, to restructure their society, no matter the cost. Not only does this mind-set influence how they read the Bible, but they believe it is their perceived connection with Jesus' revolutionary work with and for the poor that mandates their cause in the present. Their situation connects with Jesus' in such a way that his work inspires their revolutionary thought and activity; subsequently, the resultant thought and activity become the lens through which the people further understand Jesus' life and times:

> The words of the peasants as they reflect together on the gospel flesh out the Good News in the context of their own historical experience. Just as the poverty and oppression of his people called Jesus to challenge the structures of his society, so too, these elements in their lives call the people of Nicaragua into the arena of political/economic activity.[31]

In Bultmann's terms, updated historically by Käsemann and politically by Soelle, we might therefore suggest that the key life-relation for the peasants of Solentiname was their status as the economically oppressed poor of society. It was their preunderstanding that this lot was not to be accepted fatalistically, but was to be challenged with the same kind of revolutionary fervor demonstrated by Jesus in his words and actions on behalf of the poor of the first century. These are the operative interpersonal factors in their interpretative process.

This conclusion is verified visually in the pictorial presentations that accompany the interpretative dialogues. Consider again the painting depicting Jesus' birth.[32] Mythological, miraculous effects are absent—the text is successfully demythologized—and yet a kind of encoding is going on, one that has a particular political flavor. Mary and Joseph are dressed like the Nicaraguan *campesinos.* The baby is naked; no clothing for it is visible. The stable, which looks like a Nicaraguan thatched-roof hut, is populated by horses, cows, and birds, the kinds of animals native to Solentiname. The picture conveys the sense of abject poverty. There is little sense of celebration; there is every indication that survival is conditioned by struggle. In the text that inspired the drawing, we are told that Mary and Joseph stayed in the hut, not because there were no vacancies in the inns, but because poor people were unacceptable in the hotels of the time. The reader has the sense of people who are discriminated against because of their station in life. Poor, dirty, and showing little indication of having the monetary resources necessary to pay for lodging, Mary and Joseph find that everywhere they go, no one has any room *for people like them.* From the start, then, Jesus identifies with people like the *campesinos.* "He came to share the lot of the poor. And Joseph and Mary were turned away from the inn because they were poor. If they'd been rich they'd have been welcomed in." This image of rejection, of a naked infant lying among the animals because his parents were oppressed by unjust economic conditions, not only identifies Jesus with the poor, but also so enlightens him regarding the plight of the poor that he turns his energies toward improving their lot. He works for change because he believes society must and can be changed: "He was the greatest revolutionary, because being God he identified with the poor and he came down from heaven to become a member of the lower class and he gave his life for us all. The way I see it, we all ought to struggle like that for other people and be like him."[33]

Even the Spirit of God is identified with the poor of Solentiname. In the picture that describes the annunciation, once again we witness demythologization and political conceptualization.[34] The Spirit is not identified as a dove, or in some other form of mythical dress. The Spirit is another person, dressed like Mary in the clothing of Solentiname peasantry. The interaction is a fully human one, a purely political one. It is a poor human being inspired by the Spirit, who comes to human interaction in the physical guise of the economically dispossessed.

This trend of demythologization in terms of the mythical and encoding in terms of the political is also evident in the peasants' dialogues. Consider the angel who brings the good news of a savior's birth to the poor shepherds of Bethlehem. "The angel is any idea, any inspiration that you get in the woods when you're there cutting wood, like Felix says, any idea about doing something for other people, for the community." Another peasant concludes, "maybe right now when we're reading this and hearing these words the angel is coming to give us the news."[35] A similar transformation takes place when the star of Bethlehem, which led the wise men to the infant in a manger, is perceived as the talk of the townspeople who spread a great news that ultimately reaches as far as the ears of those Eastern luminaries.[36]

This procedure extends even to the understanding of the Christ-child. The holy infant, in the scene that describes Herod's vain attempt to murder him with all the other newborns of Bethlehem, is perceived as a revolutionary idea that the authorities attempt, always unsuccessfully, to quash before it gains size and stature. "Another thing: The revolutionary conscience in these countries is still a child. It's still tiny. And they persecute it so that it won't grow."[37]

This life-relation of poverty and an accompanying preunderstanding that societal revolution on behalf of the poor is both necessary and effective become the interpretative keys that influence how the textual language of the Gospels is understood. Biblical concepts take on a different meaning. Both the terms and ideas now convey understandings based more on what the text *means* than what it *meant*. Sociolinguistic context, in other words, affects, in a fundamental way, the community's interpretation of the biblical language. Fernando speaks for the entire community when he says, "And I also think that for a long time we have been misreading the Gospel, interpreting in a purely spiritual sense, eliminating all its political and social circumstances, which are certainly very dramatic; that is, we have abstracted the Gospel from its reality." Later he concludes, "I don't understand how you can read the Gospels and get spiritual lessons for your life out of it and not get involved in the Revolution. This Book has a very clear political position for anyone that reads it simply."[38] This, of course, is the critical element. To read the text "simply" is to read it through the eyes of one's own reality, without the foreign sophistication of a historical-critical or literary method that often prevents one from understanding what the text really and simply *means*. The simple reality here is poverty.

## The Subversive Design of Love

Although we do not have the space here to consider all of the reinterpreted terms and ideas in light of the new sociolinguistic context, a consideration of some key concepts will illustrate how context influences interpretation in Solentiname. Sin probably receives the most dramatic reconceptualization. It is no longer merely a spiritual crime that reflects disobedience before God; it becomes instead a fully operational social aberration. The *campesinos* call it selfishness. This selfishness is not some theoretical absolute; it is a dialectic, interpersonal reality that describes those in society who hoard what they have, which is more than they need, while others go wanting. For the *campesinos* the reality of this sin is embodied in the story of the rich man and Lazarus, Luke 16:19–31. The rich man is condemned because he is happy and content in his wealth while the poor are suffering. "The rich man's sin," Gloria remarks, "was that he had no compassion. Poverty was at his door and that didn't disturb him at his parties." Felipe agrees: "The rich man [was] damned for having squandered selfishly."[39] This reality is graphically portrayed in an accompanying painting where the rich figure eats with blind contentment while a bleeding and presumably starving Lazarus stands directly in his line of sight.[40] Yet the interpretation of the *campesinos* does not end here. They suggest that the text should no longer be read as an opiate for the poor, as if Jesus is trying to tell those who suffer the selfishness of others on earth that they must wait for heaven where justice will be served. Instead, the peasants contend that the story is designed for the ears of the rich. It is not a placation and a call to endurance for the poor; it is, rather, a striking condemnation of the rich, and a call that the poor should overthrow them.

This kind of selfishness feeds a religion based on ritual rather than compassion and concern for others. The painting of the story about the Good Samaritan makes this clear.[41] The priest and his two companions represent the established, ritualistic church in both Jesus' time and the Nicaragua of the 1970s. The road they walk leads unmistakably toward a village church whose steeple is the prominent feature of the tiny municipal skyline. The priest knows there is a problem behind them; he is looking back, even as he moves forward toward the church. He cannot be deterred from his religious destination. Only the Samaritan, the outsider, who is dressed in the marginalized clothing of Solentiname poverty, stops and gives aid. The very one who has little, shares what he does have. The others, represented by the priest and Levites and the church toward which they walk, are the images of selfishness. They are the sins of ritualistic religion that knows no compassion and therefore does not share its time or resources.

This sin of selfishness is responsible for the economic oppression experienced by the poor, and therefore becomes the target at which all revolutionary activity should be aimed. The new society that comes about as a result of a successful revolutionary effort will be exemplified by love rather than sin. Love, too, is defined interpersonally, as the opposite of selfishness; it is sharing. This sharing creates a just community of equal resources. "So it's the spirit of justice, because it's Love. The spirit of social justice, the spirit of change, Revolution. Jesus was born from this spirit."[42] A society based on the socially just ethic of sharing is one in which all people have not only equal opportunity, but also equal resources. This kind of society is symbolized by the kind of community Jesus established when he multiplied the loaves in Luke 9:10-17:

> They didn't have enough—right?—to feed the five thousand people. But then he says to them: It doesn't matter, share it. And there was more than enough!

He made them understand that no matter how little they had they had to share it. And they shared it, and with his power he made it stretch out. The lesson is that no matter how little we have we always have to give.[43]

When one has more than one needs, or even if one is poor and has little, one gives it, shares it, with someone who has less.

Because this kind of society cannot be expected to be brought about through the benevolent designs of the selfish persons who hold present societal power, the poor must unite and, through revolutionary activity, create it. This, then, becomes the basis for an interpretative rereading of the Eucharist, Mark 14:12-25. Jesus knew there would be a certain person in Jerusalem with a jug of water who would point the disciples toward the upper room when they identified themselves as followers of the master; this is an indication for the *campesinos* that Jesus had made advance plans for a hiding place. He had worked out a password, and he had planned to stay in hiding until all was prepared. The supper, based as it was on the Passover, which is commemorative of Jewish liberation, was a politically charged, subversive event:

> That Eucharist was a clandestine supper, and besides, some of them were armed. . . . The Passover supper was a commemoration of the Exodus, the liberation of the people and there Jesus is beginning another Exodus, another liberation. And an authentic Eucharist, as long as there's injustice, has to be more or less underground. Like this one that we're celebrating today.[44]

The Eucharist represents the ultimate sharing, Jesus giving his body and blood for the cause of liberating the poor and oppressed. His action, previewed symbolically in the supper, is viewed by the *campesinos* as a representation of Jesus' subversive behavior, which in turn calls for revolutionary behavior today. "But this feast was not to be a mere remembrance of the past. It was rather so that they would keep in mind that the same strength that freed them in the past would go on freeing them in the future from other imperialisms and also from internal oppressions, class struggles."[45]

This revolutionary imaging is presented pictorially in the drawing of the parable about the sower and his seeds.[46] The sower throws seeds in many places, but most of the picture represents rows upon rows of cultivated and ordered vegetation. Symbolically, society is a well landscaped, structured phenomenon. The seeds that will bring life, because they are planted haphazardly rather than in the prescribed rows, will, if they survive, interrupt the order that is already present. The effect is subversive, the conception is revolutionary.

The new society based on the subversive design of love as sharing is the reign of God (heaven) that dawns on earth as a present reality initiated by the revolutionary activity of the poor. The reign is no longer merely a divinely activated eschatological reality; it is expected that its arrival can only be precipitated by the concerted efforts of the people who operate in love. This reign will be characterized by the quality of love that will live itself out in the practical dimensions of equality and justice, which is always described in economic terms. In fact, economic justice will bring about an equality that will know no disparity between incomes of people. Economic classes will no longer exist. This picture conjures up the image of communism, and this is indeed the intention of the Solentiname *campesinos*. For them communism is a biblical concept; it is the form of societal existence preferred in the reign of heaven. When Jesus talks about the reign, about a community based on sharing and just love, he is, according to the *campesinos*, in reality talking about communism. Julio remarks, "The communists have preached what the Gospel preached, that people should be equal and that they all should live as brothers and sisters. Laureano is speaking of the communism of Jesus Christ." Rebeca agrees. "If we come together as God wishes, yes. Communism is an equal society. The word 'communist' means community. And so if we all come together as God wishes, we are all communists, all equal." [47]

Given the inequities and injustices prevalent in later-day manifestations of communist societies, it seems clear that a dialectical process has occurred. The peasants are not only interpreting the Bible out of their situation, they are understanding and interpreting their present political aspirations out of their communal situation as it is biblically processed. Their understanding of communism is refracted through a biblical lens. In the painting that depicts the crowds watching Jesus bear his cross, one of the poor holds a placard that proclaims Jesus as a communist revolutionary who is persecuted by the reactionary powers of Somoza's capitalist regime. [48] Because those who hold economic power do not want to relinquish that power, they reject Jesus, just as they reject those who at present operate in his image. Disciples of Jesus, as was Jesus himself, are therefore correctly seen as revolutionaries. Successful change can only be brought about through the sacrifices and struggles endemic to revolutionary behavior.

In this scheme the incarnation is no longer purely a christological matter. Understood interpersonally, it receives an orientation of justice; it is the materialization of a flesh-and-blood anger at economic injustice. Its very occurrence is therefore ultimately a signal for revolution. [49] God's Word, become flesh, is the realization of God's message about love that creates the community of sharing that is the reign of heaven. Because the messiah is the one who will inaugurate this reign, he is seen as a sociopolitical liberator, and the salvation he brings, a rescue from the sin of selfishness, is envisioned politically as well. In discussing Luke 2:8-20, particularly the text that reads, "to you is born this day in the city of David a Savior, who is Christ the Lord," Felix remarks:

> He's making it clear that it's for them [the poor, represented by the shepherds] that he's coming. It seems to me that they were like slaves and when they heard that a liberator was coming they were filled with joy. . . . They know that this birth was going to free them from slavery. . . . He was coming to liberate all slaves, all poor people, not just poor people of that time but those of today too![50]

Resurrection, the movement from death to life, is consequently reconceptualized politically as a rising from the death of economic oppression into a communist reign here on earth. Because Jesus worked toward these ends, so must the peasants in Solentiname. "And when there's justice throughout the earth there will come the resurrection of the dead. The error of twenty centuries of Christianity has been to believe that we can obtain the kingdom of heaven without changing the world."[51]

For this people who are bitterly oppressed by economic injustice, the Scriptures are understood as God's Word, which not only identifies with their plight, but suggests the kind of revolutionary activity necessary to change it. They truly believe that this revolutionary activity will be successful. Faith itself has become politically charged. Speaking about Jesus' calming of the storm, Mark 4:35-41, Don Tomas remarks, "Then he calmed the weather and calmed the lake, to teach them that with him they shouldn't be afraid. And so we too must have faith in all of us united, because in a community there is God. And with that faith we can make it so that in the world everything will be better." Elvis, another *campesino* agrees, "As I see it, faith is very important—the faith that we can change this world we live in. Anybody who doesn't have faith is screwed."[52]

Our discussion of the interpretations of the *campesinos* has shown how the biblical texts function as powerful hermeneutical tools in their self-understanding, providing them strength and encouragement. One would have to add that little self-critique is seen here. Their interpretations give almost no attention to the textual features of the text, but they are keenly aware of ideational features. Encouraged by Cardenal in their interpretations, they are aware of the distance between biblical times and their own. They have few interpretative tools, however, to enable them to give substantial attention to this recognition. But that is not the function of their interpretations. They are not concerned to provide historical-critical interpretations of the text, but are *engaged in* the texts. The texts become alive for them in a way they do not for scholarly interpretations, notwithstanding the concerns of Bultmann and Käsemann. Bultmann would probably have found little in these interpretations to agree with ideationally, but the ways in which the texts become alive in the Solentiname interpretations are remarkable examples of the realization of Bultmann's interpersonal concerns. The limited attention given to textual and ideational factors would certainly have an effect on the degree to which approval might be given to the details of these interpretations, but the fact remains that in these interpretations something of great interpersonal value takes place.

# 4 The Negro Spiritual

THE HISTORICAL SITUATION OF THE AFRICAN slaves in the United States conditioned the imagery and meaning of their music, in what were called "slave songs." One can understand the meaning of the music accurately only if one takes seriously the conditions that prompted it. In fact, although many of the songs were composed after the proclamation of emancipation, the condition of slavery remained the key inspiration.[1] The spiritual is an interpretative response to that particular human circumstance.[2]

The world of the black slave begins with the pain and sorrow of the Middle Passage. By even the most conservative of estimates, more than 50 million Africans perished during the centuries of American slave trading that began in 1619 when the first slave arrived on American soil. This human holocaust was the preamble to a life of perpetual misery for the individual African. Those who survived it subsequently sung of an existence so vicious that life, rather than death, became the great existential threat. "The wild sad strains tell, as the sufferers themselves never could, of crushed hopes, keen sorrow, and a dull daily misery which covered them as hopelessly as the fog from the rice-swamps."[3] The auction block decimated family relationships. Fifteen-

and twenty-hour work days debilitated the human physique. Beatings for fatigue or lack of respect crushed the spirit. In the law a slave was only three-fifths human, and the Supreme Court of the United States declared with constitutional finality that blacks had no rights that white persons were bound to respect. No wonder that W. E. B. DuBois could declare that "[the spirituals] are the music of an unhappy people, of the children of disappointment."[4]

The spiritual is not, however, a symbolic and passive acceptance of the slave's societal conditions. It is also an interpretative response to those conditions. The spiritual sings not only of degradation, but also of hope, of endurance as well as deprivation. It does not receive the historical circumstance complacently; instead it begins with that circumstance and reaches beyond it for an interpretative tool that can provide the possible parameters of hope even in the midst of despair.

## Slave Reality and the Bible

The interpretative move is from experience to biblical image, not the other way around. The slaves' critical starting point is their historical human circumstance. The biblical images become a means of understanding and enduring the pivotal reality that is their present moment. In other words, they do not first read the Bible, or speak of its images, and then interpret those images through their experience, as was done in Solentiname. They begin with the horrors of their experience and then interpret those horrors through their understanding of biblical images. Their key intent is not so much to understand the Bible as it is to understand their historical circumstance. The Bible becomes an interpretative means rather than an interpretative end.

The result is a true hermeneutical circle. The slave begins with his or her existence and the need to interpret it. The interpretation is done through song. But secular songs are insufficient to the task. Music, in and of itself, while helpful, was found to be of limited interpretative value. Further assistance was needed; the slaves found such assistance in images drawn from the Christian Bible. At this point the ideational component comes clearly into focus.

The Bible, however, was already being used by the slave owners as a mechanism to produce slave docility.[5] Biblical images therefore required further and "corrected" ideational interpretation if they were to be used in a serviceable way by slaves. Because the slaves were illiterate and uneducated in the nuances of biblical science, they had but one interpretative lens through which they instinctively analyzed the Bible: their own historical experience. Their circumstances pushed them beyond the ideational bound-

aries set for the text by white Christianity into an interpersonal engagement
with that text. The use of biblical concepts, in the final analysis, was therefore subjected to interpersonal rather than ideational control. Biblical language, in the form of conceptual ideas, was not simply used because it was
biblical—and therefore somehow sacred—but because it helped to bring
meaning and understanding to their sociohistorical circumstance.

The "texts" the slaves drew upon were orally transmitted Bible stories.
The fact that the spiritual is an oral phenomenon opens it all the more to
contextual influence; the literary controls that exist in written works are
absent. Contextual influence on the spiritual's interpretative process begins
at the moment of creative conception. The music and its accompanying
words, in order to interpret effectively the historical moment, adapt themselves to that moment. James Miller McKim, who visited blacks on the sea
islands of South Carolina in 1862, had the opportunity to see how the spiritual was created spontaneously, out of the harshness of present experience,
as a kind of responsive group-speak. The spiritual is not song sung as art; it
is song sung as emotive contextual response:

> I asked one of these blacks—one of the most intelligent I had met—where
> they got these songs. "Dey make em, sah." "How do they make them?" After
> a pause, evidently casting about for an explanation, he said, "I'll tell you; it's
> dis way. My master call me up and order me a short peck of corn and a hun-
> dred lash. My friends see it and is sorry for me. When dey come to de praise
> meeting dat night dey sing about it. Some's very good singers and know how;
> and dey work it in, work it in, you know; till dey get it right; and dat's de
> way." A very satisfactory explanation.[6]

Because of the spiritual's responsive nature individual singers had no
qualms about changing the music so that it would more appropriately fit a
new sociohistorical circumstance:

> One day when the writer was seeking to note on paper the melody of a "Sper-
> ichul" from the singing of a Negro of some musical cultivation he said to the
> singer; "you didn't sing it that way the first time." "Oh, no," said the singer,
> "that's the way we do. We don't sing it alike ev'ry time."[7]

The lyrics were equally fluid. A traveler moving through the south in 1845,
after hearing the same song sung differently almost every time he heard it,
concludes, "Slave songs, then, were never static; at no time did Negroes
create a 'final' version of any spiritual. Always the community felt free to
alter and recreate them."[8] It seems clear, then, that the spiritual was created
and continually recreated as a response to an individual slave's or former
slave's circumstances. "Those accounts and others like them make it clear
that spirituals both during and after slavery were the product of an improvisa-

tional communal consciousness. . . . They were . . . *simultaneously* the result of individual and mass creativity.[9]

As one might expect, however, there could be no textual control. Slave laws mandated black illiteracy; the slave therefore had little ability to consider the English versions of the stories, much less the Greek. Syntactic complexities were beyond their comprehension and awareness. This does not mean, however, that a "spiritual" interpretation of a biblical story must necessarily be inaccurate. There is never one single, inviolate lexical-literal textual meaning. Instead syntactic arrangements provide limitations on textual meaning; they negate impossible meanings, but cannot predict all the possible kinds of interpretative conclusions. Therefore the mere fact that the slaves could not have employed textual control in their interpretative moves does not automatically invalidate the interpretative conclusions reached in their music. Modern researchers can use textual data to determine whether such conclusions are appropriate to the language of a text (in fact, we will employ this procedure in Part Two), but they cannot predetermine that because a people is textually unskilled its conclusions are necessarily faulty.

## Slave Appropriation of Biblical Language

Indeed, an ideational consideration of the interpretative moves made in the spirituals suggests that the slave creators had a firm hold on key biblical concepts. Harold Courlander contends that the supposed naiveté for which the Negro spiritual has often been criticized is due to its literal allegiance to what modern readers now perceive as the mythological naiveté of the Bible.[10] The correspondence between biblical and spiritual imagery is so close that were one to sequence the spirituals according to the progression of biblical materials, the songs would "produce an oral counterpart of the Bible" that "if printed . . . would make a volume fully as thick as the Bible itself."[11]

The conceptual portraits in the spirituals are, in fact, so ideationally close to the biblical images that Henry Hugh Proctor labels them orthodoxy.[12] One reason for this close coherence lies in the fact that the creators of the spirituals did not experience academic anxiety caused by the Bible's mythological worldview, the kind of anxiety that ultimately provoked Rudolf Bultmann's program of demythologization. Indeed, in many ways they still lived the ancient cosmology, transplanting, without intellectual hesitation, concepts like heaven, Satan, angels, and the like directly from the biblical world onto their own historical stage. These unlettered and "naive" adherents of the oral biblical story had no awareness of a sense of dissonance between the educated thought of the late nineteenth century and the biblical imagery of antiquity. In almost all its forms, education was denied them.

Heaven, "the dominant idea in the black religious experience as expressed in the slave songs of the nineteenth century," [13] is, therefore, considered to be a spatial reality where Jesus, according to the Fourth Evangelist, prepares the many mansions of his Father's house.

God, in the spirituals, is a God-of-Encounter revealed both through natural events and directly into the consciousness of human beings. This God was no passive observer of human history, but directly and emphatically intervened into the secular, religious, and political affairs of humankind. Nathan Wright notes that this image of God "parallels or is identical with the Jehovah God of the Old Testament and with the Messiah manifestation of the New Testament." [14]

> Wade in de water, children,
> Wade in de water, children,
> Wade in de water, children,
> God's a-gwineter trouble de water. [15]

Jesus is presented in the spirituals as "God's Son come into the world to express his Father's love and to bring back the sinning world to himself." [16] The incarnation thus resulted in a man with a double nature, one part human, the other divine. Lyrics that describe him giving sight to the blind, walking on the water, and riding in the middle of the air demonstrate a furtive belief in Jesus' divinity. Further assurance of Jesus' powerful nature is evidenced in songs that proclaim his atoning ability, "I'm washed in the blood of the Lamb," and celebrate his resurrection. And yet he is still a tragic human figure, a divine servant, a man of sorrows who is acquainted with grief. His suffering is real, his death horrific:

> Were you there, when they crucified my Lord?
> Were you there, when they crucified my Lord?
> Oh, sometimes, it causes me to tremble, tremble.
> Were you there, when they crucified my Lord?

In the spirituals one also finds a belief in the Holy Spirit, the third of the divine personages. Proctor notes, however, that, like the Bible, nowhere do the spirituals use the word *Trinity*. Still, "if we examine their songs we shall find material for the doctrine." [17] The Spirit descends from heaven, is received at conversion, and evokes in the believer both the ability and the need to pray, just as the biblical authors attested.

> Ev'ry time I feel de spirit, move-in' my heart,
> I will pray.
> O, ev'ry time I feel de spirit, move-in' my heart,
> I will pray.

The spirituals' sense of eschatology was based on images derived directly from biblical mythology. The end time would be final and apocalyptic, the good would be rewarded and the wicked punished. "In dat great gettin-up mornin'" God's oppressed people, the slaves, would be vindicated.

What becomes clear in this limited ideational review of the spirituals is that in their use of biblical language to interpret their experience the slaves were overwhelmed by that language. It took them over, not only explaining their world, but at the same time helping to create it. The world of the slave had been destroyed in the slave trade, and no new reality was put in its place, except the degrading one offered by the slave system and the slave owners who perpetuated it. A new, more acceptable foundation was necessary. The slaves found it in the new linguistic reality that they appropriated orally from the Bible. As we saw in chapter 1, language shapes who we are, giving substance to our existence individually and socially. The biblical language helped significantly to create the social and thought world of the slaves, even as they attempted to use that language to explain what had been offered as their new world. The language of the biblical texts fashioned who and what they were, it gave shape to their hopes and aspirations, and in the end it helped them push beyond the symbolic boundaries placed on their reality by the slave system.

Still, even though possessing an uncritical mind, the slave songwriter did not appropriate the biblical language uncritically but reoriented it. The slave recognized a difference in world situations, if not worldview, between biblical times and the nineteenth century, and adjusted use of the conceptual imagery accordingly. Though not a demythologization, we might call what the slaves achieved an adaptive remythologization. They reoriented the biblical mythology by aligning it with a consciousness responsive to the nineteenth-century slave reality.

## The "Life Relation" and Pre-understanding of the Slave Song

It is, then, the prevailing sociohistorical circumstance of slavery that forms the primary life-relationship between the song's creator and the biblical conceptual images he or she uses as an interpretive tool. While many regional, individual, and cultural distinctions could have influenced how a spiritual took oral shape in a particular moment, slavery is the one constant that transcends all the variables. It is a part of every slave context, and thus an emotive and experiential factor in every slave song. It is what Bultmann would call the primary life-relation.

Bultmann gave us one other mechanism by which we could evaluate an interpretative process: preunderstanding. He recognized that a person's or a people's preunderstanding will influence how they interpret the biblical text. Dorothee Soelle was helpful because she demonstrated the change in preunderstanding that occurred between Bultmann's time and the latter half of the twentieth century. While in Bultmann's era societal evil was considered a fated given, in the later era it was considered pervasive, but nonetheless subject to the powers of transformation. The result was an interpretative distinction between Bultmann's more individualistically oriented biblical procedure and the more social, revolutionary approach adopted by later political interpreters. One's preunderstanding in this way becomes a reliable predictor of one's interpretative moves. It would therefore be helpful if we could establish the preunderstanding of the slaves in relationship to their life-relation, slavery, so that we can understand not only *that* it influences their interpretation of biblical language, but also *how* it does so.

We cannot establish this preunderstanding by looking only at the text of the spirituals, because the texts give mixed signals. This is especially the case since the slaves often felt the need to use symbols to fool their white masters. We must instead look at the people themselves. We look at their response to their physical condition as they sang their songs, we look at who sang the songs, and for what purposes.

It is our contention that the preunderstanding the slaves carried with them in their interpretative enterprise was one that considered their historical predicament seriously but did not believe that the evil it constituted was a fated given that could never be overturned. Because they saw God acting in history, they not only believed that there would be a divine, otherworldly revolution, but that God would, with human assistance, inaugurate revolutionary activity here on earth as well:

> There were doubtless some Black slaves who *literally* waited on God, expecting him to effect their liberation in response to their faithful passivity; but there is another side to the Black experience to be weighed. When it is considered that Nat Turner, Denmark Vesey, and Harriet Tubman may have been creators of some of the spirituals; that "Sinner, please don't let this harvest pass" probably referred to a slave resistance meeting; that after 1831 over 2,000 slaves escaped yearly; and that Black churches interpreted civil disobedience as consistent with religion; then it is clear that many slaves recognized the need for their own participation in God's liberation.[18]

Indeed, slave owners were so strict in their enforcement of the slave codes and so merciless in their beatings of slaves who sang spirituals and attended secret worship meetings precisely because it was *their* preunderstanding that the slaves were not accepting their present historical circumstance with passive acquiescence:

Whether the slaves stated their desires or intentions explicitly or obliquely, planters often felt they were singing about temporal freedom. One former slave told Lydia Marie Child of white reaction to this song "Better days are coming" around the time of Nat Turner's revolt. "The whites," the slave said, "wouldn't let us sing that. They thought we going to *rise* because we sung 'better days are coming.'"[19]

The preunderstanding evident in Harriet Tubman's use of the songs is likewise historically engaging. For Tubman, a creator of several spirituals, the music was an opportunity not for escapist musings about God's dealings in the other world, but a powerful interpretative response to the conditions of historical slavery that mandated aggressive, revolutionary behavior:

In spite of redoubled patrols, in spite of increasing rewards which began at $1,000 and finally reached as high as $40,000 (at least $.5 million in today's currency), General Harriet kept returning to slave territory, kept bringing out slaves like some omniscient, unselfish, incomparably fearless and brave Pied Piper, kept marching them along to the tune of "Old Chariot," "Go Down, Moses," "Steal Away," "The Gospel Train is Coming," "There's No Rain to Wet You," and "Didn't My Lord Deliver Daniel?" to freedom, to complete freedom on this earth, in Canada, if necessary.[20]

Nat Turner offers another engaging example. He, too, is thought to be the author of several spirituals, most notably, "Steal Away":

Steal Away, Steal Away
Steal Away to Jesus
Steal Away, steal away home,
I ain't got long to stay here.

Even if he did not write it, his conspicuous use of the song to signal clandestine slave meetings in preparation for revolt against the slave system clearly demonstrates his feeling that the song had a purpose other than a passive pining away for God's otherworldly kingdom. The lyrics declare a religious fervor, but a revolutionary spirit is firmly understood.

## A Communal Code

The interaction between life-relation and preunderstanding thus suggests that a revolutionary spirit is just as critical to the creation and singing of the spiritual as are the more traditionally understood religious affirmations. The spiritual, in this manner, becomes an interpretative response to slavery sung by people who see their sociohistorical condition as an evil that can in fact be transformed. But once again social context must be considered. Not only does it affect how the biblical language is interpreted, it also determines what kind of language must be used in the interpretative process. A slave cannot sing openly of freedom; covert symbolism must be used. We are, in other words, talking about a contextually responsive communal code. Ultimately, this is how the spiritual must be defined.

Depending on the work of Basil Bernstein, Albert Bergesen recognizes what we have already determined, that music is a kind of language whose symbolism is capable of communicating information as well as feeling.[21] Bergesen notes that music therefore operates, like language, according to code. The codes are of two basic types, restricted and elaborated. In the elaborated codes the syntax is more complex and there is more flexibility. Restricted codes, like slang or jargon, rely on more condensed symbols and phrases comprehensible only to those in the in-group. Words like *we* and *us* are preferred, whereas in the elaborated codes the pronouns are the more individualized *I* and *me*. In this way the elaborated codes are able to express more individualized and complex feelings, while the restricted codes tend to be used for more communal feelings that are predicated on a common set of assumptions shared by the in-group. Restricted codes thus contribute to group solidarity, but because they are limited in vocabulary and use a simpler syntactical system, they cannot make sense on their own. They are like a gesture, clue, or sign that only makes sense to those who know what the cryptic symbols mean.

Bergesen found that the differentiations of these codes also apply to music. "More restricted musical codes should have a simpler rhythmic, harmonic, and melodic structure and should employ more collective symbolism in their lyrics." This description fits the spirituals exactly. As Bergesen recognized, the circumstance of slavery created a high degree of community solidarity in the black populace. This resulted in a musical language whose codes were highly restricted. "During slavery, restricted musical codes appear: work songs, field songs, rowing songs, and spirituals." The spirituals tell of community problems and community salvation and "the specific images are highly condensed symbols carrying large amounts of collective information."[22] Indeed, these same symbols—Canaan, the promised land, pharaoh, and so on—are used in white spirituals and are universally acknowledged in broad Christian circles. The spirituals, however, make particular use of these universal symbols so that their relevant meanings in the slave community are altogether different than the meanings they hold in the broader society. According to Bernstein this is how a restricted code carries out its covert linguistic program. "Using these concepts, a restricted code is *particularistic* with reference to its meaning and so to the social structure which it presupposes. However, it is *universalistic* with reference to its models, as such models are generally available."[23] In this manner the engaged preunderstanding of the slave singers could be brought out in the music in a way that was understandable to those in the community, but cryptically confusing, and yet nonthreatening, to everyone else. Language that on the surface appeared pietistic and otherworldly, could in this way conjure up a revolutionary spirit.[24]

Sociohistorical context not only caused a more restricted language, it also influenced the slaves' communal interpretation of its symbols to become more temporally and spatially fluid. Within the confines of their communal understanding, the notion of the sacred is radically expanded. This occurs because of the cognitive and spiritual dissonance imposed on the slaves by their sociohistorical circumstance. The sacred implies the presence and power of God or God's divine representation. The spirituals proclaim God's sacred control over time and history. And yet, paradoxically, those who create the spirituals are entrapped in slavery, an injustice that cannot be if indeed this just and righteous God is in control. Their context thus denies that God's sacred presence intervenes presently in human history. It appears that God will intervene only in the future, as God once intervened through the likes of Moses and Jesus in the past. Their preunderstanding, however, suggests otherwise, that God will intervene through their own revolutionary actions in the present. The conflict can only be resolved through an adaptive change in their use of language. This is exactly what happens in the lyrics of the spiritual:

> They [the slaves] extended the boundaries of their restrictive universe backward until it fused with the world of the Old Testament, and upward until it became one with the world beyond. The spirituals are the record of a people who found the status, the harmony, the values, the order they needed to survive by internally creating an expanded universe. . . .[25]

This adaptation in the use of language suggests that when the slave talks about the past deeds of God or looks to the future deeds of God, the slave is not attempting to escape into another time. The opposite is true: the slave, in the moment of his or her singing, brings that time and its liberating meaning and effect into the present. In the spiritual the lines between dimensions of time and place are collapsed; past and future become present. In this manner an oppressive historical context could not destroy a revolutionary preunderstanding. The slaves adjusted their language so that it could appropriately respond to their context:

> . . . the sacred world of the slave was able to fuse the precedents of the past, the conditions of the present, and the promise of the future into one connected reality. . . . In this respect there was always a latent and symbolic element of protest in the slave's religious songs which frequently became overt and explicit.[26]

The past became present so that the slave did not merely sing about the circumstance of Jesus' crucifixion; the slave participated in that moment, and its liberating meaning brought a kind of defiant and celebratory spirit into the present, even a present weighed down in the mire of oppression. Through their pain and suffering the slaves find themselves at Jesus' side, dying in crucifixion, but triumphantly expecting that Jesus' victory, like his death, would also be theirs. "If Jesus was not alone in his suffering, they were not alone in their slavery. Jesus was with them! He was God's Black slave who had come to put an end to human bondage. Herein lies the meaning of the resurrection."[27] This is what the language of the spiritual conveys when the slave sings, "Were you there when they crucified my Lord?"

Through Jesus' resurrection the future also becomes more than an expected reality; it has already taken place in Jesus' marvelous rising from the dead. The present, in the moment of singing, is eschatologically marked by God's liberating power. So when the slaves talk about the willingness to step on board the "gospel train," they are in reality talking about the willingness to step into the future, into God's future, right now.[28] Certainly, on the lips of someone like Harriet Tubman, the gospel train steaming toward the promised land can have only one ultimate meaning.

## Liberation on a Road of Pain

Thus, the language of the spiritual, as an interpretive response to the sociohistorical circumstance of slavery, is a language of liberation rather than accommodation. This can be seen in three specific ways. First, the spiritual conveys a language of hope, and not merely metaphysical hope, but a liberating hope that helps the singer persevere and push against the boundaries of his or her present situation. It is this kind of hope that could allow the slave to sing in one verse, "Oh nobody knows de trouble I've seen," and in the very next proclaim what appears on the surface to be a contradiction, "Glory Hallelujah!"

Second, the spirituals are an affirmation of dignity in a world that was bent on denying it. This self-affirmation in the face of explicit degradation is a clue to the resistant preunderstanding that pervaded the linguistic background of the spirituals. As James Cone argues:

> The basic idea of the spiritual is that slavery contradicts God; it is a denial of his will. To be enslaved is to be declared a *nobody*, and that form of existence contradicts God's creation of people to be his children. Because Black people believed that they were God's children, they affirmed their *somebodiness*, refusing to reconcile their servitude with divine revelation.[29]

This clarification helps us specify the kind of preunderstanding the slaves employed. In our discussion on *The Gospel in Solentiname* we detected an explicit, overt revolutionary preunderstanding. In the spirituals that sense is, to be sure, more covert. What is more overtly present is this sense of "somebodiness" and "personhood," a kind of preunderstanding that is a powerful self-affirmation in a world determined to treat the slave as a non-person. This is the revolutionary germ that grows beneath the surface of the music and lyrics of the slave songs.

Finally, the spirituals ultimately look not to metaphysical liberation, but physical justice and freedom. Indeed, James Cone declares that although the emphasis is hidden behind biblical symbols, the concept of the divine liberation of the oppressed is the central theological theme in the spirituals. The songs sing of a God who is on the side of the downtrodden and oppressed and who brings judgment on the oppressor:

> Children, we shall be free
> When the Lord [as Messiah] shall appear.
> Give ease to the sick, give sight to the blind,
> Enable the cripple to walk;
> He'll raise the dead from under the earth,
> And give them permission to talk.[30]

Frederick Douglass provides an eyewitness account of the slave's understanding of the spirituals' language:

A keen observer might have detected in our repeated singing of

> "O Canaan, Sweet Canaan,
> I am bound for the Land of Canaan,"

something more than a hope of reaching heaven. We meant to reach the *North* and the North was Canaan.

> "I thought I heard them say,
> There were lions in the way,
> I don't expect to stay
> Much longer here.
> Run to Jesus—shun the danger—
> I don't expect to stay much longer here."

was a favorite, and had a double meaning. In the lips of some, it meant the expectation of a speedy summons to a world of spirits; but, in the lips of *our* company, it simply meant, a speedy pilgrimage toward a free state, and deliverance from all the evils and dangers of slavery.[31]

This contextual adjustment in language had a direct influence on the interpretation of the biblical conceptual language by the song's creator. The concepts of the biblical evangelists were now given a potent, if covert, socio-political emphasis. Starting from his or her experience, the creator of a slave song interpreted the biblical images in a way that supported the spirituals' linguistic program. "They [the slaves] found in Jesus Christ and in Christian-ity a theology and a new orientation towards the hostile and mean world. In so doing, they adapted the Christian faith to their own psychological, social, and spiritual needs."[32] Jesus, the son of God, is now emphasized as a deliverer, a ruling King whose liberating power is available to his followers. "Ride on King Jesus!" they would sing, "No man can hinder him." True, Jesus was God's son, but the slaves enjoyed a kinship with him that they believed no white person could boast. They had suffered as Jesus had suffered, they had been on his hard road of pain and anguish. The effect of this identification was revolutionary in its own way.

It is for this reason that the slave sings so passionately of Jesus' passion, death, and resurrection. In the singing of the spiritual the slave is there with Jesus, not only doomed to struggle, but destined ultimately to overcome. This is why the incarnation is such a significant historical event. God did not come simply to be with humankind; God came to liberate humankind from physical as well as metaphysical oppression. The slave therefore sang in joy as well as expectation, "Go tell it on the mountain, Jesus Christ is born."

Other notable biblical concepts are reinterpreted as well. Heaven now takes on decidedly sociopolitical implications; it becomes not only a symbol of otherworldly transcendence, but a place of physical freedom. Heaven came to symbolize Africa, Canada, and the northern United States.[33] As a future promise that broke into present time and space, heaven was also a powerful present assurance of the slaves' sense of "somebodiness" that en-couraged both endurance and resistance. "[Heaven] enabled blacks to say 'yes' to their right to be free by affirming God's eschatological freedom to be for the oppressed."[34] So when the slaves sang about "making heaven my home," the implications were not always otherworldly:

> I am a poor pilgrim of sorrow.
> I'm tossed in this wide world alone.
> No hope have I for tomorrow.
> I'm trying to make heaven my home.
>
> Sometimes I am tossed and driven, Lord.
> Sometimes I don't know where to roam.
> I've heard of a city called heaven.
> I started to make it my home.[35]

Satan becomes more than a personal devil or a symbolic representation of metaphysical evil; he is seen as both the grand architect of the slave system and as the individual whites who maintain and perpetuate it.

Angels, too, are transformed in the interpretative cosmology of the spirituals. Not only are they instruments of divine deliverance, they are also otherworldly models for those who would secure this-worldly physical liberation. Under orders from God, they became the inspiration and work of freedom.[36] James Cone makes particular note of a spiritual sung by Harriet Tubman, "Swing Low, Sweet Chariot," which features angels in a primary role:

> I look'd over Jordan, an' what did I see
> Comin' for to carry me home,
> A band of angels comin' after me,
> Comin' for to carry me home.

On first reading one figures that the imagery is otherworldly, the emphasis purely escapist. But the contextual reference to Tubman implies a radically different preunderstanding:

> In this context "Swing Low, Sweet Chariot," referred to the "idea of escape by chariot, that is, by means of which a company could employ to proceed northward." When black slaves sang, "I looked over Jordan and what did I see, coming for to carry me home," they were looking over the Ohio River. "The band of angels" was Harriet or another conductor coming for him; and "home" was a heaven in the free states or Canada.[37]

As John Lovell recognized in 1939, for the creator of a slave song the entire linguistic world of the Bible is altered. Symbols of religion become symbols of freedom:

> Satan is not a traditional Negro goblin; he is the people who beat and cheat the slave. King Jesus is not just the abstract Christ; he is whoever helps the oppressed and disfranchised, or gives him a right to his life. Babylon and Winter are slavery as it stands—note "oh de winter, de winter, de winter'll soon be ober, children;" Hell is often being sold South, for which the sensitive Negro had the greatest horror. Jordan is the push to freedom.[38]

The black slaves, then, in an effort to bring meaning to their tortured existence, create a unique language of song whose restricted codes are fully comprehensible only to those who are members of their oppressed community. This language and its context predict how they will interpret Scripture, defiantly. The linguistic transformation is nothing short of miraculous. The biblical conceptual language is forced on the slave as an opiate; the slave sees in it instead the symbolism of freedom:

> The existence of these songs is in itself a monument to one of the most striking instances on record in which a people forged a weapon of offense and defense

out of a psychological shackle. By some amazing but vastly creative spiritual insight the slave undertook the redemption of a religion that the master had profaned in this midst.[39]

We may conclude, therefore, that the Negro spiritual interprets the New Testament language interpersonally. Textual and ideational factors have limited influence, if for no other reason than the forced illiteracy of most slaves, which disallowed a rigorous attention to the written text language. The slaves actualized the text by refracting their oral understanding through the lens of their sociohistorical circumstance. In this way their lives gave meaning to the text, an interpretation that provided the strength to endure their circumstances and the impetus to act for change.

Critics of the Negro spirituals attack their interpretative moves, arguing that the biblical interpretations belie a naive and faulty understanding of the textual and ideational problems in the story language. But like the *campesinos* at Solentiname, the slave composers were not concerned with historical-critical detail. It was never their intent to provide textual and ideational allusions that might hold up in academic debate. They were concerned with the preservation of the human spirit. They were concerned with the empowerment of a disenfranchised people. They were preoccupied with the invigoration of a people's spirit even as the debilitating institution of slavery sought to crush it. The song became the instrument of their resistance, a defiant cry echoing in hope and comfort, even as its coded images summoned a thunderous call for change and confrontation. But this song was not created *ex nihilo*; it was fashioned out of the biblical story. From the stories they heard, the slave composers created (interpersonally) a world of faith that was established one lyric at a time, until fully grown in song, it overwhelmed even (and perhaps especially) its creators. The songs interpreted the text out of a life-relation of bondage and in the process created a linguistic world that not only stood over against the institution of slavery, but fostered in the songs' writers, singers, and listeners the spiritual energy that would one day destroy it.

# 5 The Sermon in the Black Church

PREACHING IS A COMMUNICATIVE ACT WHOSE effectiveness depends on sociolinguistic responsibility. A preacher must be responsible to the context in which the sermon is offered. The preacher must not only, in a broad sense, speak the language of the listeners, but must also, in a more specific sense, use that language according to the particular linguistic prescriptions, verbal and nonverbal, of the cultural or subcultural group with whom he or she is conversing. To be sure, a preacher's spoken word will be nonsensical if he or she speaks in English when the linguistic capabilities of the congregants are limited to German. And yet, to summarize briefly what we stated more fully in chapter 1, simply because the congregation and the preacher share a theoretical knowledge of a language such as English, there is no guarantee that the congregation will hear exactly what the minister intends to say. Different cultural groups have distinct uses for the same language. Indeed, even within single cultural groups, such as a nation-state with a single primary language, distinct subcultural linguistic emphases can create unique meanings for identical linguistic forms or complex combinations of such forms.

## Preaching in the Vernacular

In other words, the language of the church is culturally sensitive. First, it is a product of its cultural environment. Preachers who are raised in a cultural or subcultural region, when they are effective in their communicative endeavors, utilize the cultural linguistic keys of their community's colloquial speech in their sermons. Second, the language of preaching must adapt itself to its cultural environment; preachers who are invited guests in a subcultural milieu that is distinct from their own, in order to be effective communicators, must be aware and respectful of the cultural distinctions that affect the meaning of language. A white preacher who speaks to a black congregation with the same language he or she uses for a white congregation may indeed convey information, but will most likely miss the communicative interchange that is part of the black spiritual moment. This is not to say that preaching cannot challenge cultural norms and thereby call for progressive cultural change; but even if such change is needed and suggested, whether it is initiated by a preacher from within or outside the cultural or subcultural group, the call must be issued in language appropriate to the particular culture toward which it is focused.

Henry Mitchell, quoting Gerhard Ebeling and John Dillenberger on the New Hermeneutic, recognizes that preaching must be allowed to make textual translations appropriate to the culture or subculture in which the word is spoken. Dillenberger is of particular assistance. "This . . . does not mean the relativity of all truth, but it does mean that the absolute truth of God is always known to us concretely and appropriately in the forms of the world in which we live."[1] Such a statement has a tremendous interpersonal impact on preaching in general and black preaching in particular. Because the experience of blacks in the United States has been unique, one would expect, given the previous remarks, that black preaching would employ a language all its own. Mitchell claims that it does:

> Bluntly put, the Black preacher, whether in folk mode or working from a background of professional training, has been apt to trade "learned" language for indigenous vocabulary, familiar images and metaphors, and common experience. This has been thought of as making it plain, which is the same as the existential meaningfulness for which the New Hermeneutic strives.[2]

In so doing the black preacher adheres to the first of the two basic rules of the New Hermeneutic; the preacher, as the spirituals did, declares the gospel in the vernacular of the people.[3] Black vernacular contains two essential components. The first, described at length by Mitchell, is its unique use of the English language. This "black" language, he contends, is more than mere words; it employs its own unique experiential frame of reference, its own visual images, and its own kinds of typical sounds. Stylistically, Mitchell has found that several distinctive characteristics of black speech are employed by the preacher in the black church: a slower rate of delivery, a simpler sentence structure, a velvety drawl with softened consonants, and specialized uses of prepositions as function words.[4] None of these indicates limited intellectual capability; instead they represent an awareness of cultural distinctiveness in use of language. Dr. Martin Luther King, Jr.'s sermons are a case in point. Although Dr. King was well trained in both the professional and academic arenas, his "cadences . . . were unashamedly Black" and impressive to all segments of society.

Problems occur because the use of language is evaluated ideologically. Although we have recognized that there is no single language in any culture because subcultural linguistic distinctions always exist, often a culture elevates one kind of language above others. This "standard language" thereby becomes the norm against which all other linguistic uses are judged. A person is considered completely literate only if he or she can perform publicly according to the rules of this standard language. "In America, however, a diabolical combination of racism, class snobbery, and naivete has caused Blacks as well as Whites, to assume, consciously or unconsciously, that there is a single proper American English, and that the language spoken by most Black people is a crude distortion of it."[5]

A dilemma is therefore created in the black church. Most mainline seminaries train ministers according to the linguistic guidelines of standard American speech—what Mitchell refers to as North, midland, white middle-class. Black seminarians who learn to interpret the text through the sermon in this linguistic mode often find themselves unable to communicate effectively with black congregations. The problem can be so severe that black churches will often choose untrained clergy over those who have seminary educations. "The results have been disastrous for the church of the black masses, because the vast majority of black-culture churches have found it difficult to understand or relate to trained Black clergy preaching Whitese to them."[6] The answer must be, as Mitchell suggests, that black clergy develop a bilingual, bicultural affectation that will allow them to communicate effectively with their church, but also direct the church in such a manner that it can communicate effectively with the wider community. The key is that the language connected with black culture must not be discarded or discounted. Without it, not only communicative effectiveness, but the very identity of the black church, will be imperiled.

The second component of the black vernacular is the black experience. Stephen Reid's work is helpful because he gives a quantification of this experience.[7] The black experience, as he understands it, has three traits. The first is unity of life. The black preacher readily includes sociopolitical issues in sermonic material because there is no dichotomy between sacred and secular realms in the black experience. "God's activity in the lives of black people spans culture, religion, and politics."[8] The second is the paradoxical demonstration of patriotism and loyalty despite the recognition of ever-present racism. This patriotism is not a blind loyalty to the nation to perpetuate itself, but is instead a loyalty to the ideals that the nation espouses, especially justice and freedom for all.[9] The third is a critical awareness of racial issues that leads to race pride and activism.

The combination of these distinct elements of experience and language ensures that effective black preaching is relevant to the issues, needs, and linguistic requirements of the black community. The black sermon cannot be properly understood, therefore, unless one fully appreciates the fact that it is a working part of the black church. And the black church exists as a specific response to the socio-religio-political situation in the antebellum and post–Civil War United States. The founders of the first black churches acted in response to the racial limitations placed on their worship in the established white churches. Their very existence was sociopolitically contrived:

> It is important to note that what these and countless other expressions reveal about Afro-Christian communities is that they understood and explained their existence not through exclusive theological propositions or dogma, but chiefly on account of social—here including political and economic and educational—realities.[10]

Because of this sociopolitical frame of institutional reference, the black church, chiefly through the interpretative moves of the black sermon, emphasized issues of racial equality, freedom, and justice. It was in the black church that such sociopolitical notions first found an enduring biblical foundation in U.S. society:

> The black Christian tradition became institutionalized in the independent black churches. Prior to their emergence, the desire and quest for freedom, together with their concomitant resistance to slavery and racism, had no enduring public form. The principle of freedom and equality of all persons under God is not an abstract idea but a normative condition of the black churches, wherein all who participate can experience its reality. That is to say, the institutionalization of this principle in the black churches reveals its empirical status.[11]

Today, even though strides have been made in the integrative status of many blacks into mainstream economic, political, and educational society, the majority of blacks in the United States remain economically, politically, and socially oppressed and educationally limited. The core problems of racial prejudice and class intolerance continue to inhibit possibilities of progress. The societal context of the black church remains much the same, or as Mitchell puts it, "this life-style retains a number of constants which outweigh the apparent changes." [12]

The black church, particularly through the sermon, continues to address these issues. In so doing the black sermon meets the second principle of the New Hermeneutic; it addresses the urgent needs of the congregation to which it speaks. Since those needs are so profoundly sociopolitical, it is no wonder that much of the interpretative process of the black sermon deals with issues of sociopolitical import. This is not to suggest that more "religious" or "spiritual" texts and issues are not appropriately addressed, only that even these are not studied in isolation, but through the interpretative lens of the congregation's sociopolitical concerns. The process is highly interpersonal.

## The Structure of the Black Sermon

This secular, sociopolitical—interpersonal—orientation can be seen through structural studies of the black sermon. Gerald Davis, after studying the composition of black sermons in a variety of geographical regions and denominations, arrived at the conclusion that black sermons are of a single structural design: "To be sure, there are quasi-theological differences between the various African-American denominations and church bodies. But these differences are not, by and large, manifest in the narrative structures of the preached African-American sermon. . . . That sermon structure is cultural." [13] Davis's research demonstrates that the black sermon is a multiphase composition. In the first phase the preacher puts "before his congregation, in a coordinated framework, the syntactic [textual] and theological [ideational] ideas and structures from which the full sermon performance will be generated." In other words, the preacher establishes the biblical theme for the sermon by using textual and ideational controls. Phase two begins the interpersonal phase of the sermonic presentation; the preacher interprets the biblical theme in a manner appropriate to his or her personality. Davis describes it as a process of "restating the sermon's thematic bridges and moving progressively to a demonstration of his own idiosyncratic style." [14] The final interpersonal interpretative move is accomplished in phase three. Here the preacher interprets the text by means of secular examples that make modern illustrative contact with the biblical materials. The biblical theme is thus interpreted by means of secular sociopolitical images. This phase is so integral to the makeup of the black sermon that Davis felt compelled to assign it a formulaic designation; he calls it the weighted secular factor. It is this constant that makes an "African-American sermon preached in Oakland,

California . . . sound similar to an African-American sermon preached in Boston, Massachusetts."[15] Indeed, this element is so significant that it leads Davis to the conclusion that the black sermon always exhibits a balanced tension between the sacred and the secular; the sacred, though important in and of itself, in order to be meaningful for the interpretative needs of a black congregation, must demonstrate clear secular implications.

This structural observation has vital implications for content. The weighted secular factor indicates not only the need for secular illustrations, but also demonstrates the powerful desire to provide a secular interpretation of the biblical language in the black sermon. The illustrations are not present simply to give colorful commentary on the text; they are the present sociopolitical means through which the ancient text is to be interpersonally understood.

This sociopolitical foundation has two concrete implications for the interpretative moves of the black preacher. First, the sermons in the black church are predominantly christocentric. Even when the texts are taken from the Hebrew Bible, the connection with Christ is drawn. Often, the climactic sermonic note is allowed only after this connection has been made.[16] Again cultural context is important. A Christ figure who suffers and is redeemed because of and in spite of his trials has great meaning for a community that undergoes similar unwarranted and perpetual affliction.

Second, and perhaps more important, the sermons in the black church demonstrate a high degree of prophetic awareness. Because the church's very existence is based on the sociopolitical inequities that plague the black community, these inequities form the context in which the church's voice is heard. Present-day struggles serve as the lens through which the preacher interprets the biblical text. In turn, the biblical interpretation helps the parishioners interpret and survive their own present circumstance. Again, the process is highly interpersonal:

> That is why black theology is, in a real sense, situational in nature. It is grounded biblically, theologically, and existentially in the real world of black people. In an attempt to come to terms theologically with the black situation, black theology seeks to interpret the gospel in such a way that the situation of blacks will begin to make sense.[17]

## Prophetic Enough?

An objection is raised by many observers of the black church in the United States. These critics charge that the black church, given the circumstances of the majority of its parishioners, is not prophetic enough. Indeed, many wonder whether it is accurate to call the black church prophetic at all. The poem "The Preacher and the Slave" by Joe Hill admirably illustrates the point:

> Long-haired preacher come out every night,
> Try to tell you what's wrong and what's right;
> But when asked how 'bout something to eat
> They will answer with voices so sweet:

> You will eat, bye and bye,
> In that glorious land above the sky;
> Work and pray, live on hay,
> You'll get pie in the sky when you die.[18]

The gist of the complaint is that the black church, led by the black preacher, has been either too escapist and otherworldly in its hope for change[19] or too socially conservative and accommodating when it did recognize the societal injustices that plagued the black community.[20]

While the critics have reason for their skepticism, global conclusions are inadequate for two reasons. First, it is necessary to distinguish between what has been identified as the "Negro church" and the "black church." It is the Negro church that Manning Marable indicts in his work.[21] E. Franklin Frazier is equally concerned about the Negro church:

> And, on the whole, the Negro's church was not a threat to white domination and aided the Negro to become accommodated to an inferior status. The religion of the Negro continued to be other-worldly in its outlook, dismissing the privations and sufferings and injustice of this world as temporary and transient.[22]

The black church is a different entity. Born in the crucible of strife that was the civil rights movement of the 1960s, this church, and the sermons that proceeded from it, set the standard for a sociopolitical interpretative process:

> The "Negro Church" that Frazier wrote about no longer exists. It died an agonized death in the harsh turmoil which tried the faith so rigorously in the decade of the "Savage Sixties," for there it had to confront under the most trying circumstances the possibility that "Negro" and "Christian" were irreconcilable categories. The call to full manhood, to *personhood,* and the call to Christian responsibility left no room for the implication of being a "Negro" in contemporary America. With sadness and reluctance, trepidation and confidence, the Negro Church accepted death in order to be reborn. Out of the ashes of its funeral pyre there sprang the bold, strident, self-conscious phoenix that is the contemporary Black Church.[23]

This is the sociopolitical context that radically affects the sermon language about which we have been speaking.

Our second observation deals with the distinction between prophetic awareness and prophetic activism. Life-relation is a constant in both the Negro and the black churches; it is responsible for the prophetic awareness of societal injustice and inequity. Two consequent options are available. A church either responds by challenging the sociopolitical situation, or by claiming that only God can respond appropriately. The latter option, which is still based on a prophetic awareness, encourages an orientation to other-worldly faith, an escapist apocalypticism where justice will be served, but only in a future time and place.

The distinguishing factor is preunderstanding. In Rudolf Bultmann's pre-understanding, for example, social evils were a fated given that could not be humanly changed. He therefore turned his interpretative focus toward the existential human situation where options of change were available. The result was that his interpretative moves did not treat history seriously. In the preunderstanding of Solentiname, we found that social evils were not considered a fated given. The interpretative response was therefore revolutionary. Something similar happened with the slaves and their spirituals. Slavery was not seen as a fated given to be endured forever, but an evil that could be resisted, escaped, and even overturned. This preunderstanding led to a particular kind of interpretative meaning in the slaves' songs. In the antebellum Negro and black churches, a similar hermeneutical process is involved. If the preunderstanding is that social evils are not a fated given but can be changed through human enterprise, then the texts will be interpreted accordingly. If, however, as in the case of the Negro church, the preunderstanding declares that evils will be changed only by the apocalyptic actions of God, then, while the problems will still be seen (the life-relation guarantees they will), texts will be interpreted in a substantially different manner. The prophetic awareness of a sociopolitical evil will, however, remain.

In the period of the antebellum sermon, as we have seen from our study of the spirituals, the preunderstanding was oriented toward liberation. The social evil of slavery was not considered a given to be perpetually endured. Preunderstanding and life-relation thus interacted in such a way as to effect sermons whose hermeneutic was oriented toward liberation:

> The African American preacher used the biblical text as a source to address the context of human slavery. The preacher drew a correlation between the Hebrew slaves and the African American slaves. Confrontation grew out of the relevance of the biblical Word in terms of divine creation and human liberation. The intent was to provide consolation, to empower the slaves with their daily insults and burdens, and to give them hope for deliverance.[24]

Paul Lawrence Dunbar's poetic recreation of the antebellum sermon illustrates the point. The poem uses "the Bible to give immediate comfort to the hearers by affirming liberation from slavery."[25] In fact, after an analysis of antebellum sermons, David T. Shannon concludes that the focus of these orations was not restricted to a heavenly expectation, "a pie-in-the-sky" reward, but was founded in the desire for present social change that emerged from their understanding of God who acted as liberator for the ancient Hebrews and who reestablished this passion for justice in the ministry of Jesus. The antebellum sermon was delivered to people in exile as a sign that liberation was at hand.

Even the Negro church, we would contend, was aware of the negative sociopolitical situation of its constituents. Indeed, this prophetic awareness prompted its otherworldly and escapist leanings. The preunderstanding of its leaders was similar to Bultmann's; they believed that social injustices were a societal evil too powerful to be stamped out by human endeavor. They thus turned away from any hope of systemic societal change, and sought instead a hope for individual peace and salvation in the world beyond this one.

We find here an interesting hermeneutical cycle, prompted by critical shifts in contextual preunderstanding, where the interpretative process moves from a liberation orientation to an otherworldly accommodating orientation and back to liberation again. The transition point is the Negro church. The world that surrounded the Negro church during and following Reconstruction offered hope for positive change and then snatched it away with an apparent finality that no doubt severely affected the Negro church and its preachers:

> But their hopes and expectations were rudely shattered when white supremacy was reestablished in the South. They were excluded from participation in the white man's world except on the basis of inferiority. They were disfranchised and the public schools provided for them were a mere travesty on education. The courts set up one standard of justice for the white and another standard for the black man. They were stigmatized as an inferior race lacking even the human attributes which all men are supposed to possess.[26]

The only refuge for the Negro in such a hostile and apparently permanent world situation was the church. It offered a physical environment of affirmation and political achievement. It offered a social network based on equality of its membership. It was itself an escape from hostile surroundings. It is no wonder that its aspirations were also escape oriented; the sufferings of this world were to be overturned only in God's world to come. This preunderstanding makes the difference between the interpretative moves of the Negro church and the antebellum and black churches that historically frame it.

The Negro church sermon, reflecting a changed social circumstance that rewarded accommodation rather than challenge to institutional societal norms, was much more conservative and otherworldly in its messages. In fact, social conflict became a secondary concern. Spiritual conflict formed the basis for spiritual discussion and counsel. When social behavior was discussed it was for the purpose of illustrating matters of spiritual importance:

> Instruction is not, however, the main function of the sermon. There must be enthusiasm, even ecstasy, and the minister who is incapable of stimulating this is soon out. . . . Other more serious forms of social behavior prevailing in the community are not often touched upon, or if referred to at all it is done in a spirit of great daring.[27]

When the social circumstances changed dramatically again, so did the direction and content of the sermons in the black community. The crises and successes of the 1960s caused a change in the preunderstanding of church leaders in the black community. Positive systemic societal change became a powerful possibility. The sermonic interpretations in the black church reflect this shift in preunderstanding.

## From Biblical Metaphor to Sociopolitical Circumstance

We can see how these interpretative maneuvers are achieved in the black church by looking at a selection of its published sermons. Although the emphasis is mainly in the interpersonal arena, textual and ideational controls on interpretation are utilized as well. Since the sermon is not an exegetical paper, the black preacher does not explicitly recognize the syntactical qualities of a passage and its limitations on conceptual meaning and interpersonal interpretation. But the black preacher is keenly aware of the textual agenda.[28] In Reid's perceived three steps of the black sermonic interpretative process, step one is the critical reading of the text. Depending on scholarly insights and his or her own awareness of textual problems, the preacher first seeks to understand the material textually and ideationally. This intrinsic reading "investigates the way in which the material culture and social stratification interacted to form the community of faith that shaped the text."[29]

Textual and ideational investigation are not, however, done merely for their own sake. The black preacher pushes, interpersonally, beyond the textual and ideational boundaries. He or she uses the scholarly data creatively; the purpose is ultimately to ascertain what the text *means* rather than stopping at what the text *meant*. Textual investigation has an interpersonal purpose and focus. In Reid's three-step program, step two, the recovery of black interpretation of the text, and step three, the application of the text to the life experience of the black community, are both interpersonally oriented.[30] The interpretative moves of the black sermon are weighted toward an interpersonal focus. The focus is achieved and yet remains biblical, because biblical concepts are accepted first on their own grounds, and only then translated into the interpretative reality of the present sociopolitical circumstance:

> Again, biblical worlds should never be recreated; a biblical world can be *translated* into a force appropriate for contemporary situations-in-the-world. But such translations require a great deal of wisdom with respect to one's own physical and social world, as well as a knowledge of what is contained in the Bible.[31]

This process is achieved in two ways, both of which make use of the rhetorical device known as metaphor. Just as Jesus used familiar images to give clarity to his parables, the black preacher uses metaphor to build a biblical case for a contemporary circumstance by operating from the experience of his or her listeners. The preacher takes a biblical person or concept and uses it metaphorically to symbolize a struggle or joy in the lives of the present black Christians. In the first case the preacher makes metaphorical use of single biblical concepts.

Examples from published sermons illustrate the point. In a sermon entitled "Following Pilate's Path of Futility," Strobridge E. Hoard makes such use of Pilate.[32] Pilate remains no longer a biblical character or even a liturgical figure, but becomes a metaphor of present-day Christian futility and fear. First, the historical considerations are accounted for: "Pilate was the fifth governor of Judea. And to history, certainly to Christianity, he would have meant nothing—except that our Lord and Master stood before him to be judged."[33] Hoard goes on to discuss how Pilate, when he was appointed governor of Judea, antagonized the Jews by allowing the Roman soldiers to bring a standard bearing the image of Caesar into Jerusalem. Pilate is depicted correctly as a devious ruler who was always at odds with his constituency and who ceased in his antagonisms only when the weight of public outcry threatened to invite intervention from Rome. Pilate is depicted as a man who becomes futile before fear, and this fear is shown to be the rationale behind his ultimate execution of Jesus. He is afraid of public instability.

Pilate is the symbol of people today who, though strong in appearance, bow futilely before the sociopolitical pressures of the day. Such futility "causes us to stand before our neighbor and God in fear and trembling, sick unto death no matter how strong we are. Sometimes, we act like we don't know where to turn for power and grace."[34]

In Matthew 25:14-30 Jesus' parable demonstrates the chagrin of a wealthy man who had left a single talent in the possession of one of his servants before embarking on a long journey. Upon his return he finds that the servant, instead of investing the money for even simple interest, buried the talent and therefore wasted its potential. For William V. Guy, that servant and his underused talent become a metaphor for a present-day unwillingness to invest enough of ourselves in the sociopolitical problems that surround us:

> Christian commitment, therefore, does not encourage an atrophied mind; it demands an active one. The Christian must daily raise questions and make decisions regarding the tangled issues by which his life is surrounded: from racism to nationalism, from bombing to abortion, from building a hospital to passing a bond issue for a new sewer.[35]

In the second metaphorical case the preacher makes use of entire biblical scenes. The conceptual program of the text is reoriented so that it makes sense in the sociopolitical life of the modern black parishioner. An excellent case in point is the work done by Otis Moss, Jr., in his sermon on Luke 8:26-35. Jesus has healed the Gerasene demoniac, the one called Legion, and the populace, seeing this former madman sitting quietly at Jesus' feet, is afraid. Moss takes reverent delight in noticing that while the man was mad and a cause for extreme anxiety, the people were satisfied. But once he was healed, and logically no longer a threat to society, they, oddly, became upset. Moss believes that the parallels for black America are frightening; Legion's world becomes a metaphor for our own:

> I see a black and white parallel here. As long as we were struggling in the cotton fields of Tennessee, Georgia, Alabama, and Mississippi with our cotton sacks across our shoulders and to our sides, picking cotton and having our fingers burning from stinging cotton worms that would hide under the cotton leaves; as long as we were barefoot, actually and symbolically, laughing when we were not tickled . . . America was satisfied. . . . But one day America saw us marching to the voting booth, sitting down at lunch counters, and all of America became afraid.[36]

After black people are healed of their "madness," after they know who they are and pursue a societal recognition based on this rehabilitated state of awareness, American society, like Legion's, becomes afraid.

In "The Drum Major Instinct," Martin Luther King, Jr., searches Mark 10:35-45, where James and John request the privilege of sitting at Jesus' right and left hands in the kingdom. In this passage about being first in Jesus' religious movement, King finds a metaphor for contemporary race-related societal ills. "Do you know that a lot of the race problem grows out of the drum major instinct—a need that some people have to feel superior, or need that some have to feel that they are first, to feel that their white skin ordains them to be first?"[37]

Mary Ann Bellinger makes similar metaphorical use of Jesus' healing of an infirm woman on the sabbath in Luke 13:10-17. The woman becomes a metaphor for present social ills that must be changed. Jesus challenges the religious norms of Jewish society, which Bellinger expands to a challenge of negative sociopolitical norms. The indictment of the leaders because of their unwillingness to allow healing on the sabbath becomes an indictment of present-day unwillingness to promote social activism:

> In the case of the bent-over woman, the synagogue community had been content to give her handouts. They had been inclined to keep her as their "pet cripple." She enabled them to feel a little sorry and a little superior. She was to them what the neighborhood drunk, the wife beater, and child abuser are to us—they enable us to feel better than they, but we don't do much to change their lives.[38]

Other specific examples abound. These demonstrate that the black preacher is aware of the key conceptual images of Christianity in their proper textual and ideational modes. These concepts are, however, interpreted and processed interpersonally. Effie Clark, for instance, while recognizing the historic significance of Jesus' resurrection, understands it anew in light of the present historical circumstance of black Christians. Christological imagery becomes directly related to modern situations of social oppression. Biblical resurrection becomes a metaphor for economic liberation:

> They (an oppressed people) must organize themselves to struggle with their own weaknesses and the whole spectrum of their oppressed condition. It is at this point that such a people are no longer slaves; they are no longer dead to this world. As Brother Marcus Garvey said, "They now live a resurrected life."[39]

Cheryl Sanders in a like manner sociopolitically reconfigures the incarnation:

> Christ did not come as a Jew to the Jews, to be revealed, exclusively among Jews. Christ did not come as a black Messiah to the black nation, to be revealed exclusively among blacks. And despite what might be depicted by the art and films and Sunday School literature of Europe and North America, Christ did not come as a white man to the white race to be revealed exclusively among whites. Christ, the anointed one of God, came, yes, as a Jew (only because he had to come as somebody) but to *all* nations—to all colors, all races, all classes, and to both genders—to be revealed openly and inclusively across the world.[40]

This kind of sociopolitical interpretative move operates on virtually every key New Testament theme and concept. It is not necessary to go into them all; it is the process, not the individual cases, that concerns us. By now that process should be clear: The black preacher, operating from a sociopolitically charged life-relation, interprets the biblical text interpersonally through a sociopolitical lens. Biblical concepts become metaphors for understanding the modern social circumstance, and in the process they are invested with a new meaning. The New Testament, while remaining a repository of historical truths, has become a contemporary interpretative guide. Once again, sociolinguistic context radically affects the way in which the language of the New Testament is interpreted. In the actualization of the text in the life of the community, textual and ideational concerns, though important, become secondary. The primary move is interpersonal.

## The Interpersonal Dimension

The descriptive discussions in this and the three preceding chapters proved useful for two reasons. First, they demonstrated that communicative context does influence the reading of biblical materials. In each of the cases analyzed it became clear that the interpreter's sociolinguistic circumstance played a vital role in determining the conclusions developed in regard to text meaning. For Bultmann it was the post–World War I world. For the *campesinos* it was the socioeconomic injustices experienced at the hands of the Somoza regime. For the Negro slaves it was the debilitating and dehumanizing world of the so-called "peculiar institution." And finally, for the black preacher, it remains the socioeconomic and political world of a minority community in constant struggle. Second, by appealing to the categories of life-relation and preunderstanding, we were able to clarify how this influential process takes place.

In each case the interpersonal component played a conscious, vital role in the interpretative process. Even if textual and ideational considerations were not always given due importance in limiting the range for interpretative meaning, it is clear that the communities were aware of these functions of language and appealed to them, whether instinctively or intentionally, as a part of their interpretative process. In the case of some interpersonal analyses, the textual and ideational boundaries should be strengthened, but in other cases, as with Bultmann, the interpersonal range is not fully explored. Bultmann's lack of appreciation for the full interpersonal possibilities limited his interpretative conclusions just as inadequate attention to textual and ideational detail sometimes proved hazardous for the interpretative process in Solentiname, the spirituals, and the black church. Given our sociolinguistic argument that an interpretation remains incomplete until all three macrofunctions are intentionally considered, we remain convinced that the boundaries on the range of meaning provided by textual and ideational considerations cannot be eliminated. Interpersonally, however, an interpretation can and must be encouraged to push beyond those boundaries.

In order to demonstrate how the process can yield new interpretative perspectives on textual meaning, we propose to select a biblical text and track its interpretative history along interpersonal lines. We will find that even when an exegete intends a contextually neutral interpretation, as the context of the interpreter shifts so does the actual interpretative conclusion. The interpersonal component is at work even when an author intends to dismiss or ignore it. In this way every interpretation is an interpersonally motivated one. Nonetheless, it remains interpersonally limited, as did Bultmann's, until there is a full analectical recognition of the presence and value of interpersonal strategies and conclusions in other communities. What we look for, then, is not so much the antiseptic acknowledgment by scholars that they are influenced by their context; this already occurs. What also needs to take place is the recognition that context is a necessary interpretative ingredient that should be consciously explored and promoted so that not only the contextual influences and strategies of mainline scholars are accepted as legitimate contextual by-products of the investigative enterprise, but also that the contextual perspectives of marginalized communities be recognized as appropriate interpersonal determinants of and challenges to text interpretation. In an interpersonal-analectical atmosphere such as the one we hope to demonstrate in the next unit, text meaning does not remain static, but grows, even to the point of a perceived explosion of meaning. We will see how initial text investigations, focusing on textual and ideational criteria, do not establish a text's meaning per se, but instead begin to establish boundaries for meaning. We will see these boundaries expand interpersonally as new investigative procedures and new academic contexts are brought into interpretative play. The meaning of the text grows as the textual and ideational boundaries expand interpersonally. But, as in Bultmann's case, because there is a lack of full appreciation for the interpersonal component, the conclusions regarding meaning do not fully explore all the possibilities allowed by the textual and ideational data. For we see that when ethnographic and popular interpreters approach the texts with a conscious interpersonal agenda, new information constantly bursts on the scene, leading to meanings that push beyond the textual and ideational boundaries established by mainline scholarship. When these conclusions are analectically engaged, a process occurs whereby the full richness of the text begins to be more clearly opened, and we can see how the text comes to life in a new way in a new circumstance. The meaning of the text is changed forever.

In this next unit, then, we have three primary objectives. One, we want to recognize and affirm the interpersonal. It should not be allowed to function haphazardly or be forced to operate covertly in the interpretative enterprise. Two, we want to affirm the interpersonal conclusions of marginalized communities as they push beyond textual and ideational boundaries of meaning. And three, we want to promote an analectical engagement of interpersonal conclusions so that the rich potentiality of a text's meaning can be more fully appreciated.

# PART TWO

## Interpreting the Trial of Jesus in Mark

# 6

# Potential Meaning in Mark's Trial Scenes

Textual and ideational analyses establish boundaries on the meaning of a text.
They guide the interpreter by unequivocally
stating what the material cannot mean.
Within the boundaries, however, a full range
of possible meanings remains. They can be
accessed from beyond the textual and ideational boundaries—they can be accessed interpersonally.

This reality of *potential* meaning allows for
the principle of polysemy, the possibility that
a single acoustic or linguistic symbol, or indeed an entire text, may have a variety of conceptual implications. As Kurt Baldinger explains, a word is the additive combination of
a *signifiant* (signifier), a written or acoustic image, and a *signifié* (signified), the concept or
signification connected with that image.[1]
Polysemy recognizes that each *signifiant* has a
range of signification, called the semasiological field. As an example Baldinger refers to the
variety of meanings expressed by the Spanish
word *corona*. It can mean "kind of fortifica-
tion, halo, crown or wreath (central meaning), coin, tonsure."[2]

This semasiological reality often causes
ambiguity in textual meaning. Baldinger
notes that the syntagmatic or literary context
in which the material is found often clarifies

which meaning is appropriate. Literary context does not, however, always erase the ambiguity. In such situations an even broader context comes into play, the sociolinguistic circumstance of the text reader.

Polysemy thus implies that textual meaning cannot be defined completely; no one meaning of a word or an entire text is the correct, *complete* meaning. Meaning is more than what is found on the surface of the texts. Meaning is not limited to a single interpretation, like Rudolf Bultmann's, or interpretations like those of the spirituals, the black church, or the Solentiname community. Each interpretation is a single piece of a larger picture of potential meaning, and therefore represents the acquisition of only a segment of that potential.[3] The picture becomes ideological if such selected interpretations are considered the whole picture, within which the full and single correct meaning is resident.

Because each interpreter operates from a unique sociolinguistic background, he or she sees aspects of the potential meaning that others may not see unless they are guided to do so. A more comprehensive understanding is approached when an interpreter opens himself or herself to interpretations that originate from beyond the boundaries of his or her own sociolinguistic interpretative background. The task, thus, is not to choose for correctness between the interpretations of a Bultmann or a Solentiname peasant, but to open oneself to the light each can shed on the text by such diverse interpretations and realize that they can broaden the horizon of meaning.

If, however, we are to argue that the interpersonal function of language is as important as the textual and ideational functions, we must be ready to explain how interpersonal influences affect the way textual and ideational features are understood. Consider, for instance, the manner in which a New Testament text is interpreted. Even though text-critical variants may exist, for the most part the textual components have been stabilized because the text has been written down and codified. The lexical terms have been canonically locked in place, yet the interpretative conclusions regarding those terms vary widely because the conceptual images related to those terms are not locked in place. Interpreters can access (interpersonally) different segments of a fluid, conceptual potential of meaning even though the terms themselves remain constant. Therefore, when the interpersonal perspective changes from one text investigator to another, so do the conclusions regarding textual and ideational story features. This same phenomenon can occur when the work of a single text interpreter is considered; a change in locale, time, or physical circumstance often provokes a different interpretative conclusion for the same text. In other words, an investigator's conclusive understanding of textual and ideational features is determined by his or her interpersonal perspective.

This recognition is particularly important when one considers that the texts themselves are determined by historically contingent moral, ethical, or practical standards. In the New Testament a case in point is Paul's statement regarding the silence of women in worship:

> As in all the churches of the saints, the women should keep silence in the churches. For they are not permitted to speak, but should be subordinate, as even the law says. If there is anything they desire to know, let them ask their husbands at home. For it is shameful for a woman to speak in church. What! Did the word of God originate with you, or are you the only ones it has reached? (1 Cor. 14:33b-36)[4]

Here interpersonal considerations are particularly appropriate as a means of clarifying the link between Paul's thought and his historical situation. Paul's teaching took place within a context renowned for its religious-cultural bias against women. No doubt the bias inherent in such a life situation prevented Paul from coming to what teachers in most modern reading communities, which are often contextually marked by concerns for sexual equality and inclusivity, would consider a more reasonable understanding regarding the role of women in worship. Feminist or womanist interpreters, speaking from a different interpersonal perspective, come to the conclusion that such a statement has no authoritative meaning in a modern Christian congregation.

In fact, Paul gives mixed signals regarding the role and status of women. His reasoning shows a strong element of interpersonally determined incoherence. Because his work is so integrally affected by his sociolinguistic situation, the coherent core of his gospel message is not applied consistently throughout his argument. The interpersonal bias so influences the apostle that he violates textual and (especially) ideational constructs that he himself has established. For example, in his discussion of the silence of women, his own reasoning demonstrates how in the end he cannot argue this point ideationally. He has elsewhere established that in Christ there is no difference between male and female: "There is neither Jew nor Greek, there is neither slave nor free, there is neither male nor female; for you are all one in Christ Jesus. And if you are Christ's, then you are Abraham's offspring, heirs to promise" (Gal. 3:28-29). Realizing the problem, he appeals to the social bias of his time, showing in the process that what he tried to present in 1 Corinthians as a socioreligious and moral issue is in reality purely a sociolinguistic bias. The only basis for his reasoning in this case is therefore interpersonal. As this Pauline example demonstrates, an author's meaning, as well as the reader's interpretative response, is significantly affected by sociolinguistic context.

As we use this information in our consideration of the trial scenes in the Gospel of Mark, two key concerns will warrant primary attention. First, we intend to demonstrate that the conclusions reached by scholars operating according to the guidelines of the traditional historical-critical approach are also conditioned contextually. Even though investigators in this category consciously intend a rigorous fidelity to textual and ideational data as they are grammatically and historically acquired, they too are subject to interpersonal influence. Second, although investigators operating in the ethnographic and popular categories maintain a more conscious interpersonal objective, their conclusions should also be subject to textual and ideational restraints.

Because the amount of scholarship is vast, we cannot consider every investigation in each category.[5] We will thus work with selected authors who represent the kind of scholarship done in their respective methodological areas. We need a standard methodology for our investigation in order to ensure that scholars in each category will be subjected to the same standards in the analysis. Primarily that will mean that even though we maintain that traditional European interpreters intend to operate consciously within the textual and ideational arenas, whereas those in the ethnographic and popular categories are more interpersonally inclined, all three language functions must be engaged in the investigation of each interpreter. An investigative formula is warranted. Once again we turn to the life-relation and preunderstanding categories of Bultmann.

## Two Levels of the Interpersonal

Two investigative levels of the interpersonal function of language have to be distinguished: the macro- and the micro-interpersonal. Macro-interpersonal refers to the scholarly attempt to uncover the interpersonal factors involved in the original setting of the text; micro-interpersonal refers to the interpreters' own involvement in the act of interpretation. While an investigator operates simultaneously on both levels, he or she may at any given time consciously emphasize one or the other. It is our contention that investigators using the traditional historical-critical approach to biblical inquiry operate intentionally on the macro-interpersonal level, whereas those using the ethnographic and popular approaches operate more intentionally on the micro-interpersonal level. These levels can be distinguished as follows:

*Macro-interpersonal Level*
*Life-relation:* Scientific historico-grammatical inquiry
*Preunderstanding:* Relationship between author and original audience

*Micro-interpersonal Level*
*Life-relation:* External to interpreter. The scholar's form of research has a methodological encoding that helps determine the conclusions reached.
*Preunderstanding:* Internal to interpreter. The scholar's internal interests influence his or her interpretation.

We attempt here to formulate an evaluative mechanism that can contribute to an examination of biblical research the way Enrique Dussel's model contributes to the process of critically examining broader scientific-analytical procedures. As Dussel did for science in general, we intend to critique and categorize the two most prominent methodological approaches to biblical inquiry. Where Dussel speaks of the "centrist" scientific approach to analyzing reality, we will focus on the macro-interpersonal level of New Testament investigation. Where he specifies the marginal approach to analyzing reality, we point to the micro-interpersonal level of New Testament investigation.

Indeed, there are fascinating parallels between Dussel's model and our analysis. As does Dussel's centrist approach to understanding reality, the macro-interpersonal approach to studying the New Testament material maintains an air of scientific control and therefore superiority. Scholars who operate according to the "scientific," historical-critical method are traditionalized so that while their particular model of inquiry may be subjected to critique and sometimes derision, the historical-critical and literary foundations on which the models are built are often looked upon as unimpeachable. In order to be accepted as a credible exegete of the biblical materials, an investigator must not only learn the historical-critical program but must incorporate the main facets of its analytical process into his or her research program.

Dussel would position this approach at the center of the critical biblical interpretative process. Critical thought that arises from a peripheral position must either direct itself toward this center or be discredited. In this manner the centralized macro-interpersonal approach becomes an ideological phenomenon. It is as much perspective—so-called scientific—as it is method. And because this ideology has been adopted as the "correct" procedure by the majority of professional exegetes, scholars, teachers, administrators, and clergy, it acquires the power not only to label but also to devalue interpretative moves that do not find their locus within its conceptual and procedural bounds.

As does Dussel's centrist scientific model, the macro-interpersonal procedure specifically intends an analysis of facts that takes place in a supposed situational vacuum, uninfluenced by the social, cultural, economic, ethnic, and political context of the interpreter. The facts to which the biblical text refers do not concern the interpreter's reality, but only the biblical reality in which those facts take shape. When, for instance, the facts *temple* or *messiah* are considered in the Markan trial scenes, they can be understood only in light of the textual and ideational reality in which their use takes place. The boundaries of that reality are scientifically controlled in the macro-interpersonal analysis. It is the reality (the relationship between the author and original audience) of the biblical first-century world that establishes and uses the terms. The researcher's own reality and how it relates to the terms and their conceptual implications are considered invalid as a foundation for interpretation. The scientific task is to recreate the biblical world in which the terms were used, and then attempt to understand that recreated reality as its proper context.

An investigator who *intentionally* operates from a micro-interpersonal perspective contends that a text cannot be adequately understood if its terms and concepts are analyzed only against the background of a reconstructed first-century biblical reality. If a text is to live in the present—if its meaning and significance are to extend beyond the theoretical confines of an ancient communal setting—its terms and images must also be defined in the light of present needs and circumstances. The particular sociolinguistic situation that is immediately significant for the community presently engaging the text must be considered a viable lens through which the textual and ideational features can be studied. The objective is to determine what the text *means* in and for the interpreter's present sociolinguistic circumstance.

In fact, even when micro-interpersonal influences have an unconscious and unintentional effect, they have an effect nonetheless. The effect is realized in two ways: it is entrenched externally in the research methodology, and it asserts itself directly in the attempt to establish meaning. The first is external to the interpreter. The attempt to establish macro-interpersonally what the text meant to the original writers and readers unavoidably involves micro-interpersonal factors inasmuch as the methodological environment of the researcher has a decisive influence on the investigation. In order to determine systematically the (macro-interpersonal) historical circumstances that surrounded the author and his original audience, a "historico-scientific" investigator appeals to some form of analytical methodology. There is a particular encoding inherent to any particular investigative methodology, a coding that affects how the results it acquires are evaluated. For instance, an investigative presumption is implied in source criticism; a person who describes himself or herself as a source critic is led to ask certain kinds of textual and ideational questions, and is thereby directed toward certain kinds of answers. The source critic has a language distinct from that of the redaction critic. The very choice of an operative methodology is a contextual decision; conclusions are thereby micro-interpersonally influenced.

At a more immediate, internal level is the micro-interpersonal influence of the researcher's cultural, sociological, political, and economic background on the way in which the language of the text is understood. Instead of focusing singularly on what the text *meant* for a first-century Christian community, investigators who maintain an *intentional* micro-interpersonal orientation focus on what the text *means* for the particular sociohistorical community out of which their study arises. It is preunderstood that a reader's sociolinguistic background influences how he or she comprehends the meaning of the text language.

We should be clear here in our use of the adjective *intentional*. It is used because we are operating on two levels. The internal micro-interpersonal feature is not operative only where it is intentionally allowed to play a role— even a determinative role. It arises at every occasion where meaning is involved.

On a second level we are dealing specifically with those interpreters who *intentionally* allow internal micro-interpersonal factors to play a role in their interpretations. Investigations that are intentionally micro-interpersonally based have been chastised because their methodology allegedly lacks the sophistication of scientific procedure. We would contend, however, that at the (internal) stage of preunderstanding, micro-interpersonal investigations are based on the same sociolinguistic principles that are instrumental for investigative procedures on the macro level. The earliest Christian communities interpreted the text through their own sociolinguistic backgrounds. A meaningful dialogue was therefore established between the primitive Christian communities and the text. In the first place, effective interpretation is recognized as the direct result of this dialectical interchange between the first-century audiences and the written biblical material. More importantly, micro-interpersonal principles extend this sociolinguistic recognition in time so that the same dialogical possibilities that existed for the earliest communities may be methodologically allowed for future reading audiences.

The intentional micro-interpersonal claim is therefore the inevitable updating of what scholars agree was a fundamental part of the interpretative process in first-century reading communities. The ancient communities derived meaning sociolinguistically; modern communities derive meaning the same way. The dialectical interchange between text and reader remains the same. In traditional interpretation, however, interpersonal factors with regard to ancient communities are considered legitimate clarifications of what a text *meant;* but when those same kinds of interpersonal factors are intentionally considered from the standpoint of modern communities, traditional researchers often assume that conclusions regarding what the text *means* are biased, even though they are unintentionally involved in the same process.

We therefore contend that the micro-interpersonal process is textually and linguistically unavoidable. Its roots are found in the very macro-interpersonal procedures that pretend a scientific disregard for the influences of society and culture on text meaning. Contextual influence plays a vital role in how texts are understood.

A wide gulf remains between the macro- and the micro-interpersonal biblical approaches. It is a similar chasm to that which Dussel recognizes between centrist and marginalized analyses of reality. As we have seen in chapter 1, he argues that if there was truly to be growth in scientific endeavor, the two approaches could not settle for a mere dialectical recognition of each other. Instead he suggests an analectical engagement. Positive and meaningful analytical growth would occur as each approach learned from the other and together established a new approach that operated beyond the boundaries that limited each of them separately. We will maintain that the same must happen with the macro- and micro-interpersonal approaches to biblical analysis. If researchers beholden to either would move beyond the stage of dialectical recognition and opposition until they approached a position of analectical engagement, a positive progression in the program of biblical analysis would become possible. It is just such a progression we hope to show in our consideration of the Markan trial scenes.

## The Potential for Meaning In Mark's Trial Scenes

Before we proceed further it would be helpful to examine the Markan trial scenes textually, ideationally, and macro-interpersonally. Here we do not want to interpret the texts so much as to demonstrate, after analyzing key symbols and linguistic markers, that a vast potential of meaning exists.

### Textual Considerations

Beginning with the Sanhedrin trial (Mark 14:55-64), we find that the language of the text has an observable structure. The connection of θανατῶσαι (put to death) in verse 55 with θανάτου (death), which concludes verse 64, helps mark the scene's outer boundaries. The passage, however, includes a structural break. Not only are verses 55-59 concerned with a different theme than verses 60-64, but the grammatical patterns are distinct. While in the first set of verses verbs in the narration consistently occur in the imperfect tense (six times), in the second set we find the imperfect noted only twice.[6]

A helpful observation at this point involves the infinitive clause in verse 55, which is structurally highlighted. This emphasis on "seeking to kill Jesus" is part of Mark's overall narrative program; verse 55 bears remarkable similarity to 3:6, 11:18, 12:12, and 14:1. Each of these verses represents a situation in which conflict erupts between the Jewish leaders and Jesus to such a degree that his death is sought. In fact, in all but the first instance, the verb ζητέω (seek) is used as an imperfect plural. Throughout the Gospel the leadership is out to kill Jesus. The fact that verse 55 is the climactic presentation of this conflict-seeking theme is indicated by the difference between it and the previous conflictual encounters. "In 14:55 the form of this plan differs from the previous indications in that the aim is no longer the 'how' of the plan but its definite execution."[7] Only here does "seeking" become "planning." The basis of the plan's execution is the garnering of witnesses to testify against Jesus.

The witnessing element is also involved in the structural similarities evident between verse 56 and verses 57 and 59. There is a direct correlation between verses 56a and 57, where many (some) ἐψευδομαρτύρουν κατ᾽ αὐτοῦ (were bearing false witness against him), and verses 56b and 59, where the witness was judged as inconsistent. These parallel references serve as narrative markers highlighting the quotation that sits between them. Through this structural recognition, which John R. Donahue has identified as an example of Markan insertion technique, 14:58 is highlighted.

Verse 58 offers a structural concern of its own. It presents a contrast between the temple Jesus claims he will destroy and the one he promises to build, the latter apparently indicating some form of spiritual construction, as it is not to be built with human hands. We are immediately impressed by two structural observations. First, the statement is attributed to false witnesses, so on the narrative surface it appears to be a nontruth. It is, however, a trait of Markan irony that words described as narratively false often detail a larger truth that Mark wishes to convey to the reader. Given the thematic connection of this verse to the temple cleansing story as it is intercalated with Jesus' cursing of the fig tree (Mark 11:11-22), not to mention the repetition of the charge in 15:29, it is likely that Mark wishes the reader to pick up a larger truth here behind the obvious inconsistency of the testimonies. In Mark's narrative understanding, Jesus *is* a threat to the temple.

Second, a train of continuous thought can be traced back from verse 58 to the structural theme developed in the opening verses of the pericope, that of conflict between Jesus and the Jewish leadership. As Donahue notes, there are three major anti-temple sections in the Gospel, and each is followed by a notation that the temple leaders sought to kill Jesus.[8] "By attributing to Jesus a statement that he would destroy the Temple, Mk brings to a culmination the anti-Jerusalem and anti-Temple polemic which runs through the Gospel."[9]

We have here, then, a textual delineation of Jesus' alleged actions that are as sociopolitically oriented as they are cultically oriented. The destruction of the temple appears to be part of a highly developed political motif with sweeping social ramifications.

Verses 60-61a are also structurally connected. The double negative question uttered by the high priest in 60 is matched almost exactly by the double negative narration pattern about Jesus' silence in 61a.[10] The design establishes a vivid structural emphasis on the element of Jesus' silence. Given the connections in imagery between the traditional elements of this passage and the Isaiah corpus, Eduard Schweizer contends that Mark is emphasizing Jesus' silence in connection with themes from Psalm 38:12-14 and Isaiah 53:7.[11] The absence of verbal parallels to the Old Testament text make the observation doubtful. Better instead to see the device of silence as a dramatic technique used to prepare the way for Jesus' statement in verse 62. "Mark, in effect, says that the charge about the destruction of the temple merits no complete answer until the solemn confession of Jesus is made in 14:62."[12]

The formal questioning begins with the interrogative phrase σύ εἰ (you are). While clearly a question, the phrasing matches exactly the indicative use of the terminology elsewhere in the Gospel, where Jesus' nature is being discussed. In 1:11, 3:11, 8:29, and 15:2 we find the same construction. The pattern previous to 14:61 demonstrates that the proclamation is never uttered publicly; when it is, the speaker is enjoined to silence. Only in 14:61 does it become public, but even here it true only ironically.

We arrive finally at verse 62, a text of crucial structural significance. Not only is it the sole, direct statement by Jesus here, but it also becomes the witness capable of achieving the goal the Sanhedrin had announced at the beginning of the text. Jesus' messianic claim is highlighted with a narrative messianic formula. The verse begins with the response ἐγώ εἰμι (I am). Although several manuscripts here claim an alternative formulation, the bulk of the evidence supports the text. Despite manuscript evidence in favor of the text, J. C. O'Neill maintains that the variant, "you have said that I am" is to be preferred because this arrangement more adequately agrees with the Matthean and Lukan versions. The other Synoptists, he argues, would not have so altered Mark.[13] This argument on the surface appears to agree with the device of the messianic secret utilized by Mark throughout; the reserve would here continue to be maintained.

There is, however, a more acceptable alternative. Mark has indeed created the secrecy motif, but he has established it within the bounds of a Gospel that also designates a concept of growing conflict between Jesus and the Jewish leadership. The conflict has grown to a climax in this passage, and along with it, the messianic emphasis that Mark connects with Jesus. In other words, just as the conflict has developed to a climax here in 55-64, so also the christological images have now come to full and final expression. Mark has created dramatic tension that here reaches its resolution as he piles up christological titles in a structural density he has never shown before. The opening words, ἐγώ εἰμι (I am), direct as they are, pick up on this climactic conclusion and anticipate its full resolution later in the verse.

The response to Jesus' reply is dramatized when the high priest reacts by tearing his clothes, an Old Testament expression of horror (2 Kings 18:37, 19:1). Once the high priest signals that Jesus has become the sole valid witness against himself, the imagery that opened the pericope is picked up and completed. The testimony leads to the religious charge of blasphemy, by which Jesus is deemed worthy of death. The "seeking" of verse 55 is now fulfilled. The conflict between Jesus and the Jewish leadership has about run its course.

The cause for the denouement of this conflict, however, remains textually unclear. There are to be sure the social and political concerns of verse 58, but now these concerns have been developed so as to have a religious grounding in the charge of blasphemy. And yet, even though blasphemy appears to be the final cause for the decision against Jesus, this spiritually focused judgment is integrally connected with a sociopolitical challenge to the symbolic center of the Jewish theocratic society.

The potential field for meaning widens further when the trial before Pilate is considered. Although on the surface it appears to be thematically separate from its juridical predecessor, this trial scene maintains several structural similarities. Both trials open with a notation regarding the activity of the entire Sanhedrin, καὶ ὅλον τὸ συνέδριον (and the whole Sanhedrin). This is especially notable in the trial before Pilate since the evangelist has already, in the same opening verse, identified the three groupings that make up the official body. The additional reference is superfluous. Both trials also end with a scene of mockery. Once again the case of the second trial is notable; Luke places his post-trial mockery after the interrogation before Herod. In the Markan text a decision has evidently been made either through tradition or by the evangelist to open and close both trials with similar structural concerns.

The second trial is also bracketed like the first. Again the terminology, παραδίδωμι (hand over), has ties to earlier parts of the Gospel that were ultimately directed toward Jesus' passion and destruction.[14] At 15:1, Jesus is "handed over" to Pilate by the Sanhedrin. At 15:10, Pilate recognizes why the Jewish authorities have "handed him over," and at 15:15 he accedes to their wishes by himself "handing him over" to be crucified.

There is also a remarkable resemblance between the structures of 14:60-62a and 15:4-5, 2. The translations are presented literally so that the parallels, both approximate and exact, can be recognized:

| Mark 14:60-62a | Mark 15:4-5, 2 |
| --- | --- |
| v. 60 And having stood in the midst, the high priest asked Jesus, saying, You answer nothing? What do they witness against you? | v. 4 And again Pilate asked him, saying, You answer nothing? See with what they accuse you. |
| v. 61 But he remained silent and did not answer anything. | v. 5 But Jesus no longer answered anything, so that Pilate marveled. |
| Again the high priest asked him and said to him, | v. 2 And Pilate asked him, |

| You are the Christ, the Son of the Blessed? | You are the King of the Jews? |
|---|---|
| v. 62 And Jesus said, I am. | And having answered him he said, You say. |

Verse 15:1 is a puzzle from the start. The phrase συμβούλιον ποιήσαντες is ambiguous; it has caused concern for a host of interpreters. It can mean either "to convene a council" or "to take counsel; to make a plan."[15] Several witnesses, who Schweizer argues are as reliable as those who support the text, have offered a variation, συμβούλιον ἑτοιμάσαντες, which would assure that the reader would understand the latter meaning. In this case Mark would be spared the embarrassing redundancy of having narrated two separate trials that performed exactly the same function. In fact, Schweizer appeals to 3:6, calling our text an exact parallel of that Markan editorial insertion, and concludes that the meaning must be, as it was there, "they wrote out a decision," based on the proceedings of the night before.[16] Frank J. Matera objects that the weight of the external evidence falls to the text.[17] He then argues that Schweizer's concerns can be handled textually by an alternate reading of the text version that clarifies the problem at hand by suggesting that Mark was not introducing a new and redundant Sanhedrin trial but was merely referring back to the first.[18] Our purpose in considering the interpretive problems surrounding the phrase is not to renew questions of tradition, editing, or Sanhedrin law, but to understand how the phrase functions structurally in the overall program of the verse. We would argue that either way—whether the Sanhedrin reconvened or merely made a plan based on the earlier convening—the text functions here as a grammatical bridge that structurally connects the Sanhedrin trial to the proceedings before Pilate. The grammatical intent is the indication of a progression from one trial to the other. The reader is structurally directed to understand that the trial before the whole Sanhedrin is integrally connected to the trial played out before Pilate. In fact, the relationship is causal, indicated by the fact that the participle ποιήσαντες (having taken, made) is paired with a parallel aorist participle, δήσαντες (having bound), in relationship to the critical main verb, παρέδωκαν (they handed over). But if the Sanhedrin trial turns ultimately on the religious concern of blasphemy, the language in its parallel Pilate scene leaves no mistake that the problem with Jesus is a political one.

As was the case in the Sanhedrin trial, clear divisional markers are offered for the material that moves from 15:2-15. Verses 2-5 are bracketed by the name Pilate, and are thematically concerned with Jesus' direct witness before the Roman governor. Verses 6-15 have another marker, Barabbas. While he is not mentioned specifically in verse 6, it is clear that ultimately the personal pronoun "whom" will refer to this figure. His name is immediately picked up in verse 7.

A structural connection is also evident between the two trial segments. The emphasis here is on what is for Pilate the politically charged title "King of the Jews." It dramatically opens the first section and is on prominent display in the second, verses 9 and 12.

Jesus' messianic status, the central structural theme of the Sanhedrin trial, can immediately be designated as the key concern of the second trial as well: "it is clear that the decisive title had to be stated at the very beginning in order to make known what everything depended upon."[19]

The messianic statement is made in virtually the same syntactical form that we found in 14:61b. The same ironic presentation that follows from the revelational formula σύ εἶ (you are) is present here, making Pilate reveal a truth about Jesus' identity that Pilate appears to use as a taunt and a derision. Further, the title, positioned as it is within the same structural sentence format, which is itself in turn positioned in the same structural interrogation format, bears the same implications as "Messiah, son of the Blessed." The differences appear to be formal rather than material. Mark has used forms of title that would be most appropriate for each of the interrogators. "It is a Graeco-Roman formulation of the question which the high priest asked in a Jewish version in 14:61."[20]

Jesus' response, σὺ λέγεις (you say), does not have the same definitiveness that it had in 14:62, where he emphatically declares, ἐγώ εἰμι (I am). Various suppositions are offered to explain the dramatic departure from the use of parallel formations. Bultmann suggests that Jesus implies the affirmative but also indicates that he would have posed the question differently.[21] Martin Dibelius argues that the ambiguous answer allows the text to move forward in a way that a yes answer would not have allowed. Had Jesus admitted his guilt, there would have been no need for further proceedings.[22] Frank J. Matera concurs and goes further: "By rendering Jesus' answer in an ambiguous manner, Mark not only allows the narrator to continue, but he also presents a problem which must be resolved. In what sense is this man the King of the Jews?"[23] Matera's suggestions are helpful. Indeed, the lack of an outright denial on Jesus' part regarding his identification with this politically oriented term, combined with the continued use of it, suggests that it is an accurate description of Jesus in some way. Yet the fact that Jesus answers ambiguously highlights all the more the definitive statement in 14:62.

Part two of the trial before Pilate is concerned with the choice presented to the crowd between Barabbas and Jesus. Barabbas' introduction is highlighted in verse 7 by the bracketing of verses 6 and 8, which redundantly refer to Pilate's questioning of the crowd regarding their choice for prisoner amnesty.[24] The method of Barabbas' introduction accentuates the element of choice. C. S. Mann notes that the participle λεγόμενος (being called) is usually preceded by a personal name and then followed by a description or title. The unusual formulation here, where the participle precedes what appears to be the personal name, suggests that "what we have here is not a personal name but an epithet. *Barabbas* is the Greek rendering of *bar abba* (son of the Father)."[25] The rendering "Son of the Father" suggests a parallel with the description that Jesus accepts for himself in the Sanhedrin trial, Son of the Blessed. Even if Barabbas is not an epithet but a name, such a comparison obviously strengthens the argument that Jesus and Barabbas are offered as choices to the reader as well as to the crowd in the narrative.

In making these adroit textual connections, Mark has once again apparently confused the issue. Jesus' religious condemnation by the Jews in 14:60-64 has been placed in parallel arrangement with his sociopolitical condemnation by Pilate in a way that suggests that both judicial decision makers operate from the same allegations, when in reality they do not. Textually, then, it remains unclear whether Mark understands Jesus' crucifixion to have resulted from a sociopolitical or a religious cause. The potential for textual meaning is wide open.

## Ideational and Macro-Interpersonal Considerations

We begin our analysis with an ideational consideration of the *significant* "temple" by focusing on 14:58.[26] We have already taken note of Mark's anti-temple polemic that pits the high priests against Jesus throughout the narrative. This structural development is a clear macro-interpersonal indication that "temple" in the trial scene stretches beyond the boundaries of a purely cultic meaning.

Mark opposes two kinds of temples, one "made with hands" against one "not made with hands." The general consensus is that Mark has added to tradition with Hellenistic phraseology; neither of the two terms, χειροποίη-τον (made with hands) and ἀχειροποίητον (not made with hands), is found in other Markan uses of the saying. The phrase "not with hands" may well refer to a new socioreligious entity that stands to replace the outmoded Jewish community represented by the physical temple. The Markan interpretation of this concept suggests that the temple that Jesus, as Son of man, builds in lieu of the physical one is the gathered community of his followers (cf. 13:26-27).[27]

And yet the term *temple* as Mark uses it also has a powerful religious focus. Again one begins with the recognition of the Hellenistic imagery in the terms χειροποίητον (made with hands) and ἀχειροποίητον (not made with hands). Mark appears to be contrasting the physical temple with a spiritualized one. "The contrast between 'which men made' and 'not made by men' is typical of Hellenistic thought, where external worship in temple and sacrifice was contrasted with purely spiritual, inner worship (Acts 7:48; 17:24, cf. 2 Cor 5:1; Eph 2:11; Heb 9:11,24)."[28]

Mark's placement of the anti-temple statement in a passage concerned so deeply with eschatology enhances this view. Jesus, as Son of man, could well be interested here in the establishment of a futuristic spiritual reign rather than a human community. Indeed, the gathering of the elect promised by the Son of man in chapter 13 has powerful apocalyptic overtones. A realized earthly community need not be intended specifically.

Matera even endeavors to prove that Mark's framing of the temple cleansing with the cursing and withering of the fig tree suggests an eschatological rather than a sociopolitical messianic event. He notes that the temple imagery, the cleansing in chapter 11 and the destruction prophecy in 13:2, is bracketed by references to the Mount of Olives at 11:1 and 13:3. The references conjure up allusions to Zechariah 14:4, where the prophet presents the Mount of Olives as the location of the eschatological judgment. The resultant conceptual image would therefore suggest that Jesus' relationship with the temple is predictive more of an eschatological trial than a sociopolitical movement.

The temple in this understanding is no longer the symbol of institutionalized power in Judaism, but the locus of the divine person. Jesus' move to cleanse, destroy, and rebuild it is therefore more a religious than a sociopolitical concern. It is therefore conceptualized by the priests as blasphemy. The concern was Jesus' religious claims that led him to speak and act recklessly regarding the temple, the symbol of the deity.

Our ideational focus turns now to the key titles Messiah, Son of God, Son of man, and King of the Jews. Our concern will be to clarify the conceptual images associated with each.

Following the Markan order we begin with *Christos,* Messiah. Mark's use of the term in the rest of the Gospel helps us understand themes he is working with here. The title opens his narrative in 1:1 and is picked up again in 8:29, 9:41, 12:35, 13:21, and 15:32. John R. Donahue is helpful when he notes that in the only two instances where the title is directly applied to Jesus, 8:29, 31 and 14:61, it is qualified. In both cases, the image of a religiously oriented Son of man is paramount.[29] This connection with Son of man leads many interpreters to the conclusion that *Christos* is a *signifiant* with a primarily religious conceptual meaning.

The messianic secrecy that shrouds Jesus' ministry is publicly clarified at 14:61-62 because it is now evident that Jesus' kingdom is not of this world. He is to be a suffering, not a Davidic, messiah. In 8:31, when Peter was confused about the issue, he was severely rebuked. This messiah, as Son of man, was destined for the end narrated in 14:55-64. In fact, Joel Marcus contends that Mark has connected *Christos* with Son of God in 14:61 for precisely this delimiting reason. Rather than being a synonym for *messiah,* he contends that it indicates the kind of messianic expectation Mark has in view, not a Messiah-Son-of-David but a Messiah-Son-of-God. By this he means that Mark's emphasis is not on Jesus' identification with human political concerns, but is rather on his divine, religious identification with God. Jesus' crime is that by calling himself the Son of God he proclaims an equality with God.[30] The eschatology explicit in Jesus' confession in 14:62 heightens the intensity of his criminal predicament.

Macro-interpersonal considerations, however, suggest that *Christos* also maintains sociopolitical implications. Mark demonstrates structurally in the Sanhedrin material, and throughout the narrative, that significant conflict has occurred between Jesus and the Jewish leadership. In 15:10 he tells us that the leaders are jealous of Jesus. Tibor Horvath makes the reasoned suggestion that they have legitimate cause. He points out that Jesus' fame and reputation must have been based on his remarkable feats. Such noticeable achievement brings him recognition, allowing him to rise above his "obscure Nazarene background" and come into conflict with the Jewish leadership. "On account of his reputation, Jesus' unusual sayings and claims did not appear as simply impossible and ridiculous to the ears of the Jews."[31]

The saying, which implies a momentous feat, that Mark brings to our attention at the trial is the one regarding the temple in 14:58. It is a saying of messianic proportions. It is not the activity of a redeemer messiah that arouses concern, but the activity of a messiah whose aim is the destruction of the institutional center of Jewish religious and social life. The logic of such a conclusion arises once again from macro-interpersonal considerations: "In Jewish thought the influence of the dynastic oracle of 2 Sam 7:11-14 that the scion of David would 'build a house for my name' fostered the view that Temple building was a royal function of one designated by Yahweh. . . . Mark applies this function to Jesus."[32] Donald Juel notes more specifically that the messiah was not only the builder but also the destroyer of the temple. He then provides evidence from the Targumim and Qumran to validate his claim.[33] The 4Q Florilegium midrash on 2 Samuel 7:10-14 interests us here, for in it the messiah is clearly given jurisdiction over temple construction and destruction, and the context is eschatological. Mark's use of the traditional statement regarding the destroying and rebuilding of the temple could belie his understanding that it is a messianic claim. This hypothesis is strengthened by the fact that immediately after its presentation, the apocalyptic, messianic imagery of verses 60-62 flows forth, with its emphasis on the work of the Son of man.

While the future eschatological claim focuses on a temple "not built with hands," the claim of destruction clearly targets the physical Jerusalem temple. While this claim does not make the messiah figure in any sense a Zealot, it does suggest that, for Mark, at least as he understands the perspective of the Jewish leadership, Jesus' messianic remarks could signify an all too real negative effect on the institutional symbol of their power and authority. Jesus had taken aim, not at Rome, but at Jerusalem. The messiah who would destroy their power base promised, one day, as Son of man, to establish a power base of his own.

The second title, Son of the Blessed, which scholars have noted is equivalent to Son of God, is used in deference to the speaking of the divine name. Mark once again establishes lines of communication with the other titles. "Son of God" is picked up again in 15:39, a text preoccupied with the "King of the Jews" imagery.[34] Jesus, identified time and time again as "King of the Jews," once dead on the cross is proclaimed "Son of God." Standing as it does in such a climactic position in chapter 15, there can be little doubt that the title Son of God interprets the title King.

Marcus may be correct in his supposition that the title Son of God delimits and interprets *Christos,* but this recognition still does not solve a key conceptual problem.[35] Even if Jesus had claimed that he was Son of the Blessed, appropriately using a euphemism for the divine name, the charge of blasphemy still does not apply. It does not indicate the real problem of the Jewish leadership with Jesus, nor with his use of the title. It is only by looking at the connections between Mark's use of this title and his use of the others in the trial scenes that we can come to some sort of conclusion. As we know from Luke's Gospel, there was indeed a concern associated with Jesus' claim to the title Son of God. Luke, however, does not refer to blasphemy, but to specific sociopolitical problems when he finally narrates the trial before Pilate. The linking of this title, with its royal implications, to the title King of the Jews in the trial before Pilate suggests a similar concern. While Jesus' claim to be Son of God did not constitute blasphemy, "it provided a convenient excuse to delate Jesus to the governance on the grounds of seditious speech."[36] Indeed, the closure to Jesus' life, cloaked as it is in royal sonship imagery, confirms such a possibility. "The fact that Jesus was executed by the Romans because he claimed to have been King of the Jews (Mark 15:26,//s) suggests that something else was at stake."[37]

The Barabbas imagery reinforces this sociopolitical claim. Mark has positioned against Jesus a man whose very name, very identity, reminds the reader of the title Son of God. Barabbas is the one called Son of *Abba,* the Father. Jesus, who refers to God as *Abba,* proclaims himself to be Son of God, and he, too, is on trial. He, like Barabbas, is presented before the people—two Sons of the Father. Pilate's next actions, comparing them before the crowd, suggests that there is something ideationally comparable about them. This similarity cannot be religious, because Barabbas is not a religious figure. Jesus, who does maintain religious conceptual implications, is, by name and association, drawn into the sociopolitical narrative world in which Barabbas lives and acts.

The third title, which we have already begun discussing in connection with the previous two, is the one that holds a climactic position in 14:62, Son of man. Mark is now ready for the presentation of his *pesher* (interpretation) regarding Jesus' exaltation/parousia.[38] The two previous titles are now qualified; it is Son of man that becomes the interpretative norm and the ironical key to understanding Jesus' proper identity. Of the three Markan titles, Son of man is the only one uttered only by Jesus, and so "it becomes the designation *par excellence* by which Jesus describes his mission in Mark."[39]

The verse is therefore critical not only for this passage, but for the way in which the entire Gospel views Jesus from a christological perspective. Indeed, the conflict established in verses 55-59 is now picked up and elaborated in apocalyptic overtones. In each of the three passion predictions—8:31, 9:31, and 10:33—where Jesus predicts the outcome of his conflict with the Jewish leadership, the title Son of man is present. Connected with this conflict, which is to result in death, is the theme of resurrection, an image of vindication also climaxed here in verse 62. This, then, is undoubtedly a passage about conflict and triumph, the former waged on a human landscape, the latter engineered from the glorious beyond. The "Son of man" notation in 13:26 makes this image of glory clear.

Royal images are used as well. After categorizing the Markan Son of man sayings into three sets (sayings that refer to earthly activity—2:10, 28; sayings that refer to suffering—8:31, 9:9, 12, 31, 10:33-34, 10:45, 14:21, 41; sayings that refer to the future coming—8:38, 13:26, 14:62), Matera searches for a connecting link. He concludes that it resides in Mark's understanding of the authority, ἐχουσία, of the Son of man. It is this authority that provokes conflict with the Jewish leadership and causes misunderstanding among the disciples. They do not understand that it is an authority of service and sacrifice, not one of power and control. The future sayings about the Son of man indicate that his authority will be vindicated at his future coming. From whence does this authority come? It comes from his position as God's royal Son. Matera traces Mark's use of "authority" and finds that Jesus exercises it as God's Son.[40] But it is with the transfiguration and the Gethsemane scene that he finds his most conclusive evidence. In each case the Son of man is authoritatively identified with God's Son. The royal implications are heightened in 14:62 with the reference to the royal psalm.

This only Son, the King, suffers as the Son of man. In this way, Mark establishes a link between Jesus' role and the fulfillment of Old Testament prophecy. Here we are given a unifying motivation for the narrative program. Jesus' death in connection with these titles has for Mark the definite understanding that this King dies according to God's divine design.

The eschatological emphasis is heightened as we further consider the Markan use of Son of man. Hendrikus Boers points out, for example, that the title's connection with the other imagery of 14:62 suggests that the reign of the Son is not of this earth, but is a future, heavenly realm.[41] In fact, in the three categorizations for Son of man compiled by Matera, the third is preoccupied completely with the Son of man's future coming and the implications of the heavenly office that goes with it. Even the category that refers to the earthly activities of the Son of man (2:10, 28) is preoccupied not with matters of political and social reconstruction, but with the religious concerns of forgiving sin and teaching about the sabbath.

Matera's second category is concerned with the suffering that Jesus foresees for the Son of man. In each verse that he places in this set, Jesus' passion is prefigured as a necessity, and in 10:45 the religious reason for this necessity is plainly stated: The Son of man is to give his life as a ransom for many. This concept of suffering as fulfillment is further emphasized by Mark's use of the verb παραδίδωμι, "to hand over." A structural key to our understanding of the trial scenes, it also plays a significant role throughout the Gospel. It is connected with the title Son of man in the last two passion predictions, 9:31 and 10:33. Mark then intensifies its use in the passion proper, using it seven times in chapter 14[42] and another three in the Pilate trial scene. Once again the emphasis is religious. We are directed, for instance, to Isaiah 53:4-12 where the divine servant is sacrificed, "handed over," for the iniquities of others.

The final title, King of the Jews, has already been linked with the other three. The royal image is as important as the structural notation that this title, paralleled with Messiah, would have presented to Pilate the same conceptual meaning the other three titles presented to the high priests. This title establishes most concretely the sociopolitical implications surrounding the charge against Jesus. Its connection with the other titles, however, might suggest that here, too, Mark's aim excludes a sociopolitical intent. The supposition finds support from Mark's conceptual application of the title. Mark does not appeal to kingship language until chapter 15. Why? Because only now will it be apparent to the reader that Jesus' royal claim is not to a sociopolitical throne or cause, but to a religious realm and purpose.

Still, the kind of kingship imagery presented is crucial. Jesus suffers and dies as the messianic son who is King of the Jews. A macro-interpersonal consideration now proves useful; the perspective of Jesus' opponents must be considered. How would a Roman react to such a title? The soldiers reacted by taunting Jesus, by mockingly attributing to him the station and privileges of a political king (cf. 15:16-20). Pilate reacted with a sentence of crucifixion, a punishment uniquely suited for crimes of sedition rather than for crimes of offense against a subject people's God. Even the governor's language implies a sociopolitical concern. "The latter's question *You are the king of the Jews?* (emphatic σύ), suggests surprise; the Galilean teacher had none of the appearance of a revolutionist."[43]

Yet Pilate appears not to have trusted appearances. At 15:26, Mark notes that "King of the Jews" is the criminal charge he appends to Jesus' cross. He takes the charge seriously because he recognizes that Jesus' activities have produced an envious concern on the part of the Jewish leadership:

> Pilate would hardly have taken these charges seriously unless they had included a political matter—some threat to peace and public order—and some of the Jewish leaders may, of course, have been genuinely afraid that Jesus' popularity with the crowds might produce a dangerous popular revolt.[44]

The Jewish leaders would therefore choose Barabbas to be released since his activity was geared against Rome rather than them. Pilate could accede to their wishes since Barabbas did not attach to himself the title king. D. E. Nineham is right to point us now toward 15:12. "Pilate's next question is also very strange; surely he was able to pardon the accused."[45] The fact that he did not, even though the narrative surface suggests that he thought Jesus innocent, surely indicates that he did sense a problem with Jesus.

The Jewish leadership and Pilate would have been well founded in their conclusion that Jesus had attributed to himself the prerogatives of a sociopolitical king. When Jesus entered Jerusalem for the first time in chapter 11, he did so amidst all the trappings of a figure who was sociopolitically inclined. Boers points out that 11:7-11 encourages for the Jewish observers a recollection of the imagery in Psalm 118 about a messianic king coming in the name of the Lord:

> If Jesus' entry was anything like the one described in the account, the conclusion that he had been a messianic pretender would have been inescapable. If, furthermore, the entry had been followed by an incident such as the reported cleansing of the temple, the Jewish leaders would indeed have had every reason to be apprehensive.[46]

## Conclusion

Our brief analysis of the trial scenes from textual, ideational, and macro-interpersonal perspectives shows that a great deal of potential meaning exists in the passages. We have presented the evidence without favor for any particular position in the hopes that the reader will better understand our use of the linguistic categories as they refer to the material at hand. We will now turn to a consideration of particular researchers who have taken specific positions regarding the meaning of the passages. We intend to show through this survey how each researcher manipulates the textual, ideational, and macro-interpersonal evidence according to particular micro-interpersonal predilections. Textual, ideational, and macro-interpersonal evidence remains just that, evidence with many potential possibilities of meaning. Those possibilities are delimited micro-interpersonally.

# 7 Jesus the Redeemer

IN MARK'S ACCOUNT, RELIGIOUS CONCERNS mobilized the Jewish leadership against Jesus of Nazareth. Jesus' religious claim to be the Son of God who would effect human salvation was a blasphemous self-attestation cultically and legally punishable by death. On this matter, the earliest twentieth-century investigators of the Markan trial scenes are in general agreement.

As we have shown, there is no doubt that the textual, ideational, and macro-interpersonal information provided in the Markan trial scenes justifies such a conclusion. We have also shown, however, that the attribution of the religious motive does not exhaust the potential meaning of the text. We would argue that the investigators, who will themselves momentarily be investigated, arrived at the conclusion that it was the single most significant factor precisely because their sociolinguistic contexts preconditioned them to access and value the religious language markers above any other. In other words, though they appeal to varieties of historical, historical-critical, and form-critical principles, they are, ultimately, all micro-interpersonally driven.

## Radical Historical Skeptics

Two of the earliest twentieth-century interpreters of the trial scenes, Julius Wellhausen and Hans Lietzmann, consciously intend to limit themselves to textual, ideational, and macro-interpersonal considerations.[1] Both are radical historical critics who contend that Mark is not conveying an accurate historical accounting of Jesus' trial, but that he has manufactured an account that meets the spiritual and social needs of his faith community. These radical skeptics are preoccupied with the question, What historical reality might have inspired the nascent Christian community to narrate a fiction as though it were historical fact? In other words, what is the historical motivation behind the literary lie?

For Wellhausen the focus of the Sanhedrin passage is 14:58. Pointing to 13:2, and to a lesser degree to 15:29, he contends that Jesus did indeed speak against the temple during his ministry. This anti-temple pronouncement was the blasphemy for which Jesus was condemned in 14:64. Wellhausen is highly critical of 14:61-62, the high priest's question and Jesus' reply. His evidence is, however, neither textual nor ideational; it is rather his own intuitive historical reaction. His operation is, at this point, purely intuitive, micro-interpersonal. "Es is wenig glaublich, dass er das überhaupt getan hat, und am wenigsten dass er es vor dem Synedrium getan hat."[2] Wellhausen therefore does not believe that the verses originally belonged to the text; in order to ascertain the text's original sense one must remove them. The key ideational signifier for him thus becomes the temple. It is the center of religious life for Jewish society; therefore, to speak against it is to commit the supreme religious crime. He has built his central ideational theme from an intuitive, micro-interpersonal observation.

In order to sustain this thesis, Wellhausen must explain logically why the suspect verses are out of place in their present context. He reasons, macro-interpersonally, that the passage's original anti-temple posture was too harsh for the early Christian community. Jesus' claim to be the messiah was less troubling. Verses 14:61-62 are therefore offered as an apologetic for 14:58. He therefore solves the problem of the relationship between 14:58 and 14:61-62, not through textual analysis, but by hypothesizing the presuppositions of the early faith community.

Wellhausen argues that this same community concern is responsible for Mark's attribution of the anti-temple statement to *false* witnesses. Indeed, in this scheme, by the time Luke writes, the statement is so problematic that the third evangelist omits it altogether, as he omits the parallel reference in Mark 15:29.[3] There were such strong reservations in the community about the anti-temple statement that Mark was compelled to attach an apologetic to it and Luke was compelled to omit it. Again, Wellhausen offers no independent ideational, historical, or textual verification. He uses the historical presuppositions of his method, which are themselves based on personal intuition, to determine his findings. He is operating micro-interpersonally.

Hans Lietzmann argues that there are five internal textual and ideational reasons why the Sanhedrin trial must be considered historically suspect.[4] First, 14:58 reflects Hellenistic imagery and is therefore late. Second, Jesus' silence is based on Isaiah 53:7. Third, the title Son of the Blessed in 14:61 is "unJewish" and therefore a Christian title that the high priest would not have used. Fourth, no blasphemy occurred during the trial according to Sanhedrin law. And finally, John 18:31 was legally inaccurate—the Jewish high court did have the right to pronounce and carry out capital judgments. The fact that 14:64 shows such a judgment, but then presents Jesus' death as the consequence of a Roman decree, demonstrates that the Sanhedrin trial could not have taken place as presented.

Having therefore concluded that no Sanhedrin trial took place, Lietzmann proceeds to ascertain the macro-interpersonal and ideational foundations on which the fabrication was based. The conceptual model, he argues, is the scene in Acts 6 where Stephen, arraigned before an angry mob, is stoned because of his anti-temple stance and his vision, which is similar to the visionary statement uttered by Jesus in Mark 14:62.

Lietzmann argues that the motive behind this ideational re-creation and reproduction of the Stephen episode with Jesus at the center is the early faith community's need to present Jesus' death as redemptively precipitated. Once again the macro-interpersonal need for a community apologetic takes center stage. In Lietzmann's case, however, it is not a mere desire to let Pilate and the Romans off the hook; there is also a desire to connect Jesus' demise with the prophetic literary traditions of the Jewish people. Lietzmann searches the literary history and finds ample reason why the Jewish leadership should be presented as the architects of Jesus' destruction:

> Aber die Gemeinde wusste, dass es die Juden sind, die immer die von Gott gesandten Propheten töten, und sie bewahrte ein leidenschaftlich herbes Wort Jesu, dass er wie alle Propheten in Jerusalem sterben müsse (Luk. 13,33). So formten sie die Passionsgeschichte mit unbewusster Selbstverständlichkeit nach ihrer Theologie und entlastete den Pilatus immer mehr.[5]

Clearly, he believes Mark to be a creative author whose motivations are micro-interpersonal.

The real trial, Lietzmann claims, is the one before Pilate, which Mark begins recording at 15:2. Here Jesus is condemned explicitly for political reasons. Lietzmann bases this claim on the historical recognition that Jesus was crucified; therefore he was killed by the Romans. The title on the placard above his head read "King of the Jews," a political charge that would have given only the Romans real cause for concern. This macro-interpersonal argument, he feels, is given textual and ideational support in that the text puts this political charge on conspicuous display throughout the confrontation with the Roman prefect.

Having established his case on a macro-interpersonal foundation, Lietzmann now seeks to illustrate what happened historical-ideationally. He argues that the political charges go all the way back to the temple cleansing episode, which aroused, not Jewish, but Roman concern. Mark, through a creative literary rereading, makes it a religious affair that concerned only the Jewish leadership. The evangelist altered the historical circumstance by connecting the Sanhedrin trial to the temple cleansing and other anti-Jewish leadership speeches (11:27-33, chapter 12) so that the whole work would, on a literary level, point not to Roman political concerns, but to Jewish religious concerns. Historical-ideationally, Lietzmann argues, even the messianic claim was a politically potent self-designation for Jesus. Jesus was handed over to Pilate as a messianic pretender who was guilty of disturbing the peace.[6] In 14:64, however, Mark, bowing to the anxiety of the early faith community, made it a purely religious concern of blasphemy.

Lietzmann's work represents progress compared with Wellhausen's efforts. Macro-interpersonal investigation has become far more sophisticated, building clearly on historical-ideational and textual evidence. Micro-interpersonal influences play a less perceptible role. Even so, a strong degree of micro-interpersonal influence remains in both authors. At the first micro-interpersonal level their work is influenced by the methodological presumptions encoded in the skeptical approach to biblical inquiry. Conclusions are in many ways prefigured by the foundational questions that orient their scholarship. Radically critical questions direct them toward a highly skeptical view of the text.

This micro-interpersonal predilection becomes particularly problematic when micro-interpersonal and macro-interpersonal features are confused. This was the case with Wellhausen's research. He substituted intuition, a resource internal to his own psychic makeup, rather than textual, ideational, or historical data to support his macro-interpersonal conclusions regarding the makeup of the primitive Christian community and the effect of that makeup on the way the text was finally formed. In effect, he asked a proper methodological question but then went about solving it in a highly personalized manner.

At the second (internal) micro-interpersonal level, Wellhausen and Lietzmann are equally bounded. When we consider their work from within the broader spectrum of biblical analysis at the turn of the century, we find potent micro-interpersonal influences. Their scholarly generation was characterized by two dominant trends in the micro-interpersonal preunderstanding of biblical scholarship. The first was the general sense of historicism that became particularly acute in the latter half of the nineteenth century and continued its influence into the twentieth. "Not only was the Bible to be treated 'objectively,' that is, in accordance with the prevailing presuppositions of secular scholarship, but it and the Hebrew history of which it was the primary source were to be treated as part of the general sweep of history."[7]

The second was cultural Protestantism, a liberal, moral-ethical approach to biblical investigation that dominated the latter nineteenth and early twentieth centuries, particularly in Germany. Appealing especially to the seminal work of Immanuel Kant, Jacques de Senarclens notes that revelation plays a secondary role in this scholarly arena of thought. The believer is instead encouraged to study the moral and ethical teachings of the biblical material. This means that, where the Gospels are concerned, Jesus' teachings are of primary importance as a guide to moral perfection. The Son of God is understood as the "incarnation of moral good, or of humanity in its moral perfection."[8]

This kind of scholarly atmosphere shows a lessening of intensity regarding the revelatory significance of the passion narrative. The passion materials generally, and the trial scenes particularly, are not the loci of key concerns for the biblical student, except as repositories of information about Jesus' moral triumph and the implications of that triumph for the believer. The spiritually significant materials are found in the chapters that focus on Jesus' teachings that annotate specific moral and ethical directives for living. Questions of historical accuracy regarding the descriptions of events in the passion are therefore redemptively insignificant. In this way the ground becomes fertile for radical skepticism as a foundation for historical biblical inquiry. Because authors like Wellhausen and Lietzmann, operating from the morally secure and historically oriented foundations of cultural Protestantism, have no redemptive stake in the historicity of the trial scenes, they are enabled—indeed, even encouraged—to challenge their presentation in the Markan account. Historical study is in this way sharpened to a radical edge. Micro-interpersonal factors thus add a new dimension to the process of text interpretation.

Despite their methodological differences, these two practitioners of radical historical skepticism agree on the key principle.[9] Analysis of the trial material must begin with the macro-interpersonal rather than the textual or ideational functions of language. Ideational testimony is used to support a macro-interpersonal reconstruction of the primary concerns of the primitive community, and textual data are called upon as final investigative evidence. The researcher attempts to determine what the text means by considering first and foremost what it most likely meant to the community for which it was intended. Meaning, it is understood, is therefore derived from a micro-interpersonal interchange between primitive audience and text.

Here we recognize how the endeavor of the historical skeptics is incomplete. Their interests suggest a necessary investigative step that they did not pursue. They theorized about the meaning of a text for various historical communities, but failed to consider how their own approaches to textual meaning were influenced by their own circumstances. Because they do not allow for micro-interpersonal interchange between text and modern audience, these interpreters assume that an exposition about what the text *meant* determines what the text *means* in any and all circumstances.

## George Dunbar Kilpatrick

George Dunbar Kilpatrick starts from a micro-interpersonal premise that consciously opposes the efforts of the historical skeptics. He believes that the passion materials give an accurate record of the events at the conclusion of Jesus' life and ministry.[10] Like his opponents, Kilpatrick is energized by macro-interpersonal concerns. This means that once again the needs and questions of the earliest Christian community must be addressed. Because his historical presuppositions are so radically different, however, Kilpatrick shifts the key investigative focus. He presumes that the needs of the community are addressed by the simple retelling of the actual historical circumstance. The material was not created to provide an appropriate understanding of Jesus' death, but was saved as tradition precisely because the events themselves shed light on the manner and meaning of Jesus' condemnation. Therefore, instead of searching the textual and ideational data for seams or gaps that demonstrate contrivance, he approaches the data with the intent of acquiring evidence for historical probability. Problems in language and structure in the text no longer indicate contrivance, but suggest the evangelist has merely retold the historical event incompletely. Because his first-century reading community already knew the facts surrounding the case, the evangelist transmitted only the pertinent, climactic details. The reader then filled in any apparent narrative gaps by turning to a pool of knowledge about the trials that he or she shared with the evangelist. Because a modern investigator lacks that shared sociolinguistic background, the final product appears to be a disjointed retelling with many gaps. By macro-interpersonally filling those gaps, Kilpatrick hopes to provide a coherent historical picture of Jesus' trials. He wants to do methodologically what the first-century readers did naturally.

Kilpatrick begins on common ground between himself and Lietzmann: acceptance of the historicity of the trial scene before Pilate. As Jesus was crucified, it seems likely that the Roman governor had a hand in the final judgment. And since Rome would have been unimpressed with religious charges assessed against Jesus, it seems equally appropriate that it was his association with the politically sensitive title King of the Jews that provoked the sentence of death. But here the focus shifts. If it was Jesus' association with a political title that prompted a political trial, the following (macro-interpersonal) question is in order: What historical purpose would a trial before the Jewish Sanhedrin have served? Kilpatrick sets out to answer this question by posing a series of ideational arguments backed up with textual data.

Appealing to Mark 14:1, 43, 55, and 15:1, Kilpatrick argues ideationally that the entire Jewish leadership had a legitimate legal problem with the itinerant preacher, one for which they could turn him over to Pilate for final prosecution. Another macro-interpersonal question follows: What historical situation could have made such a unanimous judicial assault against Jesus likely? Now the charge in 14:58 makes historical sense. "The charge was that Jesus had spoken blasphemy against the Holy Place, the Temple."[11]

A key problem remains. Mark explains that the anti-temple charge was proffered by *false* witnesses. Because his historical reconstruction cannot work if the temple charge against Jesus was false, Kilpatrick must "propose a correction in Mark's narrative."[12] Even though there are significant textual variations between 13:2 and 14:58, he appeals to the former citation as conclusive evidence that Jesus did foretell the temple's destruction. Even more problematic, he cites extratextual evidence from Matthew 26:60-61 and John 2:19.

Now a second ideational problem arises. What is the historical evidence that such a statement warranted a sentence of death? In rabbinic law the act of speaking against the temple is neither blasphemy nor any other kind of crime worthy of the death penalty.[13] Again, gaps must be filled. Kilpatrick fills them macro-interpersonally. Like the historical skeptics against whom he fights, he determines his argument by his reconstruction of the communities that served as the target environment for the Gospel story. The Mishnah, Kilpatrick advises, was written after the first century in which these events took place. Since there was no longer a temple, it made little sense to include anti-temple statements in its criminal code. Kilpatrick was convinced that during the first century, as during the time of the prophets, such statements were, in the minds of the Jewish leadership, worthy of a death sentence.[14] Here he cites Lietzmann's example of Stephen, but for the opposite reason. Kilpatrick argues that Stephen is a first-century representative of the Jesus tradition whose "blasphemous" statements against the temple incited an attack that led to his death.

A further historical question calls forth Kilpatrick's next ideational consideration. How does this condemnation for religious purposes make sense in a situation where Jesus was crucified as a political troublemaker? Here he turns to the messianic question posed to Jesus in 14:61. Why was this question necessary historically? The answer makes perfect sense in Kilpatrick's scheme: "If the council was to bring Jesus before Pilate, it was desirable to bring a charge against him which would carry weight with Pilate. This a political charge would do. . . . The question was put in order to have grounds for a political charge, to be preferred before Pilate." [15]

We are left, then, with two separate trial scenes, both historical, one that condemns Jesus for religious purposes, and the other that uses a political charge to prompt an execution. The primary motivation for Jesus' demise is the Jewish religious concern; the political element is merely a foil.

Kilpatrick discerns another textual problem. The charge in 14:61-62, Son of the Blessed, is not the grammatical equivalent of that used in 15:2, King of the Jews. Once again, in order to make his historical accounting work, Kilpatrick must fill the gap. There are two possible reasons for the difference in grammatical content. First, the exchange between Jesus and the high priest may have been rewritten in the light of later history. The real question was, Are you the king of Israel? The second possibility is that Mark's narrative is incomplete. This choice suggests that the high priest asked two questions of Jesus, one regarding his messianic claims, the other regarding his claim to kingship. Only the first survived in the tradition. "Whichever we choose the inconsistency disappears and our narrative becomes coherent." [16] The problem is that, consistently, in order to make the narrative coherent, hypothetical macro-interpersonal considerations rather than textual or ideational evidence are adduced. Kilpatrick's methodological preunderstanding demands that the gaps be filled in such a way as to prove the historicity of the scene.

A final conceptual problem remains. If the primary concern was Jewish, and if the Jews already had a legitimate cause for a death penalty, why was Jesus in the end not killed by the Jews, but by the Romans? Kilpatrick argues that the Jewish court was unable to carry out the death penalty. Here he appeals textually to John 19:31 and the Palestinian Talmud, both of which explain that the Jews of this time did not possess the power to conduct capital punishment. This supposition is affirmed by another macro-interpersonal reference. He presents capital trial requirements from Egypt, which he asserts are identical to the situation in Israel of the time. There local authorities could fully execute minor cases, but had only the power of preliminary inquiry into more severe ones. Such cases were dealt with by higher powers. A prisoner was first examined by the locals and then processed for the judgment of the prefect. "We must recognize that the trial of Jesus could, with but little modification, be fitted into this scheme."[17] The problem is that Mark gives neither textual nor ideational evidence that such a macro-interpersonal parallel is appropriate.

In the end Kilpatrick establishes exactly what he set out to demonstrate, that Lietzmann erred when he argued that the trial of Jesus before the Sanhedrin was unhistorical. He manipulates the textual and ideational evidence for his own macro-interpersonal purposes so that even when the evidence proves insufficient, he can appeal to hypothetical "gap-fillings" that make sense only within the parameters of his investigative framework.

Kilpatrick's approach is problematic because he does not realize that his macro-interpersonal presumptions are micro-interpersonally based. He wants the modern reader to abandon his or her own micro-interpersonal influences and read the text out of the historical background that was present for the ancient text writer and readers. Yet his very attempt to reconstruct that background is itself micro-interpersonally determined. His procedure is not drawn from the text. In fact, the text provides no evidence to negotiate between his position and that of Lietzmann, which he opposes. There is insufficient textual and ideational information to provide a basis for critical dialogue between the two scholars. In each case the conclusion reached is a direct result of the micro-interpersonal function of the research methods, and the influence that the methodological orientation has on their internal predispositions toward the material. In both cases the method determines how they read the text and what they look for, what questions they bring to it.

Kilpatrick's external life relationship to Anglo-Saxon methodology internally predisposes him toward a presumption of historical accuracy for the text. For him the influence of the micro-interpersonal life relation comes not so much from the time in which he writes as it does from the place in which his scholarship takes shape. Scholarship is well aware that during the late nineteenth century a fundamental cleavage in the investigative considerations of the biblical material developed into two methodological schools of New Testament criticism. In Germany, where intellectual freedom was encouraged in universities paid by the state, "there developed the school based on naturalistic assumptions; this school . . . denied the historical reality of all the supernatural events recorded in the Bible or elsewhere."[18] In the face of this attack on revelatory significance, an opposing school emerged as "defenders of revelation." Reason remained a primary tool of the investigative procedure in this school as well, but its focus had shifted: "the validation of revelation was the task of reason."[19] "Though this conservative school was not without representation in Germany, its most prominent members were the famous Cambridge trio: Westcott, Lightfoot, and Hort. . . . Their critical followers in twentieth century England, though far less conservative, claim to be following the same methods as the great nineteenth century scholars."[20]

Although Glover recognizes substantial failures in the program of the conservative school, he does perceive the longstanding result of an emergent Anglo-Saxon tradition whose principles of text investigation are distinct from those generally considered as part of the German tradition. While the more aggressive German tradition asks how biblical evidence is formed, the more conservative Anglo tradition proceeds from the Scripture as evidence. In the German tradition it is customary to challenge Scripture as data, to analyze it, to investigate the material background behind it. In the Anglo tradition, instead of questioning the background or challenging the evidence, one interprets the evidence itself. As a result, while the German tradition tends to look for the origins of the Christian religion in its quest for the sources that make up the religion, the Anglo perspective traditionally views the Christian religion as given *sui generis* and considers the Bible to be its fundamental source.

Kilpatrick internalized many of the key traits of this Anglo-Saxon scholarly tradition. For him historicity is a major methodological consideration in one's deliberations on the passion materials. Affected by such a potent micro-interpersonal life relation, his methodological preunderstanding becomes quite intentional. Framing his study at almost every turn is therefore the methodologically appropriate (encoded) question, "What purpose then would these proceedings serve, if they were historical?"[21]

## The Form Critics: Martin Dibelius

The religious emphasis on Jesus' trial and condemnation continues in the work of the form critics. While the cultural Protestants maintained that the spiritual significance of the Gospel materials lay in the ethical and moral teachings of Jesus, form-critical and tradition-historical interpreters emphasized the cultic and spiritual importance of the passion materials. Consideration of early Christian religious life under the influence of the *Religionsgeschichtliche Schule* led the form critics[22] to focus on historical-ideational and macro-interpersonal investigations of the early Christian communities.

Ideationally and textually the form critics were interested in uncovering the boundaries and historical origins of the smallest independent textual units of tradition. By tracking the units back to their most primitive oral stages they hoped to use the material as sources "for reconstructing the beliefs of the early Christian community [more] than as sources for reconstructing the actual events reported."[23] The macro-interpersonal focus now turns from questions of historicity to those of community intent. The key methodological focus is still on the discovery of what the text reveals about the past, but with the emphasis now on *what the early church thought it meant.* This new (micro-interpersonal) methodological encoding will not only prescribe the manner and direction of research, it will also influence the final determination of the significance, purpose, and claims of the material.

Martin Dibelius provides an excellent example of form-critical analysis on the trial scenes.[24] Even though he recognizes that some passages like the last supper and Peter's denial may once have enjoyed a certain independence, he maintains that well before the material units reached the evangelists they had been incorporated into a single passion story. "And that is exactly what differentiates the Passion story from the Gospel tradition as a whole, i.e., its early composition as a connected narrative."[25]

As does K. L. Schmidt,[26] Dibelius contends that community purpose demands such a conclusion. A communal need early on precipitated a connected narrative about Jesus' suffering and death. While Schmidt appealed to the need for an account of the acts of Christian martyrs, Dibelius turned to community kerygma. He was firmly convinced that in early Christian preaching there was a strong micro-interpersonal need to explain the "disgrace of the arrest and the torture of the crucifixion" if indeed Jesus was to be accepted as the Risen Lord. The demands of promulgating a crucified messiah provoked the ideational need for an apologetic sermonic device. That device was the continuous passion story, which not only described Jesus' ordeal from a perspective of Christian faith, but suggested through the careful positioning of Old Testament references that everything that occurred did so according to God's salvific plan.[27]

Dibelius' macro-interpersonal reconstruction of the early Christian community thus explains how and why the material took the shape it did. He proceeds by arguing, in keeping with the sociological preunderstanding of form criticism, that community intent is the primary factor in the positioning of events in the passion narrative. In most cases, the textual structure was there for Mark to follow, not to create.[28] It was not Mark's creative intent that arranged the textual structure for the Pilate and Sanhedrin scenes, but the apologetic sermonic needs of the earliest Christian community.

Dibelius reaches a different conclusion with regard to the internal dynamics of the trial scenes. Here Mark can be seen at work, creatively establishing direction and meaning. Once again, however, even though Dibelius begins with textual and ideational observations, his focus continues to be interpersonal. He uses his textual and ideational investigation to establish the foundation for an illuminating macro-interpersonal determination. Dibelius does not believe that the anti-temple statement was originally connected with Jesus' messianic self-proclamation in verse 62. He argues instead that Mark was determined to emphasize the kerygmatic-messianic element and included the anti-temple statement of verse 58 only because there was an early record of it. Mark then downplays its effect by noting the confusion of the witnesses so as to make decisive the question and answer of verses 61 and 62.[29] Georg Bertram, a form critic who operates from similar kerygmatic presuppositions, declares that Mark further downplays verse 58 by appending the words "with hands" and "not with hands." The alterations have the effect of making Jesus speak not about the Jerusalem temple, but about the Christian community that his work, even during his trial, is in the process of constituting. The new community is of course the cultic group for which the material is appropriated kerygmatically.[30] Mark's intent, then, is soteriological, and he makes this trial the first high point of his passion narrative[31] in order to showcase this intent textually. The key emphasis for both Mark and the primitive community is the religious concern about preaching, and thereby confessing, Jesus as messiah.

## Rudolf Bultmann

Rudolf Bultmann's differences with Dibelius over the existence of a pre-Markan passion narrative are of degree rather than kind. The early narrative was, he argues, a brief recitation of Jesus' arrest, condemnation by the Sanhedrin and Pilate, crucifixion, and death. After looking at textual and ideational incongruities in the present Markan text, he hypothesizes that this early narrative was expanded by legendary accretions. He suggests, for instance, that the account of the anointing at Bethany, the prophecy of Judas' betrayal, part of the last supper (14:22-25), Gethsemane, and Peter's denial are elements foreign to the earlier narrative. He gives a macro-interpersonal explanation to these textual and ideational observations. The interpolations, which he calls embellishments, were added later out of cultic concern.[32] Of particular interest for our study is his supposition that the Sanhedrin trial was inserted for cultic-dogmatic reasons. Originally the trial was represented only by what now surfaces as 15:1. The impetus behind the need for the original passion narrative, and indeed its expanded versions, remained the kerygmatic need of the early community.

Bultmann appeals to these observations about the passion narrative as a whole when he inspects the microcosm of the Sanhedrin trial scene. In its most primitive stage it too was a much briefer account that was later embellished. In the original tradition only the charge about Jesus' identity as messiah, the Son of God, existed. Concern about Jesus' messianic identity would have fit well with the cultic concerns of the early church. The anti-temple charge in v. 58, however, appears foreign to that concern and must therefore be considered secondary. Bultmann, as did Dibelius when he considered this verse, operates micro-interpersonally; methodological presumptions are driving his effort and thereby determining his conclusions. He does point to textual reasons for this conclusion: "But, since vv. 57-59 is a particularization of v. 56, and since v. 59 is a feeble and senseless repetition of the motif of v. 56, I hold that vv. 57-59 are secondary, and believe that the story originally was intended to record that Jesus was condemned on account of his Messianic claim."[33] His conclusion makes sense only in a methodological mindset that has already decided that preaching was the original setting for the material. A key theme, perhaps *the* key theme, of the early church's preaching was undoubtedly Jesus' messianic status. The temple references have no value in such a framework, and yet Mark obviously had something in mind by including that material. This is especially clear from the incompetent way he handled it. We have already noted that Wellhausen, Lietzmann, and Kilpatrick, operating from different methodological encodings, present textual, ideational, and interpersonal evidence in support of the view that verses 57-59 originally belonged to the text, and that (in the case of the first two) it is verses 60-64 that are most suspect.

In his discussion of the trial before Pilate, Bultmann again establishes that the scene is not a unitary composition. Verse 15:2, he contends, has been artificially inserted. The Barabbas episode is likewise considered a later addition. Both expansions are the result of the community's kerygmatic needs. The expansions occur so that the Pilate scene can be connected overtly with the Sanhedrin scene that precedes it; they are linked by the cultic concept of messianism.

Once again Bultmann's macro-interpersonal reconstruction determines that it is a micro-interpersonal, dogmatic-cultic need[34] that produces messiahship as the binding concept between not only these two texts but between all the elements in the passion narrative. "Dogmatic motifs are of particular importance. As it produced particular stories, the faith of the Christian Church brought the whole Passion under the regulative idea that Jesus suffered and died as the Messiah."[35]

The final insertions therefore have not only a cultic but also a literary plan; the latter works at the behest of the former. Therefore, as had been the case with Dibelius and Schmidt, although for different reasons, Bultmann concludes that the trial scenes focus on religious, cultic communal concerns. Historical interest in what actually happened when Jesus was arrested and crucified is replaced by the micro-interpersonal involvement of the early communities. Textual as well as ideational investigations serve to clarify that involvement macro-interpersonally. Behind all of this lies Bultmann's own micro-interpersonal involvement, externally codified in his methodology but internally grounded in his convictions about the kerygma.

Taking this argument to its logical conclusion, Bertram argues that since the Pilate trial has little kerygmatic, religious significance, it would not have been included in the earliest cultically driven narrative tradition. It is instead a conjecture of materials meant to demonstrate Jesus' treatment before Pilate as a political criminal. The very text that many of the historical skeptics concluded, micro-interpersonally, to be the only historical text, is now, micro-interpersonally, singled out as a late narrative interpolation, and, indeed, fabrication.

The form-critical argument pushes the interpersonal focus beyond the work of the evangelist back to the period in which the tradition was formulated. Perhaps at the earliest oral stage, communal needs shaped the direction of story production. Although the story may have been based on historical circumstance there is no doubt, according to the form critics, that its final production was affected and effected by the needs of the worshiping community that formed it.

This turn to the macro-interpersonal is nowhere more clear than when Bultmann points out that the question is not what happened historically, but how the early Christians conceived what happened.[36] We are therefore not surprised when Donald Juel argues that according to the form critics the literature tells us more about the beliefs of the early church than it does about Jesus' actual trial. When the evangelist utilizes the information as a key source of his Gospel, he is not depicted as merely incorporating a traditional account; he also incorporates and concretizes the once fluid interaction that took place between communal need and historical remembrance. His text therefore becomes a monument to the micro-interpersonal interchange between the earliest worshiping community and their recollections about the circumstances that surrounded the death of their Lord.

Even more than this, the form critics recognize that the evangelists often deal creatively with the traditional material at precisely the point where it must be adjusted to fit the particular needs of their specific communities. Their work therefore not only crystallizes the prior micro-interpersonal exchanges that took place between the earliest Christian communities and the historical recollections they cherished; it also demonstrates that the evangelists, realizing the earliest work had not met all the needs of their particular audience, continued the process of adjusting textual and ideational material according to micro-interpersonal needs.

At the same time it is clear that, notwithstanding differences, all the form critics were determined by micro-interpersonal factors in their interpretations. Clearly important for all of them was preaching, the kerygma. This was a decisive factor in what they found meaningful in the texts they interpreted, to the extent that they projected it onto the micro-interpersonal factors that influenced the production of the texts. In this way their own micro-interpersonal interests played a decisive role in directing (encoding) the methodologies they used to develop their macro-interpersonal reconstructions, just as the micro-interpersonal interests of the historical skeptics and George Kilpatrick drove them to substantially different macro-interpersonal reconstructions from the same textual and ideational data.

# 8 Jesus the Tragic Hero

WITH DRAMATIC SHIFTS IN THE EXTERNAL and internal micro-interpersonal perspectives of later analysts of the trial scenes comes an apparent growth in conclusions about the meaning of those scenes. This growth is not a reflection on the text, which, of course, remains static, but instead reflects the change in the sociolinguistic orientation of the text's investigators. The text remains bound by its textual and ideational markers, but the limits on meaning established by earlier scholarship are obliterated when new interpersonal perspectives encourage later scholars to access and value different components of the potential textual and ideational meaning. This new valuation pushes these later investigators beyond religious boundaries. As we investigate these micro-interpersonal shifts we will see how the allegations against Jesus also apparently shift in meaning, so that Jesus' ministry, and indeed Jesus himself, take on a new meaning. The religious figure slowly but firmly becomes sociopolitically motivated. A different Jesus begins to emerge.

## Source Criticism: Vincent Taylor

With the source-critical work of Vincent Taylor we are again introduced to the micro-

interpersonal preunderstanding of Anglo-Saxon research.[1] Taylor's first publication, *The Historical Evidence for the Virgin Birth,* demonstrates even in its
title the author's conservative scholarly orientation. No doubt this internal
preoccupation with evidence prompts his search for sources. Taylor believes
that it is only through critical work with the sources that one can establish
the historical reliability of the Synoptic texts. Like Kilpatrick, he is preoccupied with uncovering the facts. This is the (micro-interpersonal) methodological encoding that guides, and indeed prefigures, his consideration of
the trial scenes.

Taylor proceeds historical-ideationally, using textual information as sup-
porting evidence, to establish a macro-interpersonal background against
which the text can be analyzed. He concludes that there are three passion
sources, each of which comes out of and addresses the needs of a particular
Christian community, the Markan, Lukan, and Johannine. This allows him
to maintain the passion narrative's overall historical reliability, while simultaneously accounting for the textual and ideational variations in the different
Gospel accounts.

Innovative operational questions help prefigure Taylor's conclusive responses. The Gospels are no longer understood to have been created as uniform, monolithic wholes in the manner of a modern novel. The key questions are, What were the sources, and how might they be isolated? One is
then compelled to ask, How historically accurate were the sources? Conclusions drawn in this way will predetermine one's position regarding the historical legitimacy of the final scenes. Questions of meaning are relevant as
well, but it is a meaning that is methodologically prescribed. How did the
evangelist compile and organize the existing sources, each with a specific,
independent meaning, so that they would create a new and unique meaning?
The whole is considerably more than the sum of its traditional parts. The
implication is that the evangelist is not really an author weaving a story from
the mix of historical circumstance and creative inspiration, but an editor—
creative perhaps in the organization and arrangement of the material, but an
editor nonetheless—who creates meaning by aligning formerly independent
units of traditional material into story-form wholes.

Like the form critics, Taylor believes that the passion material was the
first part of the primitive Christian tradition to attain the form of a continuous narrative.[2] This conclusion did not, however, suggest to him that the
narrative as it now stands in the Markan text is synonymous with the earliest
form of the narrative in the tradition. Building from textual observations, he
posits two ideational stages in the composition process, designated *A* and *B*.
*A* contains those sections that have a certain narrative continuity and are
distinguished by a lack of Semitisms and a preponderance of classical words
and Latinisms. Taylor contends that this *A* material formed the foundation

of the first passion narrative, into which the shorter, traditional reminiscence accounts from Peter (*B*) were later intercalated. "The hypothesis suggested is that Mark found an account of the Passion in Rome and expanded it by the aid of Petrine tradition."[3]

Taylor's internal discussion of the Sanhedrin trial scene is similarly source-oriented. He posits a clear ideational relationship between 14:58 and 14:61-62. Against Rudolf Bultmann, he argues that verses 57-59 are not interpolations because they agree fundamentally with the central thematic focus of the passage, messiahship. "The saying on the rebuilding of the Temple implies a claim to Messiahship and thus prompts the high priest's question, while this challenge evokes the explicit claim to be the Messiah which Jesus expresses in the language of Psa. cx. 1 and Dan. vii. 13."[4] Taylor concludes that the cause of Jesus' condemnation was the religious charge of blasphemy that develops from this central motif.

Taylor's ideational understanding of the thematic connections in the text suggests, however, another important emphasis that complements the religious. In discussing the terminology of verse 58 he comes to a conclusion that is as sociopolitical as it is religious:

> The former [χειροποίητον, made with hands] is a classical word, used also in the LXX (with reference to idols) and in the papyri; the latter [ἀχειροποίη-τον, not made with hands] is "probably a coinage for the occasion in the earliest source." The distinction is only partially valid, for while the saying rightly speaks of the creation of a new spiritual system or community (ἀχειρο-ποίητον); it refers, not merely to the destruction of a building (χειροποίητον), but also to the old order of which the Temple is the symbol and centre.[5]

Like Ernst Lohmeyer, Taylor comes to recognize that *temple* can signify more than one idea.[6] While taking the religious meaning for granted, he specifically points up the social and political order that it symbolizes. As a messianic threat to that entire order, the term *messiah* itself attains more than a merely religious connotation.

From here Taylor suggests a critical relationship between the Sanhedrin and the Pilate trials. "From this question [15:2, 'Are you the king of the Jews?'] it is clear that the Jewish hierarchy had decided to base their charges on the political aspect of the claim of Jesus to be the Messiah."[7] Taylor in effect makes a conceptual connection between the two signifiers, *Messiah* and *King of the Jews*. The textual distinction would appear to be that while *Messiah* is the more appropriate signifier for a Jewish trial, it is a term that would have little meaning for a Roman governor. A different term that contains a critical conceptual equivalence must therefore be appropriated: *King of the Jews*. *Messiah* thus appears to have a broader field of signification. In both trials a political as well as a religious anxiety about Jesus' ministry appears evident.

Although the two trial scenes consist mostly of *A* material,[8] Taylor insists that the core of each is constituted by historical remembrances of actual occurrences. The scenarios were not manufactured by Mark, but were found by the evangelist already intact in the Roman narrative. He argues concerning the Sanhedrin trial that "in general the narrative is historical, and there is no need to explain it as a secondary expansion of 15:1."[9] Instead, 15:1 is explained as redundant; Mark did not reconcile two separate sources (15:1 and 14:55-64) even though he placed them so close together.[10] Conclusions regarding the Pilate scene are similar: "Mark's narrative has greater simplicity and realism. While not the narrative of an eyewitness, it rests probably on primitive testimony."[11]

Taylor concedes that both sets of material appear to play well to the theological needs of the communities to which Mark was oriented. He insists, however, that apologetic and theological interests did not play a role in the creation of these scenes as "the story as it happened was itself apology enough."[12] Further, one need not posit doctrinal interests as the motivation for the creation of such materials because "Jesus Himself was conscious of the parallel between His situation and that of the servant of Deutero-Isaiah." Thus, he argues against Wellhausen that 14:61-62 need not have been inserted by the church because "the answer was perfectly in accord with Jesus' spirit and manner of speech."[13] Indeed, some such statement was necessary to provoke the high priest's tearing of his garment; silence would have been insufficient motivation.

Taylor maneuvers around the problem that no real blasphemy is indicated in the text by suggesting that the earliest Christian communities knew that the conception of blasphemy was ideationally enlarged by the Sanhedrin uniquely for this particular trial. This shared understanding, which Taylor's hypothesis assumes existed between evangelist and first-century reading audience, allowed Mark to transmit the tradition without formally notifying the audience that something special was going on with the blasphemy charge. They filled in information where there appears to be a gap in the logic of the story for the modern reader. Taylor attempts to fill this hole by supplementing historical information macro-interpersonally, information that he suggests the original readers shared micro-interpersonally. Once again we see that where textual and ideational evidence is lacking, macro-interpersonal theory, borne by methodological (micro-interpersonal) presuppositions, provides the basis for drawing conclusions. The hypothesized historicity of the sources guarantees that the final trial scenes, which are composites of the sources, would be historically accurate as well. The task of the investigator is to explain how it is so, as Taylor tries to do.

Ultimately, the critical difference between the form critics and Taylor is neither textual nor ideational; it is Taylor's (internal) micro-interpersonal interest in the historical accuracy of the traditional material. Taylor adopts the form critics' external, methodologically codified micro-interpersonal relationship to the text. He asks the kind of operational questions the form critics ask of the text. His procedure, then, has a similar methodological encoding. But that methodological orientation becomes decisively modified under the influence of his internal (Anglo-Saxon) micro-interpersonal involvement in the text. Indeed, we have found that his internal disposition is also externally interpersonally codified in the historically oriented methodology that he shares with George Dunbar Kilpatrick. Kilpatrick, however, does not share with Taylor many of the micro-interpersonal kerygmatic concerns of the form critics. Therefore, unlike Kilpatrick, Taylor also understands that the evangelist is not merely recounting history, but is adjusting the account so that it responds to the particular needs of the community to which he is writing. Taylor's internal and external micro-interpersonal investment in the text is, therefore, as it was for Kilpatrick and the form critics, a determining and enriching influence on the way in which he goes about his analytical process.

## Redaction Criticism: John R. Donahue

With the advent of redaction criticism, methodological presumptions focus the investigator's attention on the narrative properties of the text. Textual observations become an investigative foundation on which critics like John R. Donahue endeavor to build complex ideational and macro-interpersonal observations.[14] It is Donahue's contention that the passion narrative is a combination of Mark's creative compositional efforts and his selective use of traditional materials.

For example, verses 56 and 59 have all the textual earmarks of the Markan insertion technique. Mark, Donahue claims, uses this technique in the same way that a modern author would use italics, to highlight designated material. What is more, the material so highlighted is what Mark has picked up from pre-Markan tradition. Mark 14:58, methodologically speaking, must therefore be traditional material.[15]

But the text functions in such a way that the traditional material assumes Markan conceptual implications. The textual evidence reveals an ideational agenda. Donahue demonstrates this by giving a detailed analysis of verse 58. He suggests that it existed in the tradition in two forms rather than one. Mark not only added the hands imagery, but also brought together as protasis and apodosis what were originally separate statements. He has created a single saying by joining a saying that opposed the temple and the cult it represented to a saying that points to the establishment of the eschatological community as the substitute for the destroyed social and religious entity. The "new" saying fits appropriately into the ideational theme the text established early on. "We will suggest that from 11:1 forward Mark portrays Jesus in growing opposition to the Jerusalem cult center, and, at the same time, Jesus is pictured as preparing the eschatological community which will function as a substitute for this place."[16] Jesus' role, as it did for Taylor, but in this case because of Donahue's literary analysis of the signifier *temple*, begins to push beyond its religious boundaries.

Donahue's textual inspection of 14:60-62 operates along the same parameters. After ascertaining to what extent Mark was active in the composition of these verses, he considers their relationship to the rest of the Markan text. He makes the ideational observation, for example, that even though the silence motif of Isaiah 53:7 is operative in the text, Mark adds his own unique flavoring. While 14:60-61a and 15:4 are part of the traditional materials, Mark adds the σιωπάω (be silent) statement. This verb is a Markan trait, Donahue argues, by which the evangelist connotes a religious silence in the face of Jesus' power.[17] Mark thus adds it here to prepare the way for the solemn christological statement in 14:62.

Verse 61 shows other signs of Markan creative activity. Donahue argues that σὺ εἶ (you are) is a Markan formula that presents in an ironic way a truth statement about Jesus' person.[18] The narrator presents the truth statement about Jesus even though this truth is not understood by the person who utters it.

Ἐγώ εἰμι (I am) is another redactional formula presented by Mark. It, too, is revelational. The final Markan formula, ὄψεσθε (you will see), designates the future expectation of the parousia. The formulae indicate that Mark is responsible for the exact makeup of the two verses, and indeed, in his intention of revealing the christological nature of Jesus, also responsible for the piling up of titles in a density unparalleled in the rest of his Gospel.

Indeed, then, ideational and macro-interpersonal arguments follow from textual conclusions. For example, ideationally, two key images give meaning and focus to the trial scenes: the temple and the Son of man. For both, conceptual content is derived from textual data. In the case of the temple, Donahue, as we have shown, emphasizes restoration together with a narratively established picture of social and political conflict. Donahue's textual observations demonstrate that Mark throughout his Gospel has presented Jesus in conflict with the cult in such a way that the tension comes to a climax in this scene. The signifier *temple* then has more than a mere physical conceptual content designating a religious building. It appears that in the Gospel of Mark it has been given the conceptual mark of cultic and social community as well.

Donahue subsequently turns to the macro-interpersonal element to eluci-date the temple imagery. Mark, he argues, chooses to balance the temple that is destroyed, not with a physical structure in 14:58, but with a believing community. Mark is writing for a community that is coming to terms with the destruction of the temple and looks to the return of Jesus as the founder of a new community that will substitute for it.[19] However, because there was no preexisting understanding that the messiah was to both destroy and re-build the temple (the right belonged exclusively to Yahweh), Mark has cre-atively used traditional materials with separate meanings to establish a different meaning of his own. That creative ability, however, is informed by the contextual circumstances that affected both Mark and the community to which he wrote. In other words, Donahue believes that Mark is operating micro-interpersonally.

In a similar way, textual findings regarding the significance of the term *Son of man* in its relationship to the other christological titles provide the argumentative foundation for Donahue's ideational and macro-interpersonal observations. For instance, his textual findings argue against the probability that 14:62 comes from some messianic traditional source. Instead, he sug-gests that the Christology represented is more in line with the belief of the church community of Mark's time. Depending on the work of Norman Perrin, he concludes that in 14:62 we have the end product of a Christian *pesher* tradition that has integrated Daniel 7:13 and Psalms 110:1.[20] The all-important Son of man statement as it stands in the trial scene climaxes the use of the titles, and thereby gives content to the titles preceding it. It is only now in Mark's Gospel that the titles Son of God and Christ are given their proper meanings. Son of man thereby becomes for Mark the key ideational description of Jesus' messianic authority. Just as the conflict themes in the Markan Gospel come to a climax in 14:58, so Markan Christology climaxes in 14:62.

The ideational content of this all-important title is given its final determi-nation only after its macro-interpersonal reality is clarified. Donahue argues that Son of man was not an independent title but part of the early Christian use of the Old Testament. He found through his research that other commu-nity sources like Q, L, and M included sayings about the future Son of man. In these sources, however, the Son of man sayings did not include apocalyp-tic imagery like power, glory, and clouds of heaven. He notes three such communal uses: (1) Jesus coming in judgment, (2) the Son of man in associa-tion with Jesus' resurrection and exaltation and, (3) the παραδίδωμι (to hand over) tradition regarding the passion of Jesus as the suffering Son of man. "Thus Mark uses Son of Man precisely because it was not a fixed title but rather a symbol or evocative term to which he could give content in terms of his own purpose."[21] To such an end Mark specifically combines the future element of the sayings with apocalyptic imagery. "The *Christos* for Mark is the Jesus who must suffer, but his suffering looks beyond the passion to the *parousia* at which time Jesus receives the fullness of the messianic office." [22] In this manner Mark has created a term that relates to every phase of Jesus' existence and ministry, past, present, and future. Son of man relates to the earthly ministry of Jesus as the epiphany of the Son of man. The title also relates to the call to follow Jesus in suffering and death. And finally, through the apocalyptic future sayings, we find that the real meaning of Jesus' ministry and suffering is only known at the Son of man's return. Again, macro-interpersonal reconstruction is crucial for an appreciation of the full meaning. This ideational content is verified only in light of the tumultuous existence endured by the Markan community.

Donahue, because he cannot find any literary clues to an understanding of blasphemy on the surface level of the text, turns one final time to the macro-interpersonal. The charge is not about what happened to Jesus, but what is happening to the Christian community of Mark's time. "Therefore the charge of blasphemy in the trial narrative serves to clarify the Christology of 14:62. It speaks to a Christian community which is called on to undergo the same suffering as their master when they confess who he is." [23]

Such a historical, macro-interpersonal reconstruction leads to Donahue's overall conclusion about the final literary form of the unit as a trial. Mark, operating micro-interpersonally, Donahue concludes, has taken the traditional material of 14:53 (leading Jesus away to his death), 14:56-57 (the rising of the false witnesses), 14:60-61 (silence), and 14:65 (mocking), and creatively composed a scene that betokens a Jewish trial. Why did he choose the trial as his structural format? Once again the language is macro-interpersonal. Mark's community was itself on trial for the blasphemy of worshiping a crucified messiah. This scene, intercalated as it is within the Peter narrative, provided the ultimate positive example, along with a highly negative one, of how a believer was to respond in such a crisis.

Donahue's work demonstrates how a macro-interpersonal reconstruction can broaden one's horizon. Up to this point in our survey, scholars have concluded that, in the main, the trial scenes are apologetic efforts created to reduce the culpability of the Romans and place the blame on the Jewish leadership. The key motivation for Jesus' demise comes from the Jews, and their concern is primarily religious. Jesus is killed because of his religious claim to messiahship.

Donahue's method opens up a more literary inspection of the text in that he asks questions regarding Markan intent as demonstrated by Markan style. Thus he is structurally able to proceed beyond an isolated consideration of the trial material. Having connected the material in the trial scenes with the style and intent of the writing that precedes it, he is able to draw conclusions not only about messianic christological claims, but also about sociopolitical conflicts between Jesus and the Jewish leadership that climax in a scene of conflict in the Sanhedrin trial. The methodological encoding (external level of the micro-interpersonal) that directs Donahue's work allows him to see textual and ideational data in a new light, and thereby to reach novel conclusions about what the text *meant* for the earliest Markan readers. We can now recognize more clearly how his research operates on the micro-interpersonal level. His unique methodological direction establishes an investigative environment that creates the possibility for new and distinctive understanding. In that understanding we see clearly a new sociopolitical orientation emerging in Jesus' trial and condemnation.

In other words, the academic environment that establishes an external influence on the direction of Donahue's work is actually encoded in the methodology he chooses. In fact, he opens his work with the astute observation that an investigator's methodological environment, what we have termed the (external) micro-interpersonal life-relation, can radically influence research procedures and, therefore, conclusions. In the introduction he argues that progress in any scientific endeavor comes through two factors, the discovery of new data and "the emergence of a new methodology."[24] The methodology that emerged immediately prior to the time of Donahue's work is redaction criticism. It is his conviction that, because of its unique scientific perspective on text analysis, redaction criticism, from the mid-1950s forward, provoked significant changes in the process of biblical inquiry. The investigative landscape for an entire generation of biblical scholars was therefore dramatically altered.

An investigator now comes to the text with the question, What does the literary structure of the text narrative tell me about the theological orientation of the text? In other words, the investigator no longer assumes (*preunderstands*) that the text was merely handed to the evangelist, or that pieces of tradition were given him for a mindless patchwork construction; the investigator preunderstands instead that the evangelist used the traditions creatively. Subsequently a judgment is made as to why the evangelist does what he does; it is at this point that the theological or religious intent of the work is clarified.

Donahue recognizes the importance of addressing the textual, ideational, and macro-interpersonal functions of the narrative language. He even realizes the significance that micro-interpersonal variables have on text interpretation. But he limits his recognition of the micro-interpersonal impact. Micro-interpersonal variables determine the macro-interpersonal reconstruction that serves as the investigative background for determining text meaning. Donahue limits his consideration of micro-interpersonal variables to their influence on determining what the text *meant*. But what he writes about the micro-interpersonal function of language for the original readers demands that one consider how that process functions in the case of the modern reader as well. His work thus points to another dimension of the micro-interpersonal, one that did not yet occur to him and in which he reveals no interest. The full potential of meaning in the text therefore has not yet been achieved.

## Literary Criticism: Donald Juel

Literary criticism, another methodology that focuses on authorial activity and intent, is modeled by Donald Juel.[25] Juel, like Donahue, operates fundamentally according to textual designs. His comprehensive narrative analyses provide the investigative platform from which he launches his ideational inquiries. He connects key trial narrative information to global story emphases. These emphases, which materialize in the form of story motifs, are the structural bonds that give the trial scenes both their local and global footing. A trial scene motif can only be validly understood when it is considered in relationship to the larger themes that orient the entire Markan narrative. Once the motifs have been so established he demonstrates textually how they operate at and beneath the narrative level of the scene. Juel calls on macro-interpersonal information, when available, as corroborating evidence.

A relevant example illustrates the point. Juel observes that, unlike Luke's version of the trial, Mark's conveys a disregard for the intricacies of Jewish Sanhedrin law. This macro-interpersonal observation does not, however, stand alone; it is clarified through an appeal to the literary evidence. He directs our attention to the desire in the Markan narrative to portray a trial that misrepresents justice. After listing a catena of verses that reveal the hostility of the Jewish leadership toward Jesus,[26] he concludes that the reader has been led carefully to expect an improper proceeding.[27] The trial, in this scenario, is viewed as much more than an apologetic contrivance; it becomes instead a climactic representation of a socio-religio-political conflict between Jesus and the Jewish leadership that has been building since the early days of his ministry.

A key story motif, which Juel labels rejection/vindication, amplifies this theme of conflict. Here Juel sees connections between 12:1-12 and 8:31. In 8:31, the first of the passion predictions, Mark is concerned mostly with rejection by the Jewish leadership. Mark, Juel claims, is using the imagery from Psalm 118:22 to emphasize through the parable in chapter 12 and the prediction in chapter 8 that what happens to Jesus fits in with prophetic expectations. The trial then represents a rejection that points not to its own end, but to a vindication that the Scriptures have already prophesied.[28]

Mark, Juel suggests, has thus developed a multilevel presentation. While the actors in the story live and act on a textual surface preoccupied with rejection, the reader is expected to probe beneath the narrative topsoil and realize the different and more powerful reality of vindication. Irony is the bond that holds these two levels together in a single narrative. Because the readers are privy to information unavailable to the characters, only they are able to understand the full meaning of textual terms and situations.[29] Such an intentional declaration and examination of irony permits Juel to understand the trial scenes in a unique manner.

Consider, for instance, Juel's consideration of the prophetic motif as it plays itself out in the Sanhedrin trial. Predictably, the reader is called on to appreciate the story at a deeper level than that of which the characters are capable. In 14:58 a false prediction is attributed to Jesus. In 14:62 another false, and just as outlandish, prediction is made. At least this is the way it must appear on the textual surface. In 14:65, those mocking Jesus encourage him to prophesy, knowing certainly that he cannot; he is no real prophet. And yet, at the moment when all this is going on the reader knows that Jesus' predictions will indeed come true. As the cock crows dramatically, Peter ominously acts just as Jesus had predicted:

> The reader is expected to appreciate the irony apparent at the deeper level of the story, but he is also expected to make the appropriate inference about Jesus' prophetic statement in 14:62 [elsewhere Juel adds verse 58 as well]: despite appearances and despite the disbelief of Jesus' opponents, his prophecy will be (has been?) fulfilled.[30]

When Juel turns his attention to the key verses in the Sanhedrin trial scene, his literary observations are just as illuminating. He recognizes that although indicated as false, the anti-temple statement must be regarded as true on the second level of the text. He points to the references in 15:29 and 13:2 as evidence. But because he considers the references ironic, he does not need to—as, for example, Kilpatrick does—demonstrate a textual equivalence between the three verses. Further, like Donahue, he points to the relationship of this temple statement with the anti-temple focus elsewhere in the Gospel.

Juel, however, offers more. He recognizes clearly that *temple* is a signifier with different conceptual implications; it represents not only a thing, but a prophetic relationship. Pointing to the cleansing episode in chapter 11, he observes, "The interpretation is rather obvious. The cleansing of the temple must in some sense imply the rejection of the official representatives of Israel, the leaders of the temple establishment."[31]

Once it is recognized that *temple* entertains more than religious implications, the sense of conflict heightens and becomes sociopolitical in its orientation. In fact, the social dimension implicit in the concept *temple* is not only directed back toward Jesus' historical confrontations with the Jewish leadership, but is also projected forward toward the nascent Christian community. Juel observes that the phrase "made with hands/not made with hands" is designed by Mark to tell us something about the text. Here 14:58 finds its point of connection with 14:61-62: "The temple charge provides further testimony to Jesus as the Messiah and further defines his Messiahship."[32] Jesus is the messiah who will destroy the old temple and build a new one, not with human hands. After comparing the Greek terminology here with the same terminology in Colossians 2:11, Ephesians 2:11, Hebrews 9:11, 23–24, he comes to the following conclusion: "But the terms also point the Christian reader to a different level of understanding: the new temple, in contrast to the old, will be a temple of a different order, i.e. superior."[33] This new, superior temple will be the primitive Christian community.

Juel now appeals to the macro-interpersonal. He notes that there are multiple indications from literature of the period that communities saw themselves as a temple, and indeed in an eschatological context similar to the one encountered in the Sanhedrin trial scene.[34] He provides further evidence from the Targumim and Qumran to demonstrate that in the literature of the period it was expected that the messiah perform the function not only of building, but also of destroying the temple.[35] In the 4Q Florilegium midrash on 2 Samuel 7:10-14, the messiah is clearly given jurisdiction over temple construction and destruction, and the context is just as clearly eschatological. So Mark's use of the traditional statement regarding destroying and rebuilding the temple could well belie his understanding that it is a messianic claim. At the very least, it allows that Mark's readers would have understood it as a messianic claim that referred specifically to their faith community. This hypothesis is strengthened by the fact that its presentation is immediately followed by the apocalyptic messianic imagery of verses 60-62. Indeed, in his final appeal for corroborating testimony Juel returns to the textual connections evident in Mark's story. He ascertains in 13:26, where the Son of man will be seen coming in clouds with great power and glory, the content of the eschatological temple as community. Here, because the Son of man is to gather the elect, the temple he builds must be the community of Jesus' followers.

What Juel sees as Mark's ironic presentation of the concept of messiah initiates further distinctive recognitions. Here Juel contends that we are dealing with a Markan royal motif, the dominant theme in his Gospel.[36] The theme appears in the titles applied to Jesus in 15:2, 9, 12, 26, and 32. At 15:32 the term is used in such textual proximity to "Christ" as to suggest conceptual synonymy. Herein lies a critical connection between the Sanhedrin and Pilate trial scenes. Juel presents convincing macro-interpersonal evidence that "King of the Jews" is a specifically Roman way of speaking, since *Jew* is a term used for members of the nation of Israel exclusively by non-Jews. A taunt by Jewish antagonists, 15:32, also fits historically, as here the royal title is changed to "King of Israel." The name Israel never occurs in non-Jewish literature.[37] This recognition demonstrates that Mark understood the value of presenting the same concept with different terminology when historical propriety demanded such. The different use of "Christ" in 14:61 and "King of the Jews" in 15:2, 9, 12, 26 would indicate the same literary awareness.

By observing that *Messiah* is connected with *King of the Jews* in 15:2, Juel has directly tied the theme of the two trials together. Not only is *Messiah* thereby given a potent sociopolitical edge, but the political sense of the trial before Pilate now adds new implications for understanding the Sanhedrin scene that preceded it. Such unique observations are made possible by Juel's literary, textual approach.

Once again the distinctions between two biblical investigators rest on micro-interpersonal variables. Both Donahue and Juel operate from a textual perspective that uses ideational and macro-interpersonal evidence for support. Both of them are concerned about structural textual issues. And yet significant differences remain. These differences are not due to textual and ideational distinctions, but to the micro-interpersonal variables that influence how the evidence is read. Juel's internal desire to consider the material on a level beyond the merely compositional, combined with a methodological encoding that encourages consideration for broader literary concerns, motivates him to read the evidence in a profoundly different way. Micro-interpersonal factors thus not only guide the direction of research, they help prefigure its results.

The methodological environment has shifted; the new micro-interpersonal life-relation is founded on the critical remains of the redaction and form-critical efforts that preceded it. Form, redaction, and composition criticism became open to challenge when it appeared that the methodologies demonstrated a lack of courage with regard to their literary convictions. The procedures were followed so much in isolation that it became more and more difficult to find solutions for wider literary concerns. Donald Juel, therefore, attacks Donahue's strategy of research. He argues that one cannot begin with tradition and redaction considerations if one is to resolve literary questions. One must begin with the literature as it exists, and analyze questions of style and intent, "questions dealing with far more fundamental aspects of style than compositional techniques."[38] Such remarks are generally indicative of the internalized micro-interpersonal preunderstanding that motivates one's research.

The introduction of this subtle distinction in methodological encoding prompts a revised direction for research. Thus, when Juel turns his attention toward the Markan trial scenes he alters the focus of the pertinent investigative question and thereby assures a change in the kinds of conclusions his study will achieve. The investigator is no longer restricted to concerns about the literary structure of the specific text, but combines this interest with an exacting structural analysis of the entire narrative. The investigator still asks, What does the literary structure tell me about the theological orientation of the text? But now the realization is added that comprehending the structure of the specific text is not enough. The question must become more universal: How does the text function as an individual story that is framed by and linked to a more comprehensive story? This preunderstanding is evident in Juel's work from the start.

While Juel, therefore, recognizes the valid components of the redaction and form-critical arguments, his new methodological perspective enables him to move beyond them. He can acknowledge the value of historical information as it relates to narrative understanding. But he can also caution that "Our concern here will not be to determine the meaning of the verses within the context of the historical trial, assuming there was such a trial and such a question was asked. It is to determine what the verses *mean* in the present context."[39] Juel has employed the textual and ideational data to create an entire narrative world. The contemporary reader can "fill in" textual and ideational gaps in the trial scenes by first appealing to this narrative world that becomes the "text-linguistic" interpretive background.

Historical concerns, then, may validate the study, but they cannot initiate it. That privilege is reserved for the literary considerations that must remain primary. Literary analysis is thereby not allowed free reign, but is constrained by macro-structural, historical verification. "An interpreter must at least attempt to demonstrate that a particular idea or the development of a particular tradition would have been conceivable."[40]

In fact, because scholarship has raised this macro-interpersonal issue with regard to historical communities, similar questions are being asked about the same kind of dialectical interchange between modern communities and the text. Macro-interpersonal observations about what the text *meant* encourage micro-interpersonal questions about what the text *means*. If the reading environment made a difference in how and what the text *meant* for a primitive Christian audience, it is logical to expect that the reading environment will make a difference in how and what the text *means* for a modern audience. What is in our historical perspective a macro-interpersonal view of the material was for the ancient Christians, at the time they were interpreting what Mark had written, a micro-interpersonal act. Many modern Christian communities seek validation for their contemporary recreation of this micro-interpersonal act. They base this quest on a foundation provided by researchers like Juel and Donahue. The micro-interpersonal question regarding what the text *means* is based on the methodological principles that guide the macro-interpersonal quest for what the text *meant*. A modern community in dialogue with the text is substituted for the ancient community in dialogue with the text.

What we have seen demonstrates that such substitutions do occur. We have seen how changing micro-interpersonal influences contribute new insights into the text. When we recall the scholars considered in the past two chapters, analyzing their work on the trial scenes according to their times of publication, we see a progression of sorts. As micro-interpersonal circumstances change at both the external and internal levels, new ideas surface regarding the meaning of the scenes. New micro-interpersonal perspectives promote changes in the ways in which the textual and ideational materials are evaluated, and the changes are not always simply alternative views. The new perspectives allow for a fuller appreciation of the range of meaning that resides in the text. Issues that may appear critical for some researchers may be missed by others, because the researchers bring different, micro-interpersonally inspired questions with them to the material. The potential meaning in the text is accessed by way of those questions. New questions allow researchers to see different aspects of that potentiality. New questions bring about new kinds of interpretative conclusions. In this way interpreters move beyond the boundaries of previous interpretations. It is not that new meaning has been imposed on the text. Rather, the text has been seen in a new way so that meaning that had been overlooked before suddenly floats to the surface.

# 9 Jesus the Revolutionary

ETHNOGRAPHIC TEXT INTERPRETATIONS ARE criticized because they allegedly lack the proper awareness of and responsiveness to textual and ideational functions of language. The charge is made that they create rather than uncover meaning. Our study thus far suggests two appropriate responses to such an accusation. First, *all* interpreters are micro-interpersonally involved in text interpretation, so that the interpretative moves undertaken by ethnographic analysts are of the same kind as those utilized by more traditional interpreters. The micro-interpersonal perspective of the interpreter—of every interpreter—pushes him or her beyond the textual and ideational boundaries so that sociolinguistic context becomes as influential in history- and literary-based investigations as it is in ethnographic interpretations. Unlike the case of traditional researchers who tend to downplay the influence of their own personal ethnography, sociology, and ideology, however, scholars in this category, while adhering to the scientific principles of historical control, readily acknowledge the impact of their own cultural circumstances on their interpretative conclusions. This indicates, second, that ethnographic researchers are not *creating* text meaning, but are instead interacting micro-interpersonally with the textual and ideational data in such a way that different and heretofore uncovered elements of the potential meaning are valued. The end result is an apparently new conclusion about meaning. In reality, the conclusion is only newly recognized.

# Fernando Belo

Consider, for example, the work of Fernando Belo, a Portuguese Marxist Christian, who celebrates the fact that the micro-interpersonal preunderstanding of political transformation influences his interpretative analysis of the trial scenes. Belo's sociological footing becomes the base from which he conducts his investigations and simultaneously polemicizes against traditional investigative techniques. Thus, his passion in writing is a "body-to-body struggle with the text of the bourgeois-Christian ideology that for a number of years marked out the limits of my field of speech." [1]

This transformative preunderstanding fosters a materialist methodological approach that forms the presuppositional base for Belo's inquiry. In other words, issues of materiality are methodologically encoded in the investigative procedure that Belo uses to analyze the trial scenes. He states his point clearly, firmly believing that a transformative approach to living mandates a concern for the materiality of human existence:

> We must rather learn the difficult analyses and strategies of subversion and transformation if we are to make the earth a habitable place that can satisfy human beings and enable them to live in social relationships better adapted to the materiality of the body (hands, feet, eyes) in which the power of our bodies plays the decisive role. [2]

Once this materialist perspective is connected with Christianity, the key issue for faith will no longer be, according to Belo, "grace for the souls," but what he terms the "power (*puissance*) of bodies." The investigator is therefore conditioned to ascertain the "materiality" of the text. The consequence will be a heightened emphasis on issues of human liberation. This does not mean, according to Belo, that one places liberation issues in the text. It suggests instead that this key emphasis is already resident within the images and symbols of the material; the proper perspective of reading will recognize it.

Belo initiates his process in an almost traditional manner—he appeals specifically to the tools of the historical-critical method. He accumulates textual and ideational data and analyzes them from a literary critical perspective. Additionally, he makes abundant use of source and redaction critical techniques. In fact, at points he is so dependent on traditional principles of text investigation, his critics charge that he subverts his "materialist cause."

Materialism, it is argued, is not only significant as an ideological lens through which the text is to be viewed; it is also integral to one's understanding of how the text is to be appreciated from a literary perspective. Materiality suggests a commitment to understanding the text as a unified entity rather than as a conglomeration of interwoven layers that can be understood fully only through historical-critical dismantling.[3]

If indeed Belo's concern is primarily materialist, why does he rely so heavily on historical-critical procedure? We would argue that he feels comfortable with historical criticism because he limits its operational scope; he uses it only to justify his materialist cause. He does not mix the two procedures; he uses the former to validate the suppositions of the latter. He maintains a unified materialist perspective. But the Markan narrative does not appear to present, even to Belo, a sociopolitical concern for the transformation of the material human condition as a Marxist would envision it. The unified perspective that he brings to and expects of the text therefore requires a more sophisticated view of the text itself; there must be more to the Markan narrative than what appears on the surface, otherwise one cannot argue that Mark's text has any kind of materialist agenda. Belo, in effect, because of his own materialist agenda, needs a text composed of multiple layers rather than a single surface layer. Historical-critical tools of investigation not only help him to argue that such multiple layers exist; they enable him to delineate their origins and purpose. Belo's marriage of the two apparently contradictory methodologies therefore makes for him perfect operational sense. He imposes his materialist perspective on the text in a historical-critical manner. The result is a social semiotics radically adjusted by the ideological presuppositions of structural Marxism. His reading is clearly micro-interpersonally determined.

In building his macro-interpersonal case, Belo argues that there are two levels to the Markan narrative. The first level represents a narrative source. The second level represents the theological and narrative agenda of the Markan narrator (redactor). The former prepaschal narrative level, which represents the traditional story of Jesus prior to the Easter experience, presents a messianic account with profound materialist implications. Upon this primary narrative program, the evangelist overlays his own theologically contrary religious narrative structure and agenda. This redacted version of the story of Jesus, which is the Gospel of Mark as we presently have it, represents the theological concerns of the post-Easter Christian communities.[4] Interestingly, Belo's unique micro-interpersonal orientation has brought him to a critical conclusion that values both the sociopolitical and religious aspects of the text's potential meaning. The Jesus of the trial scenes is becoming a richer, three-dimensional figure.

The narrative source, Belo argues, is entitled "the good news of Jesus the Messiah." It is ideationally based in Jesus' teachings about the reign of God. It is textually confirmed in the language of the parables and miracle stories that establish a link between Jesus' ministry and the dawning of that reign. Its function is to present as the intention of Jesus' ministry, and therefore God's reign, the provocation and establishment of an exodus of faith to the pagans.

Unfortunately, the messianic narrative's concentration on an exodus to the pagans was a threat to the sociopolitical order of Judaism that was based on an internal maintenance of its socio-politico-religious symbolic systems. This messianic narrative, because of its radical affinity for and movement toward those who represented the socioreligious outsiders in an international sense, represents a materialist cause that was as transformative in Jesus' time as it is in Belo's.

But Belo's macro-interpersonal reconstruction offers us a Mark who, because his agenda was different from Jesus' (the needs of the community to which he directed his ministry were different), altered the emphasis of the story by overlaying his own narrative discourse atop the messianic narrative of Jesus. Scenes like the three passion predictions therefore give a structural bond to the theological position that Jesus' death was not only destined, but was foreseen in Old Testament prophecy. Indeed, the evangelist was so successful in his narrative restructuring that this sense of religious, theological necessity now appears to be the key to understanding the meaning of the story of Jesus.

Belo begins his analysis of the trial scenes much like a literary critic, establishing critical ideational connections between the target text and the Gospel as a whole. Like Donald Juel, he understands verse 55 as the climactic consummation of an ongoing theme of conflict between Jesus and the Jewish leadership. This theme has driven the narrative forward since the inception of Jesus' public ministry. The desire to find testimony worthy of securing Jesus' death has a history that Belo traces all the way back to Mark 3:20, 22-30.[5]

Predictably, Belo's materialist perspective radically alters his literary conclusions. Macro-interpersonal finds are micro-interpersonally adjusted. Since sociopolitical concerns contextualize Belo as an investigator, these are the primary concerns that guide his appeal to the literary structure of the text as a way of establishing the evangelist's sociolinguistic background. In this way he "finds" points that have been missed before in the makeup of the Markan community because the qualities of his own community inspire a unique search.

He therefore takes verse 58 as a sociopolitical statement that reflects

Mark's understanding that Jesus was in conflict not only with the religious powers but with the entire social structure of the Jewish community. In this way Belo recognizes in the temple more than a religious edifice with sociopolitical implications, which it maximally became in traditional scholarship. It is the "signifying center" of the entire Jewish social system. Polysemy is once again critical. Belo does not deny the religious signification of the temple, but he insists that it has another, more potent and primary signification, the sociopolitical. Therefore, by making use of the temple as the signifying center of the Jewish social system, Mark brings to expression a political class conflict.[6] Jesus' attack on the temple is indicative of his representation of the lower classes and his desire to reorient society so that it reflects their interests more equitably. His effort is subversive and therefore, in a classic sense, prophetic.

Belo argues that Mark's emphasis on a sociopolitical conflict in Jesus' ministry and the class antagonism it attracted are accurate representations of the historical circumstances. While the emphasis on Jesus' rebuilding of the temple in three days is a purely postpaschal theological addition, the rest of the text, according to Belo, is prepaschal. He offers ideational evidence as testimony. "At the prepaschal level, the reference here *may* be to the sequence of traders expelled from the temple, and, more generally, to the destruction of the temple and the SYMB [symbol] field and the rebuilding of a house of prayer in the field of pagans."[7]

The interrogation by the high priest, who is the signification of a state out of touch and in conflict with its constituency, is understood to be politically motivated. Therefore Jesus' reply must also be interpreted politically. In fact, the political motivations are so strongly understood throughout the trial that even the apparently religious charge of blasphemy obtains a new and more critical signification whose central emphasis is sociopolitical. "The reply [verse 62] is read as subversion that *tears* the Jewish symbolic fabric, and shatters the semantics of the dominant ideological text, to the point of attacking even the god ('blasphemy') who guarantees it."[8] The political ideologies of two classes are in conflict in this text, and it takes a reader appropriately armed with a transformative preunderstanding to recognize and comprehend the subtle sociopolitical interplay that Mark has recorded through the use of religious symbols.

At this point Belo anticipates a damaging criticism of his theory and offers a preemptive reaction. If Jesus was politically motivated by class concerns, his efforts might place him dangerously close to the position of the Zealots. Belo, however, rejects the comparison and explains ideationally that Jesus only now, in verse 62, acknowledges himself as messiah precisely because to have done so before would have opened him to the charge of being a Zealot.

Because of the "powerlessness of his body" associated with his answer in verse 62, hearers cannot associate his messianic confession with a Zealot *modus operandi*. Obviously he is a new kind of messiah. Yet he remains political, his target remains the social structure. Belo must therefore explain how Jesus' mission can remain so forcefully sociopolitical on the one hand, and yet not be associated with Zealot practices and principles on the other.

Belo's dilemma is that of a *Christian* Marxist for whom zealotic tendencies are categorically unacceptable. One can agree that Jesus' movement was not Zealot in nature, but Belo's denial is not grounded in his macro-interpersonal investigation, but in a micro-interpersonal rejection of a Zealot image of Jesus. Why could not Jesus have been a Zealot? The fact that he was "powerless of body" in 14:62 is an insufficient critical answer. We would argue that Belo is motivated by a sociopolitical ideology to explain things in a way that is sociopolitically rather than historically acceptable.

His argument betrays his interest. He begins by establishing that Jesus and the Zealots both intend a transformation of their contemporary society. Their methods for achieving change differ, however; Jesus is fundamentally opposed to the violent change espoused by the Zealots. The Zealots, Belo concluded, are "men in revolt" against the occupational forces of Greece and Rome and the ruling class of Israel that collaborated with them.

Jesus maintained three messianic goals for the transformation of his society. First, he sought a radical subversion of the contemporary societal codes. Second, he directed his transformative aim at the Jewish symbolic field centered on the temple, as 14:58 indicates. Third, he was determined to overcome the political segregations caused by the purity regulations in the Jewish law. The strategy, Belo determines, was communist.

In fact, Jesus looks suspiciously like a Christian communist. But Jesus was not a revolutionary, because his work did not entail the revolutionary design for restructuring the entire slave-based mode of production in the larger sub-Asiatic society that engulfed his own. So what exactly was Jesus? Belo explains that communism is a political program to eliminate the class system. Revolution is a strategic process for taking power. Because individuals or groups can accept one mandate without accepting the other, there can be noncommunist revolutionaries and nonrevolutionary communists. Jesus, he argues, was the latter. His tactic for achieving nonrevolutionary communist transformation of his society was the promotion of an exodus of Jewish faith principles to pagans on an international level: "It is at this intersection of communism and internationalism that the privilege of *conversion* is located, the privilege of following J[esus], the privilege of each agent bearing fruit in regard to the liberation of *bodies* (hands, feet, eyes) through the powerful work of the spirit."[9]

This is why Jesus' anti-temple statement and behavior are so threatening.

This is the messianic narrative that the priests saw operating out of his life, the one that Mark theologically covered over. It is an orientation of change that challenges the temple as a central component of the nation's sociopolitical power structure. It is an orientation of change that threatens not only to divest the temple of its political might, but threatens as well to divest Judaism itself of its singular claim to the principles of its faith. Jesus, therefore, does not look like a Zealot. Jesus looks much like a Christian Marxist. He looks, in fact, much like Fernando Belo. The macro-interpersonal reconstruction mirrors the interpreter's micro-interpersonal agenda.

This micro-interpersonal influence is also visible in Belo's interpretation of the new temple that Jesus intends to build as a replacement for the old one. Not only does the Christian Marxist Jesus intend to establish a new community; his invitation to the pagans, the outsiders, guarantees that this new community will be a communist, classless society. Not only does Jesus look like a modern Christian communist, but his goal is consistent with the modern communist goal:

> According to J[esus], the Messiah is the one who produces the space for the collective Son of Man. The latter title is the one that corresponds to a *communist ecclesiality:* to the gathering in the BAS [basileic] circle of poor people without any accompanying rich people, servants without masters, disciples without scribes, young people without adults, brothers without fathers, or, in a word, sons of man outside any relations of domination and kinship.[10]

Now Belo is presented with another dilemma. If indeed Jesus is not a Zealot and can therefore not appeal to a Zealot power base, with what kind of force will he mobilize his strategy? Belo's response is that Jesus will achieve his social and political reconstruction through his eschatological power. The eschatology of verse 62 therefore does not stand alone, but is seen anew as the divine manner in which a very human, very political endeavor will be accomplished. Jesus appeals to the power resident in this eschatological narrative when he seeks transformation of his society. His death and resurrection are not about personal salvation, they are about social revolution. "This is what the bourgeois exegesis has never been able to read, and with good reason."[11]

Like the mustard seed that grows into a great tree capable of providing shelter, Jesus' ministry will create a social structure that obtains a possibility of inclusion not only for the lowest members of the Jewish society, but for those in pagan society as well. But Jesus' goal of exodus to the pagans and the downtrodden can only be achieved at great cost to the present Jewish power structures. The representatives of that power structure recognize this fact and therefore set out to stop him. The trial before the Sanhedrin is the ultimate attempt to accomplish that goal.

Belo sees irony in the fact that Jesus' purpose of exodus to the pagans obtains for him a transference from Jewish to pagan antagonists. Irony is not, however, the only link between the two texts. They are materially connected by the concept of messiah. Belo here seems to appreciate the linguistic phenomenon of onomasiology.[12] He is arguing that the concept of messiah is, in the evangelist's mind-set, designated by both the terms *messiah* and *King of the Jews*. Both trials are therefore based on the same conceptual center, even if the individual terms appear to differentiate them. Belo explains that whereas *messiah* is a term that would adequately convey the proper conceptual content to the Jewish community, it would have no meaning for a Roman, and therefore would be, in a literary sense, out of place in a discussion with Pilate. *King of the Jews* is the appropriate, conceptually parallel designation for the same political concept. And just as it struck sociopolitical fear in the Jewish leadership, so it concerns Pilate: "The difference is rather the difference between *Jewish power* and *Roman power:* in regard to the former, the 'Messiah' stands in opposition to the politico-ideological function of the high priest; in regard to the latter, the Messiah stands in opposition to the political function of Caesar."[13]

A key component in Belo's argument is the crowd. Both Pilate and the Sanhedrin are afraid that Jesus' messianic claims and actions will inflame the people, who will then become his tool of revolutionary accomplishment. This is why Barabbas' role becomes important at the conclusion of the Roman trial; Jesus' role is clarified through it. Barabbas is an alternative to the crowd, an offering of appeasement. One revolutionary, Barabbas, whom both the Roman and Jewish powers feel can be controlled, is offered for another, Jesus, who poses the greater threat. Just as proponents of the status quo today often subvert the causes of change by singling out the hardships that any change will cause in the short term, the authorities orchestrate the crowd's choice for Barabbas by making it appear that Jesus' societal reconstructions will threaten not only the powerful, but the ordinary citizens as well. "Now, the C [crowd] of Jerusalem depended *economically* on the temple and the pilgrimages, and it was this that made it decide *against* the man whom Pilate in his stratagem presented to them as 'him whom you call king of the Jews.'"[14] It now makes sense that the one testimony brought against Jesus would be the one that alleges his position against the temple and what it signifies. From the beginning of the trial episodes the authorities have devised a political strategy to defeat a sociopolitically motivated messiah.

Belo's primary interest is the meaning of the text for his own sociolinguistic community. In that regard, he preoccupies himself with an explanation of what the text *means*. To be sure, he does so through an interpretation of what the text *meant*, but his re-creation of the Markan community is contextualized by his own micro-interpersonal position. Convinced that the position of the sociopolitically oppressed, his position as a Marxist Christian, is similar to Jesus' position and that of his followers in both his own and Mark's time, Belo in effect sees a merging between his sociolinguistic situation and that of the first-century Christian communities. He interprets the text from his own sociolinguistic situation as similar to that of the primitive Christian readers for which it was intended. Of course, there are many key differences between the two communities separated by a vast span of time and geography, but a vital link remains: both communities are oppressed socially and politically by the governing powers that control their social and political destinies. The difference is that whereas Belo's society used direct socioeconomic symbols and institutions to control the populace, the Jewish community used the religious symbols of temple and cult. The purpose is the same, oppressive sociopolitical control. The text that describes Jesus' engagement with such oppressive forces, and calls the communities who believe in him to act likewise, means the same thing for Christian communities in Belo's time and place as it did for those who encountered the messianic narrative. It is a text about transformation for a people committed to transformation.

The problem with this reconstruction is that it appears to be methodologically contrived. Jesus' situation bears an uncanny resemblance to Belo's. Instead of macro-interpersonally interpreting the linguistic clues in the text, he has done so micro-interpersonally, from the point of view of his own sociolinguistic setting. He has, in effect, substituted his own sociolinguistic situation for that of the messianic community. This does not make his approach more compromised than that of the traditional interpreters. Actually, it is contextualized in a similar way. Where traditional approaches depend heavily on macro-interpersonal constructs determined unconsciously by their micro-interpersonal situations to reconstruct the situation of the primitive Markan community, Belo does so by a conscious dependence on his micro-interpersonal perspective. For that reason it appears overt; he does not try to hide it.

The problem is that by concentrating so heavily and so quickly on his micro-interpersonal perspective, Belo does not allow the textual, ideational, and macro-interpersonal features to operate fully and, more importantly, independently. Instead of using the textual, ideational, and history-of-religion clues to establish the most likely scenario for a Markan sociolinguistic background that could subsequently be invigorated and brought to life with micro-interpersonal observations, Belo starts with the micro material and therefore appears to create, if he does not do so in fact, a Markan community that is a mirror image of his own. Allowing the data to stand initially separate from his micro-interpersonal perspective would have vastly improved Belo's critical agenda, allowing him to push beyond rather than obliterate textual and ideational boundaries. Belo's effort does have a promising micro-interpersonal base, but it would be helpful for his communicative endeavors if he could establish more firmly and more independently what the text *meant* before going on to share what it *means*.

It must be recognized, however, that Belo opens the text to contemporary communities of the oppressed for which it would otherwise have purely antiquarian interest. In his hands the text becomes more than a historical or a literary presentation; it becomes a meaningful force interpreting and directing the lives of those caught up in contemporary contexts of struggle. For this reason the new components of the potential of meaning that his study brings to life should be valued and more thoroughly integrated into any future interpretative work on the trial scenes.

## Ched Myers

Ched Myers also operates from an intentionally micro-interpersonal perspective. For him, however, conclusions based on a textual, ideational, and macro-interpersonal evaluation must stand on their own merit. We must not only understand what the text *means* to us, we must pay equal attention to how and what the text *meant* for its original readers. To that end we must attempt to uncover their sociolinguistic situation. Meaning should then occur at the point where the text influences us, not where we use our micro-interpersonal position to influence and re-create the text.

Myers establishes his internal micro-interpersonal preunderstanding in the preface to his work. He does so first through the principle of association. The foreword by Daniel Berrigan and Myers's note to Phil Berrigan imply a revolutionary social consciousness. They share a concern for change in the society of the United States based on the principle of liberation of the oppressed. Myers makes the position clear when he writes of the Berrigans and others, "Mahalo, friends; by your discipleship I continue to measure my own." He continues, "Words are not the way to liberation. In so far as this study offers any clarification or inspiration, it is done on behalf of all those nonviolent resisters presently in jail because of their witness against the imperial Goliath [i.e., the United States]." This preunderstanding facilitates a politically encoded theology "in which the truth of imperial America, with its vast disparity between rich and poor, its permanent war economy, and its institutionalized racism, is laid bare." [15] This politicized, micro-interpersonal life-relation in turn facilitates Myers's critical program of text analysis. "This commentary will read Mark as an ideological narrative, the manifesto of an early Christian discipleship community in its war of myths with the dominant social order and its political adversaries." [16]

Myers operates from a scientific perspective that is, in his own terminology, socioliterary. By this he means an investigation that applies the scientific requirements of critical literary study, but allows itself at the same time to be influenced by the pertinent sociopolitical emphases present in both text and interpreter. This investigation includes three relevant phases. He begins with an inductive literary analysis of the material. From there he proceeds to an extrinsic examination of the historical and ideological setting and prevailing social strategies in Mark's world as they are presented through the role relationships of the characters in the text. The resulting macro-interpersonal reconstruction is supplemented by a full-fledged micro-interpersonal analysis that allows Myers's own sociopolitical perspective to function as the focal point from which he observes the text. It is his intent to discover what the text *meant*. Once again, however, exegetical meaning is found to be dependent on political realities.

Myers begins his analysis by arguing that the passion narrative is an intensely political rather than a religious document. Less a statement about the origin and locus of personal salvation, it is a sketch of political intrigue that documents the end of a social subversive who dared challenge the sociopolitical institutions of his day. "It is an intensely political drama, filled with conspiratorial back-room deals and covert action, judicial manipulation and prisoner exchanges, torture and summary execution." [17]

His work begins at the inductive level of literary analysis. From the start he argues for an integral connection between the two episodes. Three devices link them. The first two are ideational. He begins with time; both trials occur within a twenty-four-hour period. The second is the triple mockery of 14:65, 15:16-20, and 15:29-32, each of which ironically confirms Jesus as messiah, prophet, and king. The third, and most important, is textual. Myers notes the parallel manner in which Mark has constructed the critical elements of the two scenes, 14:60-62 and 15:4-5, 2. "Aside from the fact that the second trial reverses the order of question/response, the two are almost exactly parallel." [18]

A problem arises, however, with the parallelism that Myers offers as textual evidence. There is a major sequential difference in the presentation of dialogue in the two trials. Myers acknowledges the difference but does not account for it. In the Sanhedrin scene the messiahship question comes at the climactic end point of the deliberations. In the Pilate scene it opens the interrogation and is followed by the charges for which Jesus offers no response. This difference in order suggests that Mark may not have arranged the material with the intent Myers proposes. Indeed, according to George Dunbar Kilpatrick, Mark is simply accounting events as they occurred. Taylor argues that the two plot lines come from the traditional sources, not the evangelist. Other scholarly opinions exist on this matter, but these few illustrations are sufficient to indicate the crux of the concern. There is no clear textual evidence that Mark intended the material to be read in parallel;

indeed, the evidence is often read in ways that leave little room for such a possibility. Further, the fact that Mark did not arrange the scenes so that their sequences would match (only a single verse, 15:2, need have been moved) seems to mitigate against the possibility of intentional parallelism. What then, if not the evidence itself, induces Myers to read the scenes as he does? It seems clear that it is micro-interpersonal perspective. The "reality" of a parallelism in the language of the trials gives his sociopolitical claims about the narrative intent their primary textual foundation. In effect, he needs the kind of parallelism that his investigation ultimately finds.

Myers uses this textual reconstruction to "prove" the key ideational point that there is a single conceptual content behind the terms *Messiah* and *King of the Jews*. Jesus is conceptually viewed as a challenge to the Jewish and Roman sociopolitical structures; in other words, he is a political subversive.

For Myers as for Belo, the key to understanding the trial scenes is 14:58. In fact, Myers is so convinced of the political-conceptual import of the signifier *temple* that he refers to ναός as "temple-state." By attacking the temple-state, Myers concludes, Jesus strikes at the very heart of Jewish social consciousness. Jesus' behavior as portrayed by Mark is manifestly subversive. It was their sociopolitical way of life, not their religious strategies of salvation, that was under attack.[19]

Myers recognizes, however, that many traditionally oriented differences of opinion have arisen regarding this matter. Most notably he refers to the impressive sociological study done by S. G. F. Brandon.[20] It is Brandon's conclusion that Jesus was indeed a political subversive. Mark, however, wishing to downplay Jesus' political troubles and thereby cover up his identity as a subversive, emphasized his religious significance instead. Therefore, when Mark came to the point of chronicling the trials of Jesus, instead of presenting the situation accurately as politically motivated, he concocted a Sanhedrin trial with religious significance. The issue became Jesus' role as redemptive messiah and the resultant charge of blasphemy. The real trial, which led to the historical crucifixion, was the one before Pilate. Mark, however, given the problems that might occur should the Roman neighbors of his reading community become offended, also wanted to present the Romans in a favorable light. The Sanhedrin trial thus served another even more significant purpose; it took the weight of complicity from the Roman governor who wanted to acquit Jesus and placed it on the Jewish leadership. The first trial therefore was included as a religious apologetic for the second one.

Myers is aware of the magnitude of the problem. "Obviously, if Mark's intention was to portray an 'apolitical' Jesus who was mistakenly condemned by a reluctant procurator, it would overturn my entire reading."[21] Operating from his socioliterary approach, he dismisses the apologia hypothesis. He suggests that the micro-interpersonal perspective of traditional scholarship has unwittingly led authors down this futile interpretive path. The concept of "blaming the Jews" is not so much in the text, he argues, as it is in the history of Western Christianity, which views the text from a long-established position of anti-Semitism. This anti-Semitic tendency is compounded by the "benign" Western view of imperial authority. Western European scholars, themselves citizens of great empires, possess unconsciously within themselves this apologetic for imperial authority and therefore are likely to see it in the text even when it is not present. The result of this micro-interpersonal influence on traditional Euro-American interpreters is the interpretative conclusion that Mark wanted to blame the Jews and exonerate the Romans. The findings are precariously similar to the presuppositions that bore them.

Admittedly operating from a different sociopolitical preunderstanding, one that is hostile to imperial power and concerned for historically oppressed peoples like the Jews, Myers offers an alternative solution. "This discourse of parallelism, far from suggesting favoritism, strongly implicates *both* parties of the colonial apparatus as equally culpable—indeed collaborative—in the political railroading of Jesus."[22] Once again he appeals to ideational literary data. He argues that Mark's use of parody and irony demonstrates his belief that both governments are responsible for Jesus' trial and subsequent death. In the highest Jewish court due process is thrown out. The hearing is rigged, and still they cannot get the testimonies straight. This would explain all the textual and ideational inconsistencies in the Markan Sanhedrin trial. "Mark *means* to portray this as a political trial in which legal constraints are jettisoned."[23] The authorities then frantically lobby the crowds, which they themselves distrust. The Roman trial once again shows parallelism; this time it is ideational in design. The issue is the same, one of political subversion, though this time the charge is the claim of kingship rather than messiahship. Pilate now consults with the Jewish crowd, which he too never trusts. In fact, he despises them. His questions are therefore to be viewed as contemptuous taunts rather than sincere quests for information and direction. "These literary hyperboles work together to indict the entire politico-legal process of the colonial condominium, not just the Jewish leadership."[24] Jesus is therefore viewed as a political threat to both the Romans and the Jews. Both are therefore shown by Mark to be unjustly plotting his downfall. A unique political perspective has obtained a unique political interpretation.

Myers now turns his ideational attention to the key objective in any seditious plot, the affections of the populace. Both the Roman and Jewish authorities are concerned about Jesus' ability to instigate revolutionary thought and activity in the crowds who follow him. Jesus must be stopped because he threatens to move the crowd to act according to his subversive designs. But because he does enjoy the temporary favor of the populace, Pilate realizes that popular support for the dissident must be neutralized before the necessary adjudication can be rendered; a propaganda ploy is called for. He decides on the release of a revolutionary figure of similar stature. Once again the macro-interpersonal evidence is called on for ideational support. Myers notes that this kind of political exchange is documented by Josephus, who notes how Albinus was blackmailed into releasing a prisoner by the Sicarii and was later bribed to release other social bandits as well. "We can conclude from this that the release of one popular dissident in order to defuse public protest over the execution of another, in the context of a politically charged atmosphere, is not only plausible but probable." [25]

Before Pilate's action can work, Jesus' stature with the crowd must be diminished so that when given the choice, Barabbas and not the "king" will be chosen. Here the deceitful alliance between the Jewish and Roman leadership is unveiled. The Jewish leaders charge Jesus with threatening not only their political power, but indeed the very socioeconomic structure on which the people depend. Jesus' attack on the temple-state is portrayed as a revolutionary call for social change that would leave everyone in socioeconomic and political disrepair. The key anti-temple charge becomes the tool that the duplicitous Jewish leaders use to lobby the crowd against Jesus:

> Certainly Jesus' talk of being "rejected by the builders" (12:10), and destruction "stone by stone" (13:2) would have incensed the thousands of laborers employed in the massive construction/restoration project. Small wonder, then, that this allegation is repeated by the crowd at the scene of Jesus' crucifixion. [26]

Jesus' messianic work thus bears a potent political charge. His adversaries confirm the sociopolitical import of his ministry in their responsive mannerisms. Indeed, even the charge of blasphemy obtains a mainly political significance. The reader is aware by now that it is only after Jesus' confession in verse 62 that the high priest accuses him of blasphemy, after he has assumed the role of the messiah, Son of the Blessed. Many traditional scholars have hypothesized that it was Jesus' acceptance of the role of divine Son that made him culpable of the death sentence. It appears therefore to be a mainly religious concern. Myers, however, pressing the parallel between the two trial scenes, turns to an etymology of Barabbas' name. His name carries, in an ironic sense, the same kind of connection to divine sonship that we see in Jesus' confession to the question in verse 62. "His name translates 'Son of the Father.'" Mark clearly offers the son of the Father as a counterpart for the Son of the Blessed; the crowd chooses the former over the latter. But the connection between them is a purely political one—two sons, two political options for societal change. The real problem with the Son of the Blessed, it therefore appears, is not so much the connection with the Father as it is what Jesus believes that connection imports, sociopolitical change. "Thus Mark's narrative concern here is to dramatize the choice. Jesus and Barabbas each represent fundamentally different kinds of revolutionary practice, violent and nonviolent, both of which have led to a common fate: prison and impending execution."[27]

Despite his effort to present an analysis that encourages a programmatic challenge to the limitations on meaning imposed by macro-interpersonal research, Myers offers a work that appears problematic in the same way as Belo's, though to a lesser degree. His conclusion early on that the commentary "*will read Mark as an ideological narrative*" based on sociopolitical presumption significantly influences his individual text investigations. Before he reaches the trial scenes a *particular* micro-interpersonal foundation has been set. Before he can independently broaden the parameters of meaning in the scenes by reevaluating the ideational, textual, and macro-interpersonal language of the text from a new interpretative perspective, his micro-interpersonal preunderstanding imposes limitations on what the text can mean. As with Belo, then, so with Myers, the macro-interpersonal information and conclusions are not given sufficient independence from micro-interpersonal perspective. Myers's work therefore appears to confirm preconceived conclusions rather than encourage new and distinct ones based on micro-interpersonal potentiality. The text is not opened up, but closes around his own interpretative perspective. In the end, instead of analectical engagement he has performed what Enrique Dussel called dialectical recognition and opposition. Instead of learning from the traditional approaches to the material, he recognizes them, challenges them, opposes them, and inserts a sociopolitical program more in tune with his own micro-interpersonal perspective in place of them. In attempting to free up the meaning he has in fact corralled it so that the text now has relevance only in an interpretative environment like his own. His sociopolitical background and the agenda it represents too clearly and too forcibly dominate the process. Instead of pushing beyond old boundaries of interpretation, he has merely replaced them with new ones. The macro must be redefined by the micro, but it must not be recreated so that it is delimited in a new, sociopolitical way.

One cannot, however, argue that Myers's work has paid insufficient attention to the text-linguistic properties of the trial scenes. Indeed, our analysis demonstrates that, like many other literary critics, he operates a textual program of analysis whose conclusions are backed up by solid ideational and macro-interpersonal evidence. He has indeed seen important meanings that are in the text even if the way he argues them is flawed. And because he recognizes that a subsequent micro-interpersonal evaluation should redirect the macro-interpersonal research in such a way that its conclusions are brought to life in modern, living communities, he at least comes close to the kind of analectical engagement that Dussel spoke of. His macro-interpersonal findings are changed because they "learn" from his micro-interpersonal perspective. They learn to access and value different components of the text's potential meaning.

# 10 Jesus, Man of the People

IN POPULAR APPROACHES TO ANALYZING THE trial scenes, we see an even greater appreciation for and influence from micro-interpersonal perspective. Since popular interpreters address the specific needs of a contemporary audience, the principal objective is an understanding of what the text *means* for the modern reader/hearer. While such an emphasis requires a background measure of methodological control, it demands even more a visible and primary role for an intensely micro-interpersonal agenda. It not only reads *from* a consciously acknowledged situation, it reads *for* such a specified circumstance. Different communities, literally, see different Jesuses. Each community accesses and values that part of the potential meaning that is uniquely responsive to its communal needs and concerns.

## The Gospel in Solentiname: A Revolutionary Rereading

The *Gospel in Solentiname* provides an excellent example. Although it depends on the Matthean version of the trial before the Sanhedrin, its inclusion in our discussion can be useful since Matthew follows Mark closely, and because the *campesinos* themselves frequently refer to the Second Gospel's version. As we observed in chapter 3, *The Gospel in Solentiname* maintains a degree of ideational control throughout. Such critical acumen, operating as it does in isolated moments during the conversations, does not, however, imply the presence of a consistent method. In fact, there is no one real critical method operative in the inquiry of the Solentiname peasants. Ernesto Cardenal provides critical assistance, but he responds more to the demands of dialogical interchange than to a need for methodological consistency. The key to understanding the *campesinos'* work lies in a consideration of their micro-interpersonal strategy. They only deal with what the text *meant* in an exegetical sense so that they can proceed to the heart of the matter for them, what the text *means* for their own circumstances.

Cardenal begins, for example, by giving the *campesinos* a historical-ideational explanation of the Sanhedrin. He subsequently describes its operation and thereby acknowledges a critical historical problem: none of the disciples would have been present at the trial. Consequently, they could know about its proceedings only through hearsay. This historical recognition does not, however, lead, as it would for Julius Wellhausen and Hans Lietzmann, to a historical-critical skepticism about the value of the text. Its historicity is never challenged. Indeed, its historicity is a secondary concern. The text is valued because it sheds light on the trials endured by *campesinos* who presently follow in Jesus' footsteps. The critical issue is not whether or how these events happened for Jesus, but how Jesus' trial and his conduct during its proceedings can give meaning to those who must stand trial before the sociopolitical powers of contemporary Nicaragua.

Without hesitation the *campesinos* observe, "This looks like the Military Court that's operating in Managua."[1] By that they mean to say first that the trial is not just, and second that what happened to Jesus is now happening to them. While their situation interprets the text, the text likewise interprets their situation. Jesus, the defendant, is an unjustly accused revolutionary like them, who answers the high priest's question the same way one of their contemporary heroes would answer the judges in a Nicaraguan political trial.

Jesus' mission, then, becomes integrally connected with their own, and they can only understand his trial, and indeed Jesus himself, by studying the text from the perspective of their program of revolutionary sociopolitical change. They are, therefore, less concerned with whether the charge in verse 58 is false or not, and more aware of the need in any political trial for false evidence as the necessary means for accomplishing a desired conviction. The adjective *false* no longer serves as a cause for methodological concern; it becomes instead a point of dramatic moral and spiritual connection between Jesus' situation and their own:

Not only here in Nicaragua, as our comrade has pointed out, but in many other countries of Latin America the same thing goes on now. Those who are struggling for freedom are taken before courts. Not to judge them and hear their defense but to condemn them. And as they can't accuse them of wanting freedom of humankind, they seek false charges. They plant weapons in their houses to say they belong to them.[2]

Such false charges have a specific purpose in the designs of the societal elite; they discredit revolutionaries by presenting them as opposed to both the codes of moral conduct and the interests of the people. The charge in verse 58 is thus understood to be an attempt by the Jewish authorities to turn the crowd against Jesus, just as Nicaraguan authorities attempted first to discredit revolutionaries before they unjustly sentenced them. In fact, it was the accomplished destruction of crowd sympathy that made the sentence, unjust as it was, enforceable.

Jesus, they argue, was, as they were, accused of being a revolutionary communist. "He had given evidence that would now be an equivalent of communism. But the Bible was communist too. He was talking about the 'kingdom,' and the prophets had described that kingdom as the perfect communist society."[3] But in the Western-oriented power structure of Nicaragua of the time, which the *campesinos* felt was tied to the imperial interests of the capitalist United States, the charge of being communist was as morally devastating as it was legally suspect. The charge, like the anti-temple one, was designed to turn the sympathies of the American people and the Nicaraguan middle class, who held decidedly American views, against the suspected revolutionaries.

*Temple,* then, is less a religious center than it is a signifier for social and political control in the early Jewish community. The anti-temple statement in verse 58 is therefore a decidedly political accusation made in a hostile political climate. "He had just taken over the temple, as we saw last Sunday. He went into the temple in a commando action, and they're probably referring to that in the trial."[4] Just as the *campesinos* use their situation to clarify Jesus, Jesus' situation gives clarity to who and what they must be as revolutionaries. Already being condemned like Jesus, they must continue to act like Jesus. This action on behalf of justice will always encourage conflict with those who have power, who benefit from societal inequities. The text, for the *campesinos,* has come alive.

If Jesus' statement about the temple's destruction is revolutionary, so too is his subsequent claim about building another in its place. The *campesinos* believe that the man who would revolutionize his world by destroying its fundamental center of social, religious, and political power would logically continue his efforts by putting in its place a more representative structure that would maintain the revolutionary aim. This is the new temple he would build, a resurrection that points not to a specific spiritual body, but to a completely changed physical world. For the community at Solentiname Jesus intended more than the creation of a localized Christian community—he was projecting a program of societal upheaval that would ultimately stretch worldwide. It is here that the eschatology in the text obtains its direction and importance. The interpretative move is a fascinating one; cosmic redemption, in their rereading, takes on a decidedly political significance.[5]

The sociopolitical emphasis established at the opening of the passage in verse 58 continues throughout the two trial scenes through the concept of messiah. Verses 58 and 62 are linked ideationally because the anti-temple statement is a messianic claim that would be appropriate to a person making the confession found in verse 62. In fact, Cardenal instructs the *campesinos* that 14:58 is so clearly imbued with messianic pretensions that the high priest's question about Jesus' identity follows logically from it.[6]

This sociopolitical messianic concern then becomes the link between the Sanhedrin and Pilate trial scenes. Jesus' design to overturn the Jewish power structures was as politically dangerous for the Romans as it was for the Jews. For the *campesinos,* then, we are no longer looking at a separate religious and political trial. Both trials are about the same conceptual problem, even if that problem is identified by the different lexical designates, *Messiah* and *King of the Jews.* They can recognize this onomasiological reality because the same duality of accusation is made against their own community:

> They did it to us when the Head of Customs in Managua sent a telegram to all the custom houses in the country forbidding the importing of the first volume of our *The Gospel in Solentiname, IV* because it was a very harmful book that "by means of the Gospel tries to preach communism to the people."[7]

At this point the *campesinos* identify for themselves the concept behind the field of designations that result in the lexical terms *Messiah* and *King of the Jews.* That concept is Jesus the liberator. They come to this conclusion by connecting all that they have considered before with the eschatological reference in Jesus' confession of 14:62. "That means he was going to come as judge, and judge in the Bible was the same as liberator: one who was coming to liberate the oppressed and take revenge on the oppressors."[8]

So Jesus' second coming is interpreted as a sociopolitical event that functions as the futuristic extension of a human ministry dedicated to the transformation of the sociopolitical situation as understood through the temple symbolism. In this way the coming is equated socially and politically to the building of a new temple:

> *Bosco:* You could interpret that coming as all the people now united—right?—who are going to judge the oppressors.
>
> *Cardenal:* He's telling them: I'm going to come like a people, like a whole community that will establish the kingdom of God on earth.[9]

Only now, after the complete sociopolitical picture is established, do the *campesinos* deal with the question of blasphemy. For them even this religious accusation maintains a sociopolitical emphasis. Blasphemy was charged, they argue, because Jesus had assumed the role of executing the divine last judgment. But since the concern about the last judgment had to do with its sociopolitical implications in the here and now rather than its salvific importance for some heavenly netherworld, the problem with this particular blasphemy was its condemnation of the present societal order rather than its claim on divine prerogative. Jesus had identified himself with the coming God, and this coming God, being identified with the "people," the disenfranchised of society, was a sociopolitical threat.

This God who becomes a "worker" community prophesied eschatologically by Jesus is understood by the *campesinos* to have been partially realized in their own sociopolitical fellowship. This is ultimately the micro-interpersonal purpose behind their interpretation of the trial scenes in particular and the biblical materials in general. They interpret Jesus' trial by viewing it through the perspective of their own sociopolitical tribulations, and they in turn allow their understanding of Jesus' work to shape their present and future work. The connection of Jesus' trial with their own trials serves two vital functions within their community. First, it means that their work is like Jesus' work; as he was "right" in his revolutionary endeavors, so are they. Their efforts must therefore continue unabated. Second, as Jesus was vindicated despite the apparent failure chronicled in the two trial scenes, so will their cause be vindicated, despite the fact that the societal powers apparently prevail at the time of their discussions. Their work is not merely informational; it is also, and perhaps primarily, motivational. Their understanding of Jesus as a political subversive on trial reaffirms their understanding of themselves.

Clearly, as we noted in chapter 3, the Solentiname peasants attend primarily to the ideational properties of the text language. This function of language forms the basis for their micro-interpersonal conclusions. Macro-interpersonal considerations play a small role, but it is their attention to the conceptual references and connections in the trial scenes that provides the foundation for their investigative enterprise. The lack of consideration for textual matters is disturbing, but understandable given the nature of popular interpretations. The intent is to avoid a preoccupation with grammatical and structural details that might take away from the primary conceptual implications that are drawn when the biblical text is used as a tool for understanding, evaluating, and directing present behavior. Still, the lack of attention to all three text-linguistic functions is reason for concern. Syntax, too, conveys meaning. In fact, it is this inattentiveness to textual controls that allows us to consider this Matthean review within a Markan study. Attention to grammatical and syntactical detail is so loose that the story presented by the peasants is an almost generic Markan-Matthean presentation. This is acceptable if—as is the case with most popular analyses—one wants to understand the story only as a broad, conceptual work about Jesus' trial and condemnation, but precise attention to specific Matthean or Markan intentions becomes highly difficult. So concerned are the peasants to understand the text for their own circumstances that a consideration for what the text *meant* specifically to either the first or second evangelist is textually and macrointerpersonally devalued in the process.

An even more damaging problem involves the perception that the Solentiname community tends to attach anachronistic labels like *communism* to biblical imagery. It appears on the surface that the peasants take terminology used in their own community and force it on the first-century trial scenes. But even here there is some justification for the move. There is a logical connection between what happens sociopolitically in Solentiname and the events presented in the biblical text. False charges brought against Jesus are seen through a lens that has encoded on it a sense of how false charges are brought against communist revolutionaries like the *campesinos*. The connection is made ideationally through the imagery of the trial and the false charges. The process starts with the text, not with communism. Communism becomes an onomasiological cipher for modern understanding of ancient textual clues. We can understand what happened to Jesus because we realize that the same things happen to Solentiname communists. Parallels in human behavior, ancient and modern, are made. Corrupt human beings in control of corrupted, power-driven institutions will react consistently when they are faced with change-oriented opponents, no matter the historical era. At this point the *campesinos*' perceptions lead to an unwarranted charge of a staged trial by the Sanhedrin. False evidence is procured; the intent is to silence the troublemaker Jesus as it would be to silence contemporary Nicaraguan troublemakers. The Solentiname peasants in this way directly impose communism onto the text. They do so because they believe that Jesus' concerns are integrally related to their concerns as political revolutionaries unjustly put on trial for their lives. The label does not corrupt the sense of what the text *meant* because the *campesinos* do not apply it there. The labeling helps them understand what the text *means* in their own lives. It is connected with Jesus because an understanding of how Jesus dealt with similar charges produces an outline for how they may deal with their own politically precarious situation.

With this popular approach, then, we see the same process that a macro-interpersonal reconstruction can discern happening in the earliest communities: a living dialectical interchange between text and reading audience. The peasants do not doubt the tradition handed to them. They merely seek to understand and apply it. But there are gaps in the text. Why is the anti-temple charge presented as false? To what does the concept *temple* refer? How is *Messiah* to be understood? What are the implications of eschatology in this context? To what does the charge of blasphemy refer? We have shown that these and other ideational problems did not pose a severe interpretative problem for the earliest readers because they shared much of Mark's interpretative background. They read between the lines and found meaning. The Solentiname community operates in the same way. They, however, do not share Mark's sociolinguistic background. Instead of attempting to fill in the gaps with methodologically reconstructed first-century historical detail, they rely on their own background as the economically oppressed of their society. Once again a concerted consideration of what the text *meant* in its own circumstance is not pursued; heightened emphasis on the present circumstance devalues the interpretative worth of the historical circumstance. They substitute the life of a twentieth-century Nicaraguan peasant, communist revolutionary for that of a first-century Greco-Roman Christian who shared with Mark a knowledge of many details of the story. The substitution is itself not problematic. Concern arises when, as is the case here, the first-century circumstance is not given independent consideration so that it can act as a restraint on the interpretative conclusions reached through the lens of the twentieth-century circumstance. The Solentiname of the 1960s and 1970s became an unrestrained interpretative screen that brought the text to life in a unique way. The gaps were filled with a sociopolitical perspective that resulted in a text and a Jesus that have a specific sociopolitical and economic bearing.

Not only does this process result in insufficient stress on the macro-interpersonal, but the emphasis on the micro-interpersonal is often overstated. The perspective of Solentiname becomes—naively, uncritically—*the* interpretative perspective of worth. Their perspective is not analectically engaged with traditional approaches, or, for that matter, with other micro-interpersonal approaches. In fact, other possibilities are not even considered. Therefore their work does not even rise to the still inadequate level reached by Fernando Belo and Ched Myers in the dialectical opposition between traditional macro-interpersonal and a specific micro-interpersonal perspective. The boundaries of meaning are not expanded, but limited to the group's own micro-interpersonal interpretative position. This is why the communist label becomes a liability. Certainly other sociopolitical groups, even capitalists, have maintained some kind of affinity with the biblical material. The *campesinos'* interpretation disallows such an interpretative possibility. It is not, however, that other perspectives are dialectically opposed and then considered inappropriate or illegitimate; they are naively ignored. If there is meaning in the text, it is meaning from, and meaning for, one particular community.

Interestingly enough, our point of critique is also the place where we celebrate the effort of the Solentiname peasants. Once again interpreters push beyond the boundaries of text meaning; a change in micro-interpersonal perspective prompts innovative and enlightening text interpretation. A provocative new component of the text's potential meaning is accessed precisely because the focus applied by this community allows its members to see what had heretofore been missed. In the process they make the text much more than a historical story about Jesus; they give it a meaningful, specific relevancy to their own situation. This kind of interpretative struggle must be affirmed despite its weaknesses in methodology. Their work serves a vital function; they forge from an ancient text contemporary meaning. The effort and objective of interpretations like that rendered by the *campesinos* must not be abandoned, otherwise we will forever suffer the threat of being unable to make the challenging transition from acknowledging what the text *meant* to celebrating what it *means*. Instead, information procured here must be analectically engaged with information derived from other micro-interpersonally driven interpretations.

## Tom Skinner: Words of Revolution

Tom Skinner's sermon/speech "To Change the System" [10] is a popular interpretative enterprise so micro-interpersonally based that he does not even pause to define which Gospel he uses for his primary reference. We can gauge from his discussion, however, that the source is Synoptic rather than Johannine, and more specifically Markan or Matthean. All the images with which we have become familiar are present.

The preface to Skinner's work provides us with a wealth of information regarding his internal micro-interpersonal preunderstanding. Like the *campesinos*, he is interested in defining what the text *means*, not only from the perspective in which he lives, but for it as well. He tells us early on that he was a leader of youth gangs, an inner-city troubled black teen whose social location was one of poverty, overcrowding, and prejudice. "I've been there," he writes. "I was born in Harlem and have lived out my life where exploitation, oppression and violence are a way of life." [11] This early life situation, conditioned by circumstances of inequity, prompted an adult preunderstanding that looked favorably on revolutionary attitudes and tendencies. "Yes, I am a radical, I am committed to revolution. I am committed to doing something about the suffering, shame, and misery in America." [12]

This revolutionary preunderstanding encodes Skinner's work and gives thematic consistency to his sermons and speeches. For him, discussion of the biblical texts must not merely provide one with scriptural and spiritual information, it must also contribute meaningfully to considerations about contemporary social ills. He therefore reads with a program in mind, a program dedicated to sociopolitical change. Revolution, he believes, because of the present sociopolitical situation of pervasive injustice, is inevitable:

> Everywhere I go people say, "The system's got to go, man," and "we gotta do away with the system." People are fed up. Blacks and whites are sick of the hypocrisy and corruption. Young people are fed up with the world their parents are handing them. Poor and middle-class citizens are reacting to the inequities they see in society. [13]

It is only the mode of the revolutionary enterprise that is in question. He believes that a proper understanding of the biblical text, given this inevitable circumstance of subversion, is one that will direct believers toward the proper kind of future conduct for inaugurating the projected social upheaval.

As was the case with the *campesinos,* Skinner's micro-interpersonal perspective is changed by what he eventually finds in the text. The former gang leader, because of what he perceives to be a revolutionary but nonviolent New Testament, moves away from a youth dedicated to violence, and embraces an adult life committed to nonviolent social change. We can see a microcosm of this journey in his sermon based on Jesus' trials before the Sanhedrin and Pilate.

Skinner establishes the sociopolitical bent of his speech immediately. When he speaks of a system in dire need of change, he is speaking of the American socioeconomic and political system that creates a reality of poverty and disenfranchisement for the bulk of its citizens. He lists a myriad of sociopolitical problems, and then he recognizes those who marched and worked and fought for change. While many kinds of people from many walks of life challenge the system, all meet a uniform response: opposition. Sociopolitical change is always opposed.

At this point he turns his attention to Jesus and the titles that are key to his confession at the Sanhedrin trial. Skinner's focus, as was that of the *campesinos,* is ideational. Jesus as messiah is Jesus as Son of God. He connects these terms not exegetically, but sociopolitically. They are connected onomasiologically, regardless of their terminological differences, because they are different lexical designations of the same conceptual reality, a Jesus who was the greatest revolutionary and radical ever to walk the earth. [14]

In what is most probably a pointed reference to the Jewish authorities who operate the temple, Skinner speaks of the "church" as a key representative of the system. He does not specifically designate the temple at this point because his work is directed completely toward his contemporary circumstances.[15] It is clear that the church represents for him the religious establishment that has acquiesced to the power designs of the larger society in the same way that the Jerusalem temple bought into the ancient Jewish sociopolitical system:

> So I had a problem. All the images that had ever been projected to me of Jesus Christ were that He too was a member of the system. In fact, the people who had messed up the system often used Jesus Christ to provide some kind of sacredness to the way they ran their corrupt institutions. So they wrapped Jesus and the American system up in the same bag.[16]

Jesus' challenge to the temple and the Jewish authority system it symbolized thus becomes a challenge to contemporary churches and the role they play in maintaining the inequities of the status quo. The text, in Skinner's hands, becomes a direct challenge to every American Christian who reads it. Jesus' anti-temple statement becomes an anti-American church statement precisely because Skinner comes to the shocking conclusion that the contemporary American church is using Jesus in the same way that the high priests used the temple, to promote stagnation rather than positive societal change.

The real Jesus, he discovered, was one who came to challenge and change the system. Referring to the conflicts with the Jewish establishment that can be traced in Mark back to the beginning of Jesus' ministry, he discovers "not a lofty Christ, but a Jesus who rubbed shoulders with people in the nitty gritty of life. He dared to mingle and talk with prostitutes, drunkards, and people of ill repute."[17] It was this Jesus who was brought to trial by the Jewish leadership, not because of his message of salvation, but because of his claims regarding social change:

> Now any time a man starts talking that strong, there are going to be problems. When a man starts shaking up the religious, political, and social system, the people *in* the system feel they have to stop him. . . . Jesus came along and began to threaten both their systems [Pharisees and Sadducees—the Jewish leadership] and denounce them both. Strangely the Pharisees and the Sadducees suddenly got together. Now they had a common enemy. They conspired to have Jesus locked up because He was "dangerous."[18]

As the Jewish leaders exploited the common Jewish people, so the Roman imperialists exploited the Jews. It was the same kind of system, Skinner charges, only a different segment of society was now in ultimate control. The key concern, however, remained the same, maintenance of the status quo. "The Romans had moved into Jewish territory and said to the Jews, 'We are here to run things and if you keep things cool, nothing will happen to you.'"[19]

But, according to Skinner, revolution was as inevitable then as it is now. He points to the Zealots, and in particular, a Zealot named Barabbas:

> And Barabbas began to rap to his people, "There is only one way to get that Roman honkie off your back—burn him out!" So Barabbas and his band of guerrillas burned Roman homes, jumped Roman soldiers on the streets, and killed Roman soldiers whenever they could do it without great risk.[20]

Jesus, Skinner has already pointed out, was a revolutionary too. But Jesus had a different program; his way was one of nonviolent confrontation. Jesus and Barabbas agreed there was a problem; they even agreed on the nature and magnitude of the problem. In fact, as far as Skinner is concerned, Jesus would have agreed with present-day revolutionaries: "*I'm not so sure that Jesus Christ is interested in preserving a corrupt [American] heritage.*"[21] At the point of choosing a response, however, Jesus and Barabbas came to a radical difference of opinion. Jesus recognizes that the victims of societal oppression could be as evil as the perpetrators of that oppression. It was therefore necessary to change more than systems alone; people themselves needed to be altered.

Skinner now comes to the point of decision, for the people of Jesus' time as well as those of Skinner's time. There will be revolution—societal injustice demands it. The question is, What kind of revolution will it be? Who's going to lead it? "*We do have an option.* We can decide between Barabbas and Jesus. Either one of them will change the system. One will do it the wrong way and one will do it the right way. Either way the system will be changed. It's up to you to decide who will do it."[22] The choice belongs as much to us as it did to the crowd gathered that Passover season in Jerusalem.

Pilate knows there is a choice to be made, and he knows the crowd must be allowed to make it. So he allows them a prime opportunity. Even so, in Skinner's interpretation the governor is not a sympathetic figure. Recognizing the parody and irony in the text, Skinner interprets at this point with a literary, ideational skill worthy of academicians like Donald Juel and Ched Myers. Mark, he argues, is not trying to make the Romans look good at Jewish expense. His offerings of amnesty are in reality calculated taunts:

> [Pilate] gets up in front of the Jews and says, "Look, I've got two revolutionaries in jail. And you know how much I love you dear Jewish people. I've always loved the dear Jewish people. In fact, some of my best friends," says Pilate, "are Jews. And not only that, the guy who ran my bath last night was a Jew. I even had lunch with one last week. So I have nothing against you dear Jewish people."[23]

Pilate's taunting betrays a scheme. The choice he offers is really no choice at all. He wants the crowd to opt for Barabbas, the more visibly active revolutionary. This is because Barabbas, for all his terrorizing, is a part of the status quo. The Romans know they will always have a Barabbas. They are prepared to deal with a Barabbas. They are confident that their armies will always be able to defeat a Barabbas. So freeing Barabbas will appease the large festival crowd, it will make them feel as if they have made a difference, and in the end that liberating act will have maintained the very oppressive system against which the crowd thought they were mounting a challenge:

> You can always stop Barabbas. But the question is: *how do you stop Jesus?* How do you stop a Man who has no guns, no tanks, no ammunition, but still is shaking the whole Roman empire? How do you stop a Man, who—without firing a shot—is getting revolutionary results?[24]

The question is as pertinent for Skinner's contemporary readers as it was for the Roman governor. In fact, Skinner's interpretation of this ancient text, as we can see from the references to tanks and ammunition, is designed to shed light on his world. He switches from the ancient to the modern context without seeing any real change in meaning. The choices presented to the Jerusalem crowd are presented anew in the twentieth century. This present meaning is the one that becomes critical for Skinner's evaluation.

The Jerusalem crowd selects Barabbas to be the recipient of amnesty. Pilate is pleased; he has maintained the peace and assured the continuity of the status quo. The Jewish leadership is pleased as well, for this now completely politically motivated Jesus also represented a formidable threat to their sociopolitical system.

Jesus was therefore consigned to die. It appears that his effort was lost. But his eschatological claims, voiced in 14:62, were initiated with his resurrection, a resurrection that for Skinner becomes a political event. Jesus' resurrection, like his ministry, as seen through the lens of the trial scenes, is significant not because of its salvific religious value, but because of its sociopolitical significance. The new thing this revolutionary, this messiah, this son of God brings is a world and a people changed in his image:

> Three days later Jesus Christ pulled off one of the greatest political coups of all time. He rose from the grave, saying, "All power is given unto Me in heaven and in earth. And with this power, I'm prepared to radicalize men for God. I'm prepared to make revolutionaries and radicals for the kingdom of God."[25]

As did the *campesinos* in Solentiname, Skinner's micro-interpersonal approach to the text has established a potent present meaning for an ancient text. Where macro-interpersonally oriented research saw gaps and inconsistencies in the language of the text, Skinner finds meaning in precisely the same way the primitive communities determined meaning. What are perceived as gaps in the logic or texture of the story are filled with information from the reader's sociolinguistic background. The earliest readers used their own ancient backgrounds; Skinner, making the case that the situation of oppression faced by Jesus and his followers remains ideationally constant, figures that his own background, too, shares sufficient variables with the earliest communities and the evangelists who cared for them. He is therefore as confident about using his background as an interpretative lens as the earliest Christians no doubt were about using theirs. He demonstrates little doubt that he can and should make interpretations by involuntarily applying his own sociolinguistic background as the guide for reading and interpreting the linguistic clues in the text. It is a living dialogical interaction between reader and material.

This approach carries inherent problems, however, similar to what we saw in our review of the Solentiname interpretation. Like Myers, Skinner envisions but a single layer—the sociopolitical—to the text of the trial scenes. We have found, however, that there are religious implications like the resurrection or the eschatological plan of the Son of man that differ from Barabbas' primarily political plans. In fact, Skinner's own work points out these implications. But instead of allowing them to stand independently, Skinner immediately evaluates and reorients them through his micro-interpersonal perspective. The religious concerns are merged into the sociopolitical in such a way that this multifaceted text becomes a single-emphasis statement about a political cause and the change it demands. The result is that we have an interpretation that applies specifically to the urban American situation with which Skinner is familiar. Sociopolitical emphases establish boundaries around the text's potential meaning in the same way that religious ones once did.

## John Killinger: A Traditional Popular Approach

To balance the popular interpretations of the text given from such a revolutionary perspective, a brief look at a sermon that comes out of a more mainline church setting might be useful. Even a brief look will lend credence to our suggestion that a different micro-interpersonal perspective, particularly at the popular level, yields a different, contextually appropriate Jesus.

John Killinger was the senior minister at the First Congregation Church of Los Angeles at the time this sermon, "Jesus and the Temple Religion," was published.[26] While Skinner's micro-interpersonal preunderstanding encouraged a revolutionary understanding of the text, Killinger's more mainline circumstance as the pastor of a Christian community encourages a different preunderstanding. Killinger immediately relates the text to the situation of his contemporary hearers. Like Skinner he identifies his Christian hearers with the temple followers of Jesus' time. He, too, believes that Jesus' anti-temple statement has as much to say against the modern church as it did against the Jerusalem temple. Jesus is, in effect, attacking modern Christianity:

> And most of our church buildings are looked upon as modified temples, for they are our centers of religious faith and practices just as the temple in Jerusalem was a center for the Jews. . . . It comes as something of a shock, therefore, when we really hear the gospel and realize that Jesus and the early Christians were basically anti-temple.[27]

It is no wonder then that the crowd, both past and contemporary, turns against Jesus:

> Imagine how we would feel today if a country preacher came into Lynchburg and went around to all our churches—all our beloved temples—saying that our trust is in the wrong things, that all of this brick and mortar, all of this beautiful stained glass, all of these mighty organs and hand-rubbed pulpits and brass lecterns and expensive pieces of communion ware, get in the way of our seeing God, which is, after all, the object of most religion.[28]

Here the difference in Killinger's social location becomes critical. While Skinner and the *campesinos* saw the temple as a representation of the sociopolitical system of Jewish life, Killinger sees it as the center of Jewish religious life. For the ancient Jews, and for the latter-day Christians, therefore, the issue is one of religious rather than sociopolitical challenge. "It was its [the temple's] very centrality in the spiritual life of the people that allowed it to become the strongest citadel of evil. . . . If Israel had been led astray, it was because those in charge of its spiritual life had failed as leaders." If dysfunctional symptoms existed in the culture, they were the outcome of an inherently spiritual, rather than sociopolitical, temple disease. The temple is problematic because it has become a religious idol. "Why were Jesus and his early followers so set against the temple? It was because they saw the temple as a mislocation of faith."[29] Rather than appealing to God for salvation, the people had become dependent on institutionalized religion. It is a dependency that is equally threatening to contemporary mainline Christianity.

Killinger's new micro-interpersonal preunderstanding allows him to see something new in the text. He sees the contrast of the temple built with hands and that not built with hands in a new light. The temple must fail because it has become itself an idol; people no longer look to the real temple, God's Spirit, the real dwelling place of God. Killinger therefore also sees the reality of polysemy in the term *temple*. But the field of signification is radically different. The temple is no longer a physical building, a religious symbol, or the representation of a sociopolitical way of life; it is instead a physical building and a religious symbol. The new temple is therefore no longer a new social and political entity; it is a new spiritual relationship with God effected through the new spiritual temple that is the resurrected body of Jesus Christ. Here Killinger's traditional influence is laid bare. His interpretation of the temple as a spiritual entity betrays through its language and thought a special affinity with the commentary on this text by Eduard Schweizer. "The contrast between 'which men made' and 'not made by men' is typical of Hellenistic thought, where external worship in temple and sacrifice was contrasted with purely spiritual, inner worship."[30] Killinger does not allow the new Christian community to be the new temple, because it stands accused of the same charge brought against the temple. "The religion that is centered in the physical temple would be destroyed, for it was idolatrous; but the religion that is centered in the resurrected Jesus—the temple to be raised in three days—would live forever."[31] Ultimately, then, the new temple becomes completely spiritualized. The social location of the popular interpreter has contributed to a popular understanding of what and how the text *means.* Jesus is literally now a different Jesus.

Killinger's sermon is brief. He limits his consideration to the material immediately surrounding the anti-temple statement of 14:58. It is therefore more difficult to make a comprehensive analysis of his use of all three text linguistic functions. But even here we can recognize the popular interpreter's attraction to engaging the text ideationally. Killinger focuses on the conceptual imagery contained in the term *temple* and connects a brief macro-interpersonal study of how it might have been understood in the first century with an in-depth consideration of its contemporary application. At this point we can see how powerfully the micro-interpersonal position of the interpreter affects his or her conclusions. It is not coincidental that Killinger, a religious leader preaching to a worshiping congregation, understands *temple* to be a religious concept. The micro-interpersonal perspective has altered the conclusion about the central meaning of the text imagery precisely because the community to and for which the interpretation is made has changed. Killinger's observations are in line with Skinner's until he comes to the point where he must explain the key ideational concept that the text does not itself clarify. *Temple,* as a conceptual image, has a range of significations, as we have seen. Which *signifié* is key to the evangelist's discussion? The text does not itself offer a definitive answer. An interpretation must be made. Skinner turned to his micro-interpersonal background for interpretative assistance; Killinger turns to his. Since those backgrounds are so different, the conclusions, and the Jesus portrayed through them, are different as well.

Indeed, it is precisely this difference in conclusion and the micro-interpersonally oriented manner in which it is achieved that instructs us. One person's or one community's interpretation must not be placed in a position superior to all others. Interpretations are highly contextualized. Not only must there be a dialectical recognition of the value of other interpretative methods and conclusions, but if we are to truly push beyond interpretative boundaries, there must also be true analectical engagement among varying micro-interpersonal interpretative perspectives. As Enrique Dussel's model shows, such an encounter would allow for a learning process in which different approaches could not only acknowledge each other, but in fact learn from each other and change as a result of a new awareness. In this way the different presentations of Jesus might more beneficially become fuller presentations of the one Jesus.

# 11 Beyond Interpretative Boundaries

A MAN STANDS ALONGSIDE A PEACEFUL LAKE in beautiful mountain surroundings. Escaping, if only momentarily, the stress and noise of the city, he has driven a great distance to get here. He has come seeking the solitude, the peacefulness, and the pleasure that fill him visually and aesthetically as he stands on the shore. He feels the breeze as it carries leaves across the shimmering surface that reflects the sunlight like a mirror. He receives from the lake the beauty and calm he came seeking.

High above him an eagle circles. She has left behind a nest of young. Her journey brings her here with another purpose in mind. She seeks from the lake not its beauty but its sustenance. She seeks what the man neither searches for nor misses. Her target identified, she dives on the breeze, breaks the water's calm surface, retrieves a fish, and then, satisfied, climbs out of sight.

The change is one of perspective. This change allows, perhaps even demands, a change in what is seen. The eagle does not place fish in the pond, neither is the man's visit here problematic because he has missed the fish. Each of them has seen something unique in the vast array of possibilities because each has come to this place with different questions. It is for this reason that while they see clearly, they also see differently.

Analogies can be taken to a certain point, beyond which they fall apart, and this one is no exception. It is useful, however, in illustrating the central point we wish to make. The biblical text harbors a vast potential of meaning. A researcher's questions codetermine his or her final conclusions regarding which segment of that potential meaning to access. It is not necessarily the case that a new meaning is placed in the text, but that meaning may be interpersonally and therefore contextually extracted from it. For this reason we come to the conclusion that the fullest possible meaning can be achieved only by drawing from the variety of interpretations, not understanding them as alternatives, but as providing a complimentary range of meaning. Encouraged by Enrique Dussel, we conclude that an analectical engagement that precipitates a recognition and appreciation for the different kinds of sociolinguistically determined evaluations can push us beyond the boundaries that attempt to place limits on the possibilities for text meaning.

Several years ago the seeds for this research were sown when I was challenged with the idea of considering the different ways in which different peoples use language. The motivation for such an analytic move came from my observation that the black church and the black community it serves interprets biblical language in a demonstrably unique manner. I had two concerns. First, I was chagrined by the inability of traditional approaches to biblical interpretation to bring the text to life in the midst of my circumstances as a black Christian. Second, I was often stung by the criticism of black interpretations that, it was alleged, imposed a foreign ideology on the text. When I widened my perspective on this matter I found that the black church was not alone in the kind of interpretative independence it demonstrated. Other religious, ethnic, political, and social groups also interpreted the biblical texts in ways that were sensitive to their particular communal circumstances. What were the factors, I wondered, that determined the form of interpretation that characterized the sociopolitical and religious groupings that did not abide by these principles? How could one identify those factors? Was there legitimacy in the procedures involved? The sociolinguistic theory of M. A. K. Halliday seemed the most promising vessel for eliciting the answers I sought.

Before proceeding I considered a related concern. If we were to establish that there is legitimacy to each of the interpretative moves in these sociopolitical settings, how are we to find some means of mediating among them? How do we find a way of opening communicative channels that promotes accommodation rather than opposition among the interpretative camps? The model of analectical engagement offered by Dussel provided me with a mechanism uniquely suited for the task.

This research began with the specific aim of finding a way to affirm the work done by what we have referred in this study to as the micro-interpersonally oriented text interpretation. Our research has demonstrated that there is a basis for such an affirmation. We have found that black, liberation, and other kinds of micro-interpersonally oriented text interpretations cannot be dismissed, because all research must deal with the fact that micro-interpersonal factors determine how the text is interpreted. Traditional, historical-critical research is determined by the same kinds of internal and external sociolinguistic factors that influence intentional micro-interpersonal interpretations.

We also found that micro-interpersonally oriented research provides a valuable service to believing communities. Their work enables the text to come to life in a way that the fruit of traditional research does not. Instead of focusing purely on what the text *meant* in the past, the intentional micro-interpersonal investigation offers itself as a reliable gauge of how and what the text *means* in a particular community's circumstance. For this reason we conclude that black interpretations as well as others that perform like them provide a valuable service to those within and outside their communities. It is valuable for those within because it brings the text to life in a manner that takes into consideration the community's particular needs and concerns. It is valuable to those outside when they approach such interpretations analectically. When such micro-interpersonally based interpretations are viewed not as an opposing alternative to meaning, but as a new, previously undiscovered component of the text's potential meaning, it will transform the ways in which people inside and outside the community understand the material. The new interpretation becomes a part of the interpretative process and thereby changes that process instead of appearing as an imposing view.

Dussel's model of analectical engagement, when applied specifically to biblical analyses, helps us recognize an important fact. Interpretative approaches can benefit from an awareness of and affiliation with other approaches, leading to change in the conception of investigation. Analectical engagement promises that as one approach honestly encounters another and learns from it, its very conceptual existence will change, as will the manner in which it views the biblical reality it is designed to investigate.

The analectical process as Dussel envisions it, however, is a limited interpretative technique. It is based on the assumption that one interpretative approach, the traditional, will engage another specific approach, the Latin American liberation, and thereby create a new and complete reference for meaning. It was his hope that a complete and comprehensive meaning of the text could ultimately be achieved in such an additive manner. Our analyses of the trial scenes demonstrates that such a limited engagement is insufficient if the vast range of a text's potential meaning is to be appreciated. In other words, while the analectical approach provides us with a useful model of engagement, its concentration on two approaches stops short of what we now see to be the necessary concern. The full spectrum of meaning available in a text can only be appreciated by allowing a multitude of communal interpretations to engage each other in the analectical manner that Dussel proposed. No final, complete, comprehensive text interpretation can result from this process because changes in sociolinguistic circumstance are perpetually inviting new ways of approaching and therefore evaluating the text. A text can therefore never be interpreted completely; it can only be more comprehensively appreciated once it is understood that what is determined to be its meaning is dependent on a variety of sociolinguistic factors. A text can be envisioned as a rainbow of potential meaning whose individual colors, while visible to one interpreter or community, are invisible to many others.

Our analysis of interpreters who worked on the Markan trial scenes proved to be an illuminating case study. The analysis demonstrated that traditional researchers typically concentrate on all but the micro-interpersonal text-linguistic features in their analyses. Textual, ideational, and macro-interpersonal factors are consciously considered in the interpretative process. Traditional investigators recognized that textual and ideational considerations are by themselves insufficient to the task. A determination of what the text *meant*, which tends to be their objective, is impossible unless the language is also analyzed macro-interpersonally. These researchers recognized that because modern readers do not share a common sociolinguistic background with the authors and original readers of the texts, gaps in textual and ideational meaning arise. An author uses the language of the text according to textual and ideational norms of a particular first-century community, making use in that way of the interpersonal function of language. Therefore, to understand properly what the author intended when he used a term such as *temple* or *messiah*, the interpreter must reconstruct the context in which the author derived terminological and ideational meaning. And because the first readers of the text often did not share the same historical circumstance as the author, most traditional interpreters also recognized the need to clarify the sociolinguistic situations of each of the primitive reading communities. This kind of knowledge would allow the interpreter to predict how different primitive communities might have comprehended terms and concepts whose meanings are not exhausted by a consideration of textual and ideational features alone.

Traditional researchers recognized that the earliest readers interpreted the material micro-interpersonally, while the researchers investigated macro-interpersonally, that is, without allowing for the involvement of micro-interpersonal factors of their own in the investigation. They hoped to recreate the micro-interpersonal circumstances of the authors and original recipients of the texts as clearly as possible, figuring that in the process they would obtain a clearer picture of what the text *meant* to those earliest reading communities. In other words, wherever there are textual and ideational gaps in the meaning of the story, traditional researchers turn to a macro-interpersonal reconstruction of the micro-interpersonal factors that determined the earliest reading communities (and so also the authors of the texts), hoping that an awareness of the original sociolinguistic circumstances would allow a better understanding of what the text *meant* at the time it was written.

Our findings demonstrated that other variables were also at work in the interpretative process of the traditional researchers. While they concentrated on textual, ideational, and macro-interpersonal features of language, they were also heavily influenced by micro-interpersonal variables of an external and an internal kind. Researchers who reached different conclusions were found to have appealed to the same textual and ideational-historical evidence. Our analyses demonstrated that in each case the differences in their interpretations arose from micro-interpersonal factors of which the researchers were rarely aware. For them, too, changes in micro-interpersonal influences contributed to new insights into textual meaning. Their inability to consider intentionally micro-interpersonal variables in their own interpretations not only contributed to a lack of interpretative control; their macro-interpersonal focus tended to suggest that there could be no comprehension of what the text *means* unless such meaning was extrapolated directly from a declaration of what it *meant*. Since every suggestion of what the text *meant* was itself contextually defined, there is no escape from the reality that what the text was expected to *mean* contributed to what it was perceived to have *meant*.

We therefore found that the full spectrum of the text's meaning can only be appreciated if one's analysis is not limited to an individual interpreter or a single group of interpreters. The complete "rainbow" becomes visible only when each of the micro-interpersonally oriented investigations is considered. For example, a review of the Anglo-Saxon researchers, George Dunbar Kilpatrick and Vincent Taylor, helped us to appreciate the possibility of the text's historicity. We were presented with various scenarios that increased the likelihood that the first-century Palestinian and Roman figures may have acted in a trial setting in the manner that Mark described. However, the perspective of the historical skeptics, Julius Wellhausen and Hans Lietzmann, encouraged us to attend to other elements of the potential meaning. At that point the possible biases of the evangelist came to light. We gained a clearer picture of how the needs of the early Christian communities may have induced the evangelist to alter his presentation of the events that surrounded Jesus' death, and thereby change how those events were ultimately understood. On the assumption that the primitive communities were religiously motivated, the historical skeptics argued that Mark formulated the Sanhedrin scene so that its redemptive concerns could be enhanced at the expense of what may have been a political trial before the Roman governor. The primary truth exhibited by the Sanhedrin trial was therefore Jesus' politically charged anti-temple statement in 14:58.

Still, all of the "rainbow" was not yet visible. The form and tradition historical critics, Martin Dibelius and Rudolf Bultmann, motivated by a completely different set of micro-interpersonal concerns, saw within this same set of texts an indication of the early Christian communities' worship designs and motivations. The text was understood differently because its meaning was integrally bound up with its most probable communal use. Now the trial scenes told us less about Jesus' ordeals or the author's intentions than it did about the primitive Christian communities. Because the early communities were worship oriented, these critics concluded that the material in 14:60-62 represented the earliest traditions since it was most applicable to that communal need.

To this point the concepts of messianism and anti-temple polemic had been viewed mainly as separate entities in competition with each other. Operating from a source-critical perspective, Taylor saw a link between the two trial components. His work presented the case that Jesus' anti-temple stance and the titles applied to him were complementary aspects of what the Jews and Romans perceived to be Jesus' problematic behavior. The concept of messianism was expanded to include social as well as religious concerns.

Still, it was not until we turned to practitioners of literary exegesis that we saw within the text a comprehensive sociopolitical concern. Once again, the change in micro-interpersonal perspective provoked an ability to see a new section of a constantly unfolding rainbow of meaning. In Juel's work the conceptual understanding of *temple* broadened to such a degree that its sociopolitical implications were as vital as its religious ones.

In each case we found that the change in communicative context allowed for, and even demanded, a new investigative perspective that in turn provoked new questions and therefore new answers about the meaning of the material. It was therefore virtually impossible to obtain a final, complete meaning, even by way of adhering to historical-critical principles of research. As internal and external micro-interpersonal perspectives changed so did the conclusions regarding meaning.

The ethnographic and popular researchers we investigated shifted the focus of their text investigations to the needs and concerns of their present communities. The shift in perspective once again compelled a shift in the comprehension of a text's meaning. New pieces of the meaning rainbow were coming to light. Communities caught up in contemporary sociopolitical turmoil saw in Jesus' trial a primary sociopolitical motivation. He was killed because he had sought too energetically to transform society, just as their own contemporary communities were seeking such transformation. Jesus became a revolutionary on trial who could even, as in the case of the Solentiname *campesinos,* condone violence should the situation warrant it. Jesus' activities in ancient Palestine were viewed through the eyes of twentieth-century Marxists, communists, black civil rights activists, and— most importantly—impoverished persons suffering from the same kinds of inequities that haunted Jesus' world. The text was no longer considered an ancient historical document that once spoke in dialogue with ancient communities but had long since gone silent and thus ought to be analyzed in a situational vacuum; it became a living entity that applied itself specifically to contemporary needs and concerns. The text came alive. With this new life came new meaning. In each community, from the Marxist Christians of Fernando Belo to the inner-city black revolutionary community of Tom Skinner, a different sociopolitical piece of the rainbow of meaning came into focus.

We also recognized, however, serious text-linguistic deficiencies in these micro-interpersonally oriented research efforts. The most immediate concern is that the popular approaches fail to consider carefully enough, if at all, the textual features of the language in the trial scenes. But the critique that turned out to be the most damaging came from the recognition that Fernando Belo and Ched Myers, like the popular researchers, paid insufficient attention to the macro-interpersonal features of the texts. While they made energetic efforts to establish macro-interpersonal reconstructions of the first century's sociolinguistic circumstances, their efforts were severely compromised by their own micro-interpersonal positions. Ethnographic researchers did not allow the textual and ideational-historical evidence to establish an independent contextual reconstruction of the first century that could have been effectively used as a restraint on their micro-interpersonal presuppositions. That is to say, while macro-interpersonal reconstructions should not be viewed as ends in themselves, they are necessary because they provide restraints on what and how the text language can *mean.* A micro-interpersonal interpreter cannot present an appropriate interpretation of the language if he or she gives to the language a meaning for which there is no historical precedent. Macro-interpersonal reconstruction provides a range of potential meaning in which a micro-interpersonal investigator may make interpretative moves that are faithful to the needs and concerns of his or her community. If that macro-interpersonal consideration is not allowed an independent hearing, however, the investigator will tend, as our research demonstrated, to impose modern meanings that, though micro-interpersonally significant, are not macro-interpersonally appropriate. Because these interpreters were so focused on determining what the text *means,* they did not get close enough to a determination of what the text *meant* in first-century Palestine. The result was that the ancient conditions that surrounded Jesus and his trial became a looking glass that mirrored the conditions surrounding the micro-interpersonal interpreter and his or her community.

As we found from Dussel's work, however, micro-interpersonally driven interpretations that arise from the margins, when analectically engaged with more traditional methods of interpretation, can broaden the horizon of overall meaning in the text. These studies are valuable because they show the relevance of a text for a particular community. Because the change in sociolinguistic location invites new vision, the material—in our case the trial scenes—is seen in a way that otherwise would be missed. Because the text has been seen from a new perspective, new and different components of its potential meaning can be acquired.

In fact, we have seen that this micro-interpersonal process of interpretation as practiced by Tom Skinner and the *campesinos* was also practiced by the evangelists. Mark, for instance, interpreted his source traditions in a way that was relevant for the particular community to which he wrote. The process was as necessary in the first century as it is today, otherwise the text is of only general historical interest to a community. If the text is to connect with a community, to meet its needs and direct its life, it must be seen as relevant not as a general historical account, but as a particular message to a particular people. Only an intentional and well thought-through micro-interpersonal interpretation can foster this kind of interpretative move.

Problems develop only when textual and ideational considerations are not given firm enough controls. This caution does not mean, however, that interpretation must begin with textual and ideational factors and only then consider community relevance. Micro-interpersonal considerations must be applied responsibly, in concert with textual, ideational, and macro-interpersonal considerations, from the start. In this way the text will legitimately find meaningful new life in new sociolinguistic surroundings.

We find, therefore, that in order to appreciate the entire range of possible meaning, an interpreter must listen to all (not just the traditional and the Latin American liberation) perspectives on the text before drawing conclusions. Even then, after those conclusions have been drawn, the interpreter must realize that the interpretative task is not complete. There will always be new and excitingly different sociolinguistic perspectives from which to view and develop an understanding of the text.[1] We contend then that we go beyond Dussel, acknowledging that while his analectical program lays the theoretical groundwork, it applies that theory in too limited a fashion.

We initially appealed to Dussel's methodology because it had been our intent to develop a single method that would comprehensively convey the meaning of a text. But in our study of the Markan trial scenes we found that because meaning is determined in large part by micro-interpersonal context, there is no single, final interpretation of a text that can bring out all of its meaning, past, contemporary, and future. This is why approaches must learn from each other; each approach can offer a different and valuable perspective on text meaning. As long as the human condition changes, the micro-interpersonal variables that influence text investigation will change. Therefore, new micro-interpersonally determined approaches will be continually in production, allowing for the possibility of adding to the methodological techniques of investigation and the potential for meaning. In other words, the objective of a complete interpretation is not only an illusion, but undesirable because it locks out the ways in which perpetually new experiences can shed light on what and how the text *meant* and *means*. Because the interpersonal factors do not remain the same, the text remains alive and can never be interpreted completely.

Bultmann again serves as an excellent example. His existentialist interpretation had positive meaning for the historical situation in which he lived. Bultmann took note of the micro-interpersonal factors and used them to bring new light to the biblical texts he investigated. He was mistaken in thinking that he had established a method of interpretation that could be used in every instance of the human experience. We have found that as human circumstances changed, Bultmann's existentialist interpretation lost much of its relevance for new historical micro-interpersonal circumstances. As generations change, the issues that are to be addressed in the interpretation change, demanding constantly new interpretations. At this point we find a strong measure of support for the intentionally micro-interpersonal interpretations.

Bultmann's approach retains its merit, not by holding to its contingent existentialist approach, but by analectically engaging new approaches, so that it can develop and change in response to new times and new micro-interpersonal concerns. We have tried to offer a window into the validity of such an analectical shift by demonstrating how an updating of Bultmann's methodology provides an excellent background for our own program of analyzing and categorizing the interpersonal influences on text interpretation.

J. P. Gabler had already recognized in the late 1700s the need to adapt interpretative moves to sociolinguistic situations.[2] Dogmatic theology was for him a legitimate task, but only when founded on the investigative moves of biblical theology. One first had to ascertain what the biblical text actually *meant*. We now realize that this hope is an impossible ideal. Because of our investigation of traditional approaches, however, we now know that when the micro-interpersonal variables change, not only do we see a change in what the text *means,* but our perception of what the text *meant* also changes. Coming to terms with such a recognition teaches us that there can never be one final text interpretation. We have demonstrated that micro-interpersonal variables are always determinative. Because we also know that the human circumstance is constantly changing, we can conclude that text interpretation will remain fluid. This does not mean the text changes. It obviously remains the same. But we have found that the text is multivalent. There is no single meaning. Textual, ideational, and macro-interpersonal investigations establish limits on a text's meaning potential. But within that limited range of potential meaning is a rich field of possibilities that are gleaned differently, according to the ways in which the textual and ideational information is micro-interpersonally viewed.

At the end then, we come back to the contention that opened our work. For an interpretation not to be considered deficient, each of the three text linguistic features must be fully considered. Every interpretation must engage with the text distinctively in terms of all three functions of language. Even then, a proper understanding of the interpersonal feature brings us to the recognition that an interpretation can never be complete. Therefore, the only way to expand interpretation beyond the boundaries of a single interpretative move or a group of interpretative moves is to allow different approaches to engage each other analectically and therefore learn from and be changed by one another. Traditional approaches cannot continue without taking note of micro-interpersonally oriented interpretations; conversely, micro-interpersonally oriented interpretations cannot affirm themselves against traditional interpretations, but have to engage with them. Through such recognitions we can move toward a fuller interpretation, one that we must concede will always remain incomplete.

# Notes

## 1. A Contextual Approach to New Testament Interpretation

1. Hendrikus Boers, *Who Was Jesus: The Historical Jesus and the Synoptic Gospels* (San Francisco: Harper and Row, 1989).

2. Ibid., 10.

3. Cf. ibid.: "At the same time, in its present form the story shows how easily such a tradition was adapted to express a Gentile Christian conception by shifting the emphasis from Jesus' Davidic lineage to his divine sonship through the Holy Spirit."

4. M. A. K. Halliday, *Explorations in the Functions of Language* (London: Edward Arnold, 1973) 7.

5. Ibid.

6. Ibid., 27.

7. Ibid., 13.

8. Ibid., 14.

9. Ibid., 15.

10. Ibid., 36.

11. Halliday is careful to note that these are semantic categories, and that because the functional approach to language is oriented around these categories, it is an approach concerned with meaning rather than morphology or syntax. Functions will be coordinated with meaning; "We shall not attempt to assign a word or a construction directly to one function or another" (ibid.).

12. This ideational content is then given structure by ideational elements in the text such as the

agent, process, goal, or phenomenon. "The notions of agent, process and the like make sense only if we assume an ideational function in the adult language, just as 'object of desire' and 'service' make sense only if we assume an instrumental function in the emergent language of the child" (ibid., 39). Halliday illustrates this category by explaining its function of transitivity in the grammar of the clause. "The clause is a structural unit, and it is the one by which we express a particular range of ideational meanings, our experience of processes—the processes of the external world, both concrete and abstract, and the processes of our own consciousness, seeing, liking, thinking, talking, and so on. Transitivity is simply the grammar of the clause in its ideational aspect" (ibid.).

13. Ibid., 107.

14. M. A. K. Halliday, *Language as Social Semiotic: The Social Interpretation of Language and Meaning* (London: Edward Arnold, 1978) 31.

15. All language functions in contexts of situation and is relatable to those contexts. The question is not what peculiarities of vocabulary, or grammar, or pronunciation, can be directly accounted for by reference to the situation. It is *which* kinds of situational factors determine *which* kinds of selection in the linguistic system. The notion of register is thus a form of prediction: given that we know the situation, the social context of language use, we can predict a great deal about the language that will occur, with reasonable probability of being right. (Ibid., 32.)

16. Ibid., 144.

17. Halliday, *Explorations in the Functions of Language*, 64.

18. Dell Hymes, "Models of the Interaction of Language and Social Life," in *Directions in Sociolinguistics: The Ethnography of Communication*, ed. John J. Gumperz and Dell Hymes (New York: Holt, Rinehart and Winston, 1972) 42.

19. Norman Fairclough, *Language and Power* (New York: Longman, 1989) 24.

20. Ibid., 26.

21. Halliday, *Language as Social Semiotic*, 12.

22. Halliday, *Explorations in the Functions of Language*, 13–14.

23. The Sapir-Whorf hypothesis is a radical exposition of this argument. Whorf, building on the hypothesis originally established by Sapir, argued that the structure of the vocabulary and grammar of an individual's language actually shaped that person's view of the world. Language thus becomes a direct guide to social reality. Ralph Fasold notes that this controversial thesis is neither totally accepted nor totally rejected today. Most scholars agree with some version of the weak form of the thesis. It maintains that a people's behavior will tend to be guided by the linguistic categories of their languages under certain circumstances. For a summary discussion of the Sapir-Whorf hypothesis, see Ralph Fasold, *The Sociolinguistics of Language* (Cambridge, Mass.: Basil Blackwell, 1990) 50ff.

24. Ibid., 52.

25. R. A. Hudson, *Sociolinguistics* (Cambridge, England: Cambridge University Press, 1980) 12.

26. Fasold, *Sociolinguistics of Language*, 41, 42.

27. Hudson, *Sociolinguistics*, 13.

28. Halliday, *Language as Social Semiotic*, 14.

29. Halliday, *Explorations in the Functions of Language*, 49.

30. Ibid., 50.

31. Ibid., 51.

32. That Halliday's procedure can work in a textual investigation is demonstrated in the work of David Hellholm, which makes use of the three categories of text investigation from the standpoint of the reader-interpreter as well as the producer of the text. See David Hellholm, *Das Visionenbuch des Hermas als Apokalypse: Formgeschichtliche und texttheoretische Studien zu einer literarischen Gattung,* vol. 1, *Methodologische Vorüberlegungen und makrostrukturelle Textanalyse* (Sweden: CWK Gleerup Lund, 1980), especially pp. 27–51. Hellholm discusses these categories under the headings *die syntaktische Textdimension* (textual), *die semantische Textdimension* (ideational), and *die pragmatische Textdimension* (interpersonal). His specific work on the interpersonal category is found on pp. 42–52. Hellholm is influenced by a variety of linguistic and rhetorical sources in establishing his sense of text pragmatics. Although we cannot mention them all, two notable ones are W. Dressler and H. F. Plett. Among Dressler's works noted by Hellholm are *Einführung in die Textlinguistik, Textlinguistik, Current Trends in Textlinguistics.* Some of Plett's works are *Einführung in die rhetorische Textanalyse, Textwissenschaft und Textanalyse, Rhetorik.* These are merely examples of Hellholm's sources, but they indicate the strong background in rhetoric and linguistics that helps him formulate his understanding of how language works in texts from the perspective of reader as well as producer.

As does Halliday, Hellholm recognizes that the interpersonal element helps illumine the text first from the vantage point of the producer. But he also notes that the sender/writer is influenced by the needs, expectations, and perceptions of the receiver/reader of the material. The communicative situation involves both author and reader of a text. His explicit recognition of the role of the reader helps him to work more consciously with the entire communicative situation. He notes an internal pragmatic that considers the communicative situation within the text between different *dramatis personae* (this approach approximates the tenor or style of discourse in Halliday's context of situation). This internal pragmatic is analyzed by using the tools of speech competence, especially semantics and syntax. Hellholm also formulates what he calls a theory of performance. Here he recognizes that a text is never fully complete because, given the different contexts of reading, every reader understands the text differently (this concept approximates Halliday's cultural context). Furthermore, even in the case of a single text receiver, every time she or he reads a text in an altered context, a new interpretative result is achieved. From the standpoint of the reader, communicative context is therefore a vital component. With regard to ancient texts, Hellholm adds to this mix the difference between author and interpreter, the reader of the text separated by a vast distance in time from the text producer. Hellholm subsequently utilizes these tools to analyze the Hermas material, and his work is a clear demonstration that the categories are helpful in analysis of text reading and interpretation as well as text production.

33. Fairclough, *Language and Power,* 8.

34. Ibid.

35. Enrique Dussel, *Philosophy of Liberation,* trans. Aquilina Martinez and Christine Morkovsky (Maryknoll, N.Y.: Orbis Books, 1985) 2.

36. Ibid.

37. Ibid., 9–10.
38. Fairclough, *Language and Power,* 2.
39. Dussel, *Philosophy of Liberation,* 123.
40. Ibid., 125.
41. Ibid., 154.
42. Ibid., 155.
43. Ibid., 155–57.
44. Ely Eser Barreto César, "Faith Operating in History: New Testament Hermeneutics in a Revolutionary Context," Ph.D. diss., Emory University, Atlanta, 1983, 12. The chart presented by César represents the best visual representation of Dussel's complete method. César presents an excellent exposition of the model's operation in pp. 12–19.
45. Dussel, *Philosophy of Liberation,* 157.
46. Ibid., 159, 160.
47. César, *Faith Operating in History,* 12–13.
48. Ibid., 13.
49. Enrique Dussel, *Ethics and Community,* trans. Robert R. Barr (Maryknoll, N.Y.: Orbis Books, 1988) 219.
50. Enrique Dussel, *History and the Theology of Liberation: A Latin American Perspective* (Maryknoll, N.Y.: Orbis Books, 1976) 1ff., 145ff.

## 2. Existential Interpretation

1. Rudolf Bultmann, *Jesus Christ and Mythology* (New York: Charles Scribner's Sons, 1958) 19. Bultmann offers the mythical presentation of heaven as evidence. The intent is to describe God as transcendent, beyond the world. But because the thinking of the time was incapable of conceptualizing transcendence abstractly, it presented transcendence crudely as physical space (ibid., 20). A new conceptual language is necessary because of the new context. The new conceptual language must honor not mythology, but the scientific thinking of modern humanity. Thus, the conceptual idea of heaven presented by the text producer no longer has conceptual meaning in a spatial sense, but in an existential one. The idea of an upper chamber in a three-tiered universe is dismissed, while the subject matter transmitted by the idea—that of a transcendent reality wholly other than humankind—is retained.
2. Rudolf Bultmann, "New Testament and Mythology," in *Kerygma and Myth,* ed. Hans Werner Bartsch, trans. Reginald Fuller (London: SPCK, 1960) 11.
3. Rudolf Bultmann, "The Problem of Hermeneutics," in *Essays Philosophical and Theological* (London: SCM Press, 1955) 234.
4. Rudolf Bultmann, "The Problem of a Theological Exegesis of the New Testament," in *The Beginnings of Dialectic Theology,* vol. 1, ed. James Robinson, trans. Keith R. Crim (Richmond: John Knox Press, 1968) 239.
5. Rudolf Bultmann, *Jesus and the Word,* trans. Louise Pettibone Smith (New York: Harper and Row, 1969) 3.
6. Ibid., 6.
7. Ibid., 8.

8. Ibid., 10.

9. Ibid., 11.

10. Bultmann, *Jesus Christ and Mythology*, 46.

11. Ibid., 50.

12. Rudolf Bultmann, "Is Exegesis Without Presupposition Possible?" in *Existence and Faith*, ed. and trans. Schubert M. Ogden (New York: Meridian Books, 1960) 294.

13. Bultmann gives a potent example when he describes how a reader comprehends the textual notation, "joy of Jesus" (Rudolf Bultmann, "The Significance of 'Dialectical Theology' for Scientific Study of the New Testament," in *Faith and Understanding*, trans. Louise Pettibone Smith [New York: Harper and Row, 1969] 157). Historically, each of us has experienced joy in individually distinct ways. Our joy is qualitatively different from the kind of joy associated with Jesus, but our unique historical awareness of our own past joy gives us a preknowledge of joy that allows us to comprehend Jesus' joy in a potential sense. We can never understand it fully because it is an otherworldly joy, but we can know it as a possibility, because of our dialectical relationship with history. Understanding the concept of joy as it is presented in the text is therefore more than an intellectual enterprise; it is an awareness that is deepened through our own past and sharpens hope for our present and future. It is an understanding of the text language that is existentially conditioned. On p. 159, Bultmann makes a similar claim about the understanding of the term *death* in the New Testament. Each of us has a unique preunderstanding of death that influences the way we interpret the term when it is used in the text.

14. Bultmann, *Jesus Christ and Mythology*, 50.

15. Ibid., 50, 51.

16. Ibid., 57–58.

17. Bultmann, "The Significance of 'Dialectical Theology,'" 291.

18. Cf. Norman Perrin, *The Promise of Bultmann* (Philadelphia and New York: J. B. Lippincott, 1969) 13–14. "All though his career Bultmann has been concerned to interpret the New Testament historically, to determine what it *said*. He has devoted himself to the task of understanding what a given New Testament author would have meant by the words he used and how the readers for whom he wrote would have understood him. At the same time he has been concerned to interpret the New Testament existentially, to determine what it *says* today to a man involved in living out his existence in the world."

19. Walter Schmithals, *An Introduction to the Theology of Rudolf Bultmann* (London: SCM Press, 1968) 222.

20. Ernst Käsemann, *Jesus Means Freedom* (Philadelphia: Fortress Press, 1968) 132.

21. Ibid., 132–33.

22. Ibid., 133.

23. Ibid., 134. Cf. also Dorothee Soelle, *Political Theology*, trans. John Shelley (Philadelphia: Fortress Press, 1974). Soelle makes a similar point that Bultmann is guilty of reducing the question of meaning to individual existence and therefore abandoning the question of meaning in history. A correct valuation of the historical, she contends, leads one toward a theology that is appropriately aware of the political

sociolinguistic parameters of a text interpreter. Such an awareness allows an appreciation of the fact that New Testament mythology has an inherent political as well as existential concern. "By virtue of this individualistic construction, Bultmann is not in a position to demythologize or to interpret New Testament cosmology; he must eliminate it, whereas a political theology can read the political intentions inherent in those cosmological images" (p. 48).

24. Ibid., 64.

25. Christopher Rowland and Mark Corner, *Liberating Exegesis: The Challenge of Liberation Theology to Biblical Studies* (Louisville: Westminster/John Knox Press, 1989) 38.

26. Ibid., 72.

27. Soelle, *Political Theology*, 2.

28. Rowland and Corner, *Liberating Exegesis*, 39.

## 3. The Gospel in Solentiname

1. Cf. Philip Scharper and Sally Scharper, ed., *Gospel in Art by the Peasants of Solentiname* (Maryknoll, N.Y.: Orbis Books, 1984).

2. Christopher Rowland and Mark Corner, *Liberating Exegesis: The Challenge of Liberation Theology to Biblical Studies* (Louisville: Westminster/John Knox Press, 1989) 55.

3. Ibid., 56.

4. Ely Eser Baretto César, "Faith Operating in History: New Testament Hermeneutics in a Revolutionary Context," Ph.D. diss., Emory University, Atlanta, 1983) 454.

5. Scharper and Scharper, *Gospel in Art*, 13.

6. Cf. Ernesto Cardenal, *The Gospel in Solentiname*, trans. Donald D. Walsh (Maryknoll, N.Y.: Orbis Books, 1977) 4:92–101.

7. Ibid., 4:92. Translation is Cardenal's.

8. Ibid.

9. Ibid., 4:94. "The Magdalene," the student says, "was used to that perfumed life, and things like that, and so she's being grateful according to her way of life. She's accustomed to a life of perfumes, jewels, carousing. And she pours perfume on him because that's the life she led, she thinks that's logical." Once again the act is considered wasteful and inconsiderate of the poor who could have benefited had the ointment been sold and the revenues been used as contributions.

10. Ibid., 4:97.

11. Ibid., 4:96, 97, 98.

12. Ibid., 1:15.

13. Ibid., 1:104.

14. Ibid., 1:114.

15. Ibid., 1:150.

16. Ibid., 2:154.

17. Ibid., 4:188.

18. Ibid., 1:9.

19. Ibid., 1:13.

20. Ibid., 1:85.

21. Ibid., 1:157.

22. Ibid., 3:260.

23. Ibid., 1:27.

24. Ibid., 1:76.

25. Ibid., 1:209.

26. Ibid., 3:259.

27. Ibid., 1:63.

28. Ibid., 1:96–97. They make a similar recognition when discussing Jesus' statements about how to pray (1:206). The matter of ritualism is discussed in a different manner in regard to the Good Samaritan story (3:103).

29. César, "Faith Operating in History," 463.

30. Ibid., 471.

31. Julie Miller, book review of *Gospel in Art,* in *International Bulletin of Missionary Research* 9 (1985):198.

32. Scharper and Scharper, *Gospel in Art,* 11.

33. Cardenal, *Gospel in Solentiname,* 1:47–48.

34. Scharper and Scharper, *Gospel in Art,* 7.

35. Cardenal, *Gospel in Solentiname,* 1:55.

36. Ibid., 1:69.

37. Ibid., 1:73.

38. Ibid., 1:71, 85.

39. Ibid., 3:252. For other citations where sin is listed as selfishness, cf. 1:101ff., 114ff., 172, 216, 218, and 4:121ff.

40. Scharper and Scharper, *Gospel in Art,* 37.

41. Ibid., 39.

42. Cardenal, *Gospel in Solentiname,* 1:17.

43. Ibid., 2:148.

44. Ibid., 4:122.

45. Ibid., 4:123.

46. Scharper and Scharper, *Gospel in Art,* 41.

47. Cardenal, *Gospel in Solentiname,* 1:179.

48. Scharper and Scharper, *Gospel in Art,* 61.

49. Cf. Cardenal, *Gospel in Solentiname,* 1:1–12, the discussion on the prologue to the Gospel of John.

50. Ibid., 1:53.

51. Ibid., 4:255.

52. Ibid., 2:181.

## 4. The Negro Spiritual

1. William Francis Allen, Charles Pickard Ware, Lucy McKim Garrison, *Slave Songs of the United States* (New York: Peter Smith, 1867) xix.

2. A powerful connection between music, religion, and social circumstance lives

inside the spiritual, derived from the slaves' African heritage. The originators of the Negro spiritual were African in their attitudes toward religion and music. To the ancestral group from which these Africans sprang, religion did not splinter into social, political, and philosophical subdivisions; it spoke of the social, the political, and the philosophical with one voice born of the overriding desire to fathom the workings of the universe. Some critics, however, have argued that the Negro spiritual is a bland copy of white antebellum spirituals and therefore has no African musical or religio-social characteristics. James Weldon Johnson in his preface to *The Book of American Negro Spirituals* argues convincingly that because many key similarities exist between the Negro spiritual and African melody and rhythm, the connections cannot be denied. Cf. James Weldon Johnson and J. Rosamond Johnson, *The Books of American Negro Spirituals* (New York: Da Capo Press, 1977) 17–19. Cf. also Tilford Brooks, *America's Black Musical Heritage* (Englewood Cliffs, N.J.: Prentice-Hall, 1984) 32–34. Brooks also notes the African musical connection to the spirituals, and likewise demonstrates that while there was necessarily contact between Negro and white Spirituals, the impact was too minimal to deny the originality and African influence of the Negro material. He appeals to research that, in comparing Negro spirituals and African songs, demonstrated that thirty-six spirituals were either identical to or closely resembled African songs. Fifty other spirituals had formal structures identical to West African songs. "The preponderance of evidence, however, points towards the Black spiritual being primarily rooted in the African musical tradition" (p. 33).

3. Lucy McKim Garrison, "Songs of the Port Royal 'Contrabands,'" in *The Social Implications of Early Negro Music in the United States,* ed. Bernard Katz (New York: Arno Press and the New York Times, 1969) 9–10. First published in *Dwight's Journal of Music,* Boston, 9 August 1862.

4. W. E. B. DuBois, *The Souls of Black Folk: Essays and Sketches* (Chicago: A. C. McClurg and Company, 1904) 253.

5. "White Christianity" encouraged mental and physical servitude among blacks. Many owners believed that the more pious their slaves were, the more docile they would become. In fact, slave catechisms were written to insure that the message of black inferiority and docility in the face of a divinely ordained white domination would be nurtured in the slave. An example: "*Q:* What did God make you for? *A:* To make a crop. *Q:* What is the meaning of 'Thou shalt not commit adultery?' *A:* To serve our heavenly Father, and our earthly master, obey our over seer, and not steal anything." Cf. James H. Cone, *The Spirituals and the Blues: An Interpretation* (New York: Seabury Press, 1972) 23. Quoted from Donald Matthews, *Slavery and Methodism* (Princeton: Princeton University Press, 1965).

6. James Miller McKim, "Negro Songs," in *The Social Implications of Early Negro Music in the United States,* 1–2.

7. Miles Mark Fisher, *Seventy Negro Spirituals* (Boston: Oliver Ditson Company, 1926) xi.

8. Lawrence Levine, "Slave Songs and the Slave Consciousness: An Exploration in Neglected Sources," in *Anonymous Americans,* ed. Tamara K. Hareven (Englewood Cliffs, N.J.: Prentice-Hall, 1971) 108.

9. Ibid., 107.

10. Harold Courlander, *Negro Folk Music, U.S.A.* (New York and London: Columbia University Press, 1963) 39.

11. Ibid., 43.

12. Henry Hugh Proctor, "The Theology of the Songs of the Southern Slave," *Journal of Black Sacred Music* 2, no. 1 (Spring 1988): 63.

13. James Cone, "The Meaning of Heaven in the Black Spirituals," in *Heaven*, ed. Bas Van Iersel and Edward Schillebeckx (New York: Seabury Press, 1969) 61.

14. Nathan Wright, "Black Spirituals: A Testament of Hope For Our Time?" *The Journal of Religious Thought* 33 (1976): 87.

15. All spirituals, unless otherwise noted, listed from Johnson and Johnson, *The Books of American Negro Spirituals.*

16. Proctor, "Theology of the Songs of the Southern Slave," 53.

17. Ibid., 55.

18. James Cone, "The Meaning of God in the Black Spirituals," in *God as Father*, ed. Johannes-Baptist Metz (New York: Seabury Press, 1981) 59.

19. John W. Blassingame, *The Slave Community* (New York: Oxford University Press, 1972) 73.

20. John Lovell, *Black Song: The Forge and the Flame* (New York: Macmillan, 1972) 125.

21. Albert Bergesen, "Spirituals, Jazz, Blues, and Soul Music: Role of Elaborated and Restricted Codes in the Maintenance of Social Solidarity," in *The Religious Dimension: New Directions in Quantitative Research*, ed. Robert Wuthnow (New York: Academic Press, 1979) 334. Cf. also Basil Bernstein, *Class, Codes and Control*, vol. 1 (London: Routledge and Kegan Paul, 1971) 118–67.

22. Bergesen, "Spirituals, Jazz, Blues and Soul Music," 336, 337, 338.

23. Bernstein, *Class, Codes and Control*, 1:119.

24. Cf. Mike Thewell, "Back with the Wind: Mr. Styron and the Reverend Turner," in *William Styron's Nat Turner: Ten Black Writers Respond*, ed. John Henrik Clarke (Boston: Beacon Press, 1968) 80. The view that the language of the spirituals was a covert language whose true meaning was incomprehensible to the white community is supported by the work of Mike Thewell on language use by the American slaves. For his conclusions he depends on the work of Morton W. Bloomfield and Leonard Newmark (cf. *A Linguistic Introduction to the History of English* [New York, 1963] 82–83). Bloomfield and Newmark speak of a paralanguage where total meaning is conveyed in terms of silence, pitch, stress, accent, juncture, disjuncture, and terminals in oral communication. Thewell thus notes that the oral language of the African slave included two imposed types. The first was a language adopted for use by the white overseer and slave master, which Thewell says was parodied in the "Sambo" dialect of southern white humorists—even Samuel Clemens. But there was another language, a covert one, which the slaves used as a means of promoting self-worth and resistance. The duality in language described above in the spirituals thus reflects a dualism evident in the wider language of the slave community. "The only vestiges we can find of the real language of the slaves are in the few spirituals which have come down to us, which give a clue to its true tenor. It is a language

produced by oppression, but one whose central impulse is survival and resistance" ("Black with the Wind," 80). Necessarily, this language was coded.

25. Levine, "Slave Songs and Slave Consciousness," 115. Levine explains that this use of language has its roots in the slaves' African heritage. "In Africa, songs, tales, proverbs, and verbal games served the dual function of not only preserving communal values and solidarity, but also of providing occasions for the individual to transcend, at least symbolically, the inevitable restrictions of his environment and his society by permitting him to express deeply held feelings which he ordinarily was not allowed to verbalize" (pp. 108–9).

26. Ibid., 122.

27. Cone, *Spirituals and the Blues,* 54.

28. Cone, "The Meaning of Heaven in the Black Spirituals," 66.

29. Cone, "The Meaning of God in the Black Spirituals," 57.

30. Cone, "The Meaning of Heaven in the Black Spirituals," 58.

31. Frederick Douglass, *My Bondage and My Freedom* (New York: Miller, Orton and Co., 1857) 278–79.

32. Carl Marbury, "Hebrews and Spirituals: Soulful Expressions of Freedom," in *God and Human Freedom,* ed. Henry James Young (Richmond, Ind.: Friends United Press, 1983) 81.

33. Cone, "The Meaning of Heaven in the Black Spirituals," 62.

34. Cone, "Black Spirituals: A Theological Interpretation," in *Music and the Experience of God,* ed. Mary Collins, David Power, and Mellonee Burnin (Edinburgh: T. & T. Clark, 1989) 49.

35. Cf. ibid., 49–50.

36. Lovell, *Black Song,* 238.

37. Cone, "The Meaning of Heaven in the Black Spirituals," 63.

38. John Novell, Jr., "The Social Implications of the Negro Spiritual," in *The Social Implications of Early Negro Music in the United States,* 136.

39. Howard Thurman, *Deep River: Reflections on the Religious Insight of Certain of the Negro Spirituals* (Port Washington, N.Y.: Kennikat Press, 1945) 36.

## 5. The Sermon in the Black Church

1. Henry H. Mitchell, *Black Preaching: The Recovery of a Powerful Art* (Nashville: Abingdon Press, 1990) 18–19. Cf. John Dillenberger, "On Broadening the New Hermeneutic," in *The New Hermeneutic,* ed. James M. Robinson and John B. Cobb, Jr. (New York: Harper and Row, 1964) 2:162.

2. Mitchell, *Black Preaching,* 18.

3. Ibid., 20.

4. Ibid., 81.

5. Ibid., 79.

6. Ibid. A similar situation occurs in rural white church communities like those in Appalachia. Educated ministers who preach in an educated language, though white like their congregants, will be viewed with suspicion. This sociolinguistic phenomenon is not restricted to any particular subcultural group or ideological stance.

7. Stephen Breck Reid, *Experience and Tradition: A Primer in Black Biblical Hermeneutics* (Nashville: Abingdon Press, 1990) 16–17. See also 54, 85–86.

8. Ibid., 16.

9. Ibid., 54.

10. Vincent Wimbush, "Biblical-Historical Study as Liberation: Toward an Afro-Christian Hermeneutic," *The Journal of Religious Thought* 42, no. 2 (1985–86): 12.

11. Peter Paris, *The Social Teaching of the Black Churches* (Philadelphia: Fortress Press, 1985) 10–11.

12. Mitchell, *Black Preaching*, 19.

13. Gerald L. Davis, *I Got the Word in Me and I Can Sing It, You Know: A Study of the Performed African-American Sermon* (Philadelphia: University of Pennsylvania Press, 1985) 6.

14. Ibid., 19.

15. Ibid., 61. Work done by David T. Shannon on the antebellum sermon demonstrates that this structural alignment has been a part of the African American sermon from its earliest stages. Cf. Shannon, "An Ante-bellum Sermon: A Resource for an African American Hermeneutic," in *Stony the Road We Trod: African American Biblical Interpretation,* ed. Cain Hope Felder (Minneapolis: Fortress Press, 1991) 105–111. Using the poem "An Ante-bellum Sermon" by Paul Lawrence Dunbar as an example of the earliest slave sermons, Shannon cites the development of the sermon in a manner that demonstrates agreement with Davis's structural assessment. After opening with the preliminaries of establishing the setting and purpose of the meeting, the preacher sets the theme by presenting the text and the biblical background. He explores the theme, making use of his own stylistic and imaging devices. Immediately following the stylistic phase, the preacher presents a disclaimer that he is speaking to the modern sociopolitical situation. The disclaimer, in the context of the fuller sermon, is a way of calling the congregation's attention to the fact that the situation of slavery is being addressed, but in a way that appears on the surface to be nonthreatening to slave owners and overseers.

16. Reid, *Experience and Tradition*, 22–23.

17. Carl H. Marbury, "Black Preaching: Biblical Preaching and Black Theology," in *Preaching in Ebony*, ed. J. Solomon Benn III (Grand Rapids: Baker Book House, 1981) 17.

18. Quoted in Manning Marable, *How Capitalism Underdeveloped Black America: Problems in Race, Political Economy and Society* (Boston: Southend Press, 1983) 195.

19. Cf. Walter B. Hoard, "Introduction," *Outstanding Black Sermons*, vol. 2 (Valley Forge, Pa.: Judson Press, 1979) 10–11.

20. Cf. Marable, *How Capitalism Underdeveloped Black America*, 204–5.

21. Cf. ibid., 199–205.

22. E. Franklin Frazier, *The Negro Church in America* (New York: Schocken Books, 1974) 51. First published in 1964.

23. C. Eric Lincoln, *The Black Church since Frazier* (New York: Schocken Books, 1974) 105–6.

24. Shannon, "An Ante-bellum Sermon," 123.

25. Ibid., 104.

26. Frazier, *The Negro Church in America*, 50.

27. Charles S. Johnson, *Shadow of the Plantation* (Chicago: University of Chicago Press, 1934) 157.

28. Cf. Mitchell, *Black Preaching*, 60–61.

29. Reid, *Experience and Tradition*, 19.

30. Ibid., 19–22.

31. Wimbush, "Biblical-Historical Study as Liberation," 19.

32. Strobridge E. Hoard, "Following Pilate's Path of Futility," in *Outstanding Black Sermons*, vol. 2 (Valley Forge, Pa.: Judson Press, 1979) 33–40.

33. Ibid., 35.

34. Ibid.

35. William V. Guy, "When Atrophy Sets In," in *Preaching the Gospel*, ed. Henry J. Young (Philadelphia: Fortress Press, 1976) 71.

36. Otis Moss, Jr., "Going from Disgrace to Dignity," in *Preaching the Gospel*, 52–53.

37. Martin Luther King, Jr., "The Drum Major Instinct," in *Preaching the Gospel*, 41.

38. Mary Ann Bellinger, "Upright But *Not* Uptight," in *Those Preachin' Women: Sermons by Black Women Preachers*, ed. Ella Pearson Mitchell (Valley Forge, Pa.: Judson Press, 1985) 74.

39. Effie M. Clark, "How a People Make History," in *Outstanding Black Sermons*, ed. J. Alfred Smith (Valley Forge, Pa.: Judson Press, 1976) 25.

40. Cheryl J. Sanders, "Christ in You, the Hope of Glory," in *Those Preachin' Women*, 105.

## 6. Potential Meaning in Mark's Trial Scenes

1. Cf. Kurt Baldinger, *Semantic Theory: Towards a Modern Semantics*, trans. William C. Brown, ed. Roger Wright (New York: St. Martin's Press, 1980) 14–24, 110–12, 129, 153–54.

2. Ibid., 14.

3. Meaning is also not limited to what the author intended in writing the piece. This is certainly true for quoted material, which retains meanings that may not be intended by the author who quotes it. But it is also true in original material since the author does not have complete control over his or her text.

4. Cf. also 1 Cor. 11:2-16 regarding Paul's views on the veiling of women in worship.

5. For relatively recent surveys of the literature on the passion narrative and the trial scenes, particularly the Sanhedrin scene, see the following works: David Catchpole, *The Trial of Jesus: A Study in the Gospels and Jewish Historiography from 1770 to the Present Day*, Studia Post-Biblica 18 (Leiden: E. J. Brill, 1971); Vincent Taylor, *The Passion Narrative of St. Luke: A Critical and Historical Investigation* (Cambridge: Cambridge University Press, 1972) 1–38; John R. Donahue, *Are You the Christ? The Trial Narrative in the Gospel of Mark* (Missoula, Mont.: Society of Biblical Literature, 1973) 1–51; Donald Juel, *Messiah and Temple: The Trial of Jesus in the Gospel of Mark*

(Missoula, Mont.: Society of Biblical Literature, 1977) 1–40; Joel B. Green, *The Death of Jesus: Tradition and Interpretation in the Passion Narrative* (Tübingen: J. C. B. Mohr, 1988) 1–14.

6. Indeed, these imperfect tenses appear to be functionally equivalent to the aorist.

7. Donahue, *Are You the Christ?* 69.

8. John R. Donahue, "Temple, Trial and Royal Christology (Mark 14:53-65)," in *The Passion in Mark: Studies on Mark 14–16*, ed. Werner Kelber (Philadelphia: Fortress Press, 1976) 69. Cf. Mark 11:18, 12:12, 14:1.

9. Ibid., 68–69.

10. The balance would be broken if one were to accept the variants regarding the text of verse 60 where the double negative question appears not as an independent sentence but as a clause connected to the following words by ὅτι (that). There is every indication, however, that the text, given its witness strength, is to be preferred. Bruce Metzger's conclusion appears strong: "The elliptical use of τί(τί ἐστιν ὅ), what is it that [these testify against you]?") seems to have led several copyists to replace it with ὅτι [that]" (Metzger, *A Textual Commentary on the Greek New Testament* [Federal Republic of Germany: United Bible Societies, 1971] 115). Evidence regarding Markan style supports such textual conclusions. "The double question is more in accord with Mark's style (cf. 8:17f) and its effect is vivid" (Vincent Taylor, *The Gospel according to St. Mark* [London: Macmillan and Co., 1952] 567). Given this conclusion, we would therefore contend that, despite the strength of witnesses for the variant in 61a where the double negative narration occurs, the text is to be preferred. The Markan stylistic use of tradition that opened the first scene in verses 55, 56 suggests the probability that he would be using the same technique here as he opens this second scene.

11. Eduard Schweizer, *The Good News according to Mark* (Atlanta: John Knox Press, 1970) 319–33.

12. Donahue, *Are You the Christ?* 87.

13. J. C. O'Neill, "The Silence of Jesus," *NTS* 15 (1969–70): 153.

14. Cf. 1:14; 3:19; 10:33; 14:10, 11, 18, 21, 41, 42, 44.

15. Metzger, *A Textual Commentary on the Greek New Testament*, 117.

16. Schweizer, *The Good News according to Mark*, 333.

17. Frank J. Matera, *The Kingship of Jesus: Composition and Theology in Mark 15* (Chico, Calif.: Scholars Press, 1982) 8.

18. "And immediately, early in the morning, after they had held a consultation, the chief priests . . ." Cf. ibid., 9.

19. Schweizer, *The Good News according to Mark*, 335.

20. Ibid., 336.

21. Rudolf Bultmann, *The History of the Synoptic Tradition*, trans. John Marsh (Oxford: Basil Blackwell, 1963) 636. First published as *Geschichte der Synoptischen Tradition*, 1921.

22. Martin Dibelius, *From Tradition to Gospel*, trans. Bertram Lee Woolf (New York: Charles Scribner's Sons, 1965) 415. First published as *Die Formgeschichte das Evangeliums*, 1919.

23. Matera, *The Kingship of Jesus*, 16.

24. Cf. ibid., 16, 20.

25. C. S. Mann, *Mark* (Garden City, N.Y.: Doubleday, 1986) 637.

26. There are lexical differences in Mark's use of the temple terminology. While he uses ναός exclusively in the passion materials (14:58, 15:29, 15:38), elsewhere he uses ἱερόν. The distinction between the two is well known: while the former indicates the sanctuary, the latter represents the outer dwellings as a whole. Given, however, that Mark is relying on traditional materials as regards the passion, this difference does not cause alarm. It is the temple imagery that is important, not the literal terminology. Cf. Donahue, *Are You the Christ?* 104–5: "Mark uses two terms for temple, *hieron* in 11:11, 15, 16, 27; 12:35; 13:1, 3 and 14:49, and *naos* in the above contexts [14:58 = Mt 26:61; 15:29 = Mt 27:39; Acts 6:14; Jn 2:19]. The difference does not indicate a difference between the whole temple area and the sanctuary proper, but rather connotes a difference between tradition and redaction since Mark uses *hieron* in those places which show his strongest redaction."

27. Once again macro-interpersonal considerations are illuminating. Eta Linnemann is not convinced that any evidence exists of the temple being used to designate community in the New Testament environment (see Donald Juel, *Messiah and Temple,* 146, for a summary listing of her objections). Juel, however, after adducing the New Testament witnesses where this reality is noted (2 Cor. 6:16; Eph. 2:21; and 1 Cor. 3:16-17), presents evidence from Qumran. His textual recitations (see his accounting of 1QS 8:4-7, 8:8-10, 9:3-6, 5:5-7; CD 3:18-4:10; 1QpH 12:3 on 161ff.) lead one to the biblical and extrabiblical conclusion that communities of the period did use temple imagery for self-designation.

28. Schweizer, *The Good News according to Mark,* 325.

29. Donahue, *Are You the Christ?* 92.

30. Joel Marcus, "Mark 14:61: Are You the Messiah-Son-of-God?" *Novum Testamentum* 31 (April 1989): 130.

31. Tibor Horvath, "Why Was Jesus Brought to Pilate?" *Novum Testamentum* 11 (1969): 181.

32. Donahue, "Temple, Trial and Royal Christology," 77.

33. Cf. Juel, *Messiah and Temple,* 171ff., for exposition on Qumran 4Q Florilegium and 2 Sam. 7:10-14, and 182 for information from the Targumim.

34. Cf. 15:2, 9, 12, 18, 26, 32.

35. Cf. Marcus, "Mark 14:61: Are You the Messiah-Son-of-God?"

36. Mann, *Mark,* 626.

37. Hendrikus Boers, *Who Was Jesus?* (San Francisco: Harper and Row, 1989) 75.

38. Cf. Norman Perrin, "Mark XIV. 62: The End Product of a Christian Pesher Tradition," *New Testament Studies* 12 (1965–66): 150–51. *Pesher* is a characteristic term used for interpreting the Hebrew Scriptures. Its general meaning is interpretation. The Scriptures are interpreted in light of the new historical context into which they are introduced. Christian interpreters traditionally interpreted the text through the lens of the Jesus event. Perrin suggests that two points of origin are offered for the interpretation (*pesher*) of 14:62. The first, the resurrection, would make use of Psalm 110:1 and Daniel 7:13. The second, the crucifixion, would make use of Zechariah 12:10-14 and Daniel 7:13. The first scenario details an exaltation motif, with

the "Son of Man" ascending to the Ancient of Days and sitting on the right hand. The second denotes a messianic return to earth.

39. Donahue, *Are You the Christ?* 184.

40. Cf. Matera, *The Kingship of Jesus,* 105ff. Mark juxtaposes the language of sonship "authority" at 1:11, with its background of Psalm 2:7; 1:22, 27; 3:14-15; 6:7-13; 11:27-33; 12:1-12; 12:34-37.

41. Boers, *Who Was Jesus?* 84.

42. Cf. 14:10, 11, 18, 21, 41, 42, 44.

43. Sherman Johnson, *A Commentary on the Gospel according to St. Mark* (London: Adam and Charles Black, 1960) 248.

44. D. E. Nineham, *Saint Mark* (New York: Penguin Books, 1963) 411.

45. Ibid., 338.

46. Boers, *Who Was Jesus?* 89.

## 7. Jesus the Redeemer

1. Julius Wellhausen, *Evangelium Marci* (Berlin: Druck und Verlag Von Georg Reimer, 1909). Hans Lietzmann, *Der Prozess Jesu* (Berlin: Verlag der Akademie der Wissenschaften in Kommission bei Walter De Gruyter U. Co., 1931).

2. "It is hardly believable that he would have done this at all, and even less believable that he would have done it before the Sanhedrin." Wellhausen, *Evangelium Marci,* 124.

3. Ibid., 125.

4. Cf. Lietzmann, *Der Prozess Jesu,* 5–6.

5. "But the community believed that it was the Jews who always killed the prophets sent by God, so the community established as true a passionate and harsh word of Jesus, that he must die in Jerusalem like all the prophets. So the community formed the passion story with an unconscious understanding in light of this theology and so further exonerated Pilate." Ibid., 11.

6. Ibid.

7. Willis B. Glover, *Evangelical Non Conformists and Higher Criticism in the Nineteenth Century* (London: Independent Press, 1954) 19.

8. Jacques de Senarclens, *Heirs of the Reformation,* trans. G. W. Bromiley (London: SCM Press, 1963) 59.

9. For a later example of a radical historical-critical interpretation of the Markan trial scenes, see Paul Winter, *On the Trial of Jesus* (Berlin: Walter De Gruyter, 1974); also Haim Cohn, *The Trial and Death of Jesus* (New York: KTAV Publishing House, 1977). A sociolinguistic evaluation of Winter's work can be found in Brian K. Blount, "Beyond the Boundaries: Cultural Perspective and the Interpretation of the New Testament," Ph.D. diss., Emory University, Atlanta, 1992, 292–98. Winter intends his macro-interpersonal observations to have a more solid historical-ideational foundation. He distinguishes two categories of community interest in the historical situation that prompted the evangelists to fabricate secondary trial elements and then add them as if they had belonged originally to the text. The first is hortatory: Mark is exhorting his readers to follow the example given by Jesus, not that

given by Peter. The second is apologetic: Mark wishes to blame the Jewish nation for Jesus' death and exonerate the Romans. The only historical trial was the one before Pilate, which Winter believes was politically motivated. Motivated by hortatory and apologetic concerns, however, Mark fabricated the Sanhedrin and Barabbas scenes.

We would argue that, like the work of Wellhausen and Lietzmann, Winter's work is micro-interpersonally based. Certainly he shares the same skeptical, foundational questions at the external level. At the internal level his influences, though distinct, prompt him similarly to confirm his radical orientation to the historicity of the texts. His Jewish methodological background is illustrative here. Because his methodological background is not Christianity, as was the case for the cultural Protestants (but for different reasons), Winter has no religious stake in establishing historicity for the passion materials. His background encourages a radical stance to the materials. Secondly, as Ernst Bammel points out, in terms of methodology Jewish scholarship has often tended toward the apologetic motif where Jesus' death is concerned (see Ernst Bammel, "The Revolution Theory from Reimarus to Brandon," in *Jesus and the Politics of His Day*, ed. Ernst Bammel and C. F. D. Moule [Cambridge: Cambridge University Press, 1984] 43). This motif counters any evangelistic presentation of the Jews as culpable in Jesus' death. Again tracing the line of Jewish scholarship on the trials, Bammel finds the tendency to present Jesus as a sympathizer of Zealot causes and practices, which fits in with the understanding of Jesus' only historical trial (before Pilate) as being politically motivated. On both the external and internal level, then, Winter, though writing well after his radical forebears, remains similarly influenced by micro-interpersonal factors.

10. George Dunbar Kilpatrick, *The Trial of Jesus* (London: Oxford University Press, 1952). For other examples of scholarship that fall into this historical category, see Josef Blinzer, *Der Prozess Jesu* (Regensburg: Verlag Friedrich Pustet, 1960), and Pierre Benoit, *The Passion and Resurrection of Jesus Christ* (New York: Herder and Herder, 1969).

11. Kilpatrick, *The Trial of Jesus*, 9.

12. Ibid., 10.

13. The fact that Mark's account of the trial is at variance with a multitude of Sanhedrin regulations has been widely attested. For a firsthand comparison one can consult Herbert Danby, trans., *The Mishnah* (London: Oxford University Press, 1933) 382–400. For a summary listing of the specific Sanhedrin rules broken, see John Donahue, "Temple Trial and Royal Christology (Mark 14:53-65)," in *The Passion in Mark: Studies on Mark 14–16*, ed. Werner Kelber (Philadelphia: Fortress Press, 1976) 61f. We are particularly concerned here with Sanhedrin 7:5, which prescribes that the charge of blasphemy requires a pronouncing of the divine name. Jesus' alleged anti-temple statements contain no such pronouncement.

14. Kilpatrick, *The Trial of Jesus*, 11.

15. Ibid., 14.

16. Ibid., 15.

17. Ibid., 20.

18. Glover, *Evangelical Non Conformists*, 27.

19. E. Brooks Holifield, *The Gentlemen Theologians: American Theology in Southern Culture, 1795–1860* (Durham, N.C.: Duke University Press, 1978) 94.

20. Glover, *Evangelical Non Conformists*, 27.

21. Kilpatrick, *The Trial of Jesus*, 5.

22. In future occurrences the phrase *form critic* will be used to include tradition historical work as well.

23. Donald Juel, *Messiah and Temple: The Trial of Jesus in the Gospel of Mark* (Missoula, Mont.: Society of Biblical Literature, 1977) 20.

24. Martin Dibelius, *From Tradition to Gospel*, trans. from the 2d rev. ed. by Bertram Lee Woolf (New York: Charles Scribner's Sons, 1965). Cf. also K. L. Schmidt, *Der Rahmen der Geschichte Jesu* (Berlin: Trowitzsch and Sohn, 1919). Both of their works appeared in the original German in 1919.

25. Dibelius, *From Tradition to Gospel*, 180.

26. Schmidt, *Der Rahmen der Geschichte Jesu*, 305.

27. Dibelius, *From Tradition to Gospel*, 184, 185.

28. Ibid., 181.

29. Ibid., 213.

30. Georg Bertram, *Die Leidensgeschichte Jesus und Der Christuscult: Eine Formgeschichtliche Untersuchung* (Göttingen: Vandenhoek and Ruprecht, 1922) 57.

31. Dibelius notes the second high point is the death scene. See *From Tradition to Gospel*, 192–93.

32. Bultmann, *The History of the Synoptic Tradition* (New York: Harper and Harper, 1963) 265.

33. Ibid., 270–71.

34. Cf. ibid., 284; here Bultmann states that the dogmatic motif stands in close relationship to the cult.

35. Ibid.

36. Ibid., 270.

## 8. Jesus the Tragic Hero

1. Vincent Taylor, *The Formation of the Gospel Tradition* (London: Macmillan, 1935); *Jesus and His Sacrifice: A Study in the Passion-Sayings in the Gospels* (London: Macmillan, 1937); *The Gospel according to St. Mark* (London: Macmillan, 1952); *The Passion Narrative of St. Luke: A Critical and Historical Investigation* (Cambridge: Cambridge University Press, 1972). For other references of modern source-critical work on the passion materials, see Wilfred L. Knox, *The Sources of the Synoptic Gospels: Volume I, Saint Mark*, trans. H. Chadwick (Cambridge: Cambridge University Press, 1953) and Eduard Lohse, *History of the Suffering and Death of Jesus Christ*, trans. Martin O. Dietrich (Philadelphia: Fortress Press, 1967).

2. See Taylor, *Formation of the Gospel Tradition*, 44–45, for reasons: (1) The passion story has the nature of a connected historical account more than do the rest of the materials. (2) The Gospels are in "substantial agreement" as to the course of events. (3) The tone of the narrative has a realism and sobriety that lend to its historical value.

3. Taylor, *The Gospel according to St. Mark*, 658.

4. Ibid., 563.

5. Ibid., 566.

6. Cf. Ernst Lohmeyer, *Das Evangelium des Markus* (Göttingen: Vandenhoeck & Ruprecht, 1963) and *Lord of the Temple: A Study of the Relation Between Cult and Gospel* (Edinburgh and London: Oliver and Boyd, 1961). Lohmeyer argues that *temple* has a wide field of signification, community being the common linguistic denominator. Mark 14:58, therefore, signifies the interaction of the person of Jesus with the Jewish temple in such a way that Jesus' followers, a new community, have freedom from the doomed Jewish community's cult and its practices.

7. Taylor, *The Gospel according to St. Mark,* 579.

8. Taylor notes that only 15:2 and 15:6-14 contain the quantity and quality of Semitisms requisite for qualification as Petrine material.

9. Taylor, *The Gospel according to St. Mark,* 563.

10. Ibid., 578.

11. Ibid., 577.

12. Taylor, *Formation of the Gospel Tradition,* 46–47.

13. Taylor, *The Gospel according to St. Mark,* 564, 569.

14. See John R. Donahue, *Are You the Christ? The Trial Narrative in the Gospel of Mark* (Missoula, Mont.: Society of Biblical Literature, 1973). Because there have been numerous redaction-critical studies of the trial scenes, we will limit our investigation to Donahue's work. For an excellent summary discussion of the major redaction critics, see Joel B. Green, *The Death of Jesus: Tradition and Interpretation in the Passion Narrative* (Tübingen: J. C. B. Mohr, 1988) 10–14.

15. See Donahue, *Are You the Christ?* 83, also 103ff., where Donahue argues that because of 14:58's similarity with anti-temple statements in Mark 15:29, Acts 6:14, and John 2:19, the saying is part of the pre-Markan tradition.

16. Donahue, *Are You the Christ?* 109.

17. Ibid., 86.

18. Cf. Donahue, *Are You the Christ?,* 88. Donahue notes that it is used at 1:11, 3:11, 8:29, 14:61, and 15:2.

19. Ibid., 113.

20. Norman Perrin, "Mark XIV.62: The End Product of a Christian Pesher Tradition," *New Testament Studies* 12 (1965–66): 150–55.

21. Donahue, *Are You the Christ?* 183.

22. Ibid., 178.

23. Ibid., 97.

24. Ibid., 1.

25. Donald Juel, *Messiah and Temple: The Trial of Jesus in the Gospel of Mark* (Missoula, Mont.: Society of Biblical Literature, 1977).

26. See ibid., 63. The verses cited are 8:31, 10:33, 11:18, 12:1-12; 12:13, 14:1, 14:10-11, 14:65, 15:10, 15:11, 15:31.

27. Juel, *Messiah and Temple,* 64.

28. Ibid., 54.

29. Ibid., 46–47.

30. Ibid., 71.

31. Ibid., 131.

32. Ibid., 57.

33. Ibid., 157.

34. See ibid., 146. Here Juel notes 2 Cor. 6:16; Eph. 2:21; 1 Cor. 3:16-17. Also Qumran 1QS 8:4-7; 8:8-10; 9:3-6; 5:5-7; CD 3:18-4:10; 1 QpH 12:3.

35. Cf. Juel, *Messiah and Temple*, 171ff. There he provides an exposition of 4Q Florilegium, 2 Sam. 7:10-14, and information from the Targumim.

36. Juel, *Messiah and Temple*, 49.

37. Ibid., 50–51.

38. Ibid., 35–36.

39. Ibid., 78; emphasis added.

40. Ibid., 39.

## 9. Jesus the Revolutionary

1. Fernando Belo, *A Materialist Reading of the Gospel of Mark*, trans. Matthew J. O'Connell (Maryknoll, N.Y.: Orbis Books, 1981) 1. First published in French in 1974.

2. Ibid., xiii–xiv.

3. Ched Myers, *Binding the Strong Man: A Political Reading of Mark's Story of Jesus* (Maryknoll, N.Y.: Orbis Books, 1988) 468–69.

4. Belo, *A Materialist Reading of the Gospel of Mark*, 238.

5. Belo is also convinced that the same theme appears in 7:1-24a, 8:10-13a, 9:33—10:1a, and 11:27b-33.

6. Belo, *A Materialist Reading of the Gospel of Mark*, 218.

7. Ibid.

8. Ibid.

9. Ibid., 261.

10. Ibid., 261–62.

11. Ibid., 219.

12. Onomasiology is the inverse of semasiology, which was described at the beginning of chapter 6. Whereas in semasiology a single term can have an entire field of signification, thereby allowing one term to have several possible conceptual contents, with onomasiology a single concept can have an entire field of designation. That is to say, a single concept can be expressed by several *signifiants*, or lexical terms. Once again Kurt Baldinger provides a helpful example. The concept or mental object *head* can be designated by an entire field of designations. It can denote "skull, bean, noggin, head." See Kurt Baldinger, *Semantic Theory: Towards a Modern Semantics*, trans. William C. Brown, ed. Roger Wright (New York: St. Martin's Press, 1980) 111.

13. Belo, *A Materialist Reading of the Gospel of Mark*, 223–24.

14. Ibid., 224.

15. Myers, *Binding the Strong Man*, xxxii.

16. Ibid., 31.

17. Ibid., 354.

18. Ibid., 370.

19. Ibid., 371.

20. S. G. F. Brandon, *Jesus and the Zealots: A Study of the Political Factor in Primitive Christianity* (Cambridge: Manchester University Press, 1967).

21. Myers, *Binding the Strong Man,* 370.

22. Ibid.

23. Ibid., 372.

24. Ibid., 371.

25. Ibid., 374.

26. Ibid., 375.

27. Ibid., 380.

## 10. Jesus, Man of the People

1. Ernesto Cardenal, *The Gospel in Solentiname,* trans. Donald D. Walsh (Maryknoll, N.Y.: Orbis Books, 1977) 4:201.

2. Ibid., 4:202.

3. Ibid., 4:203–4.

4. Ibid., 4:204–5.

5. Ibid., 4:206.

6. Ibid., 4:207–8.

7. Ibid., 4:207; emphasis added.

8. Ibid., 4:209.

9. Ibid.

10. See Tom Skinner, "To Change the System," in *Words of Revolution* (Grand Rapids: Zondervan Publishing, 1970) 61–78.

11. Ibid., 7. See also p. 65 where he outlines the conditions of poverty, families without fathers, prostitution, police brutality, and despair.

12. Ibid., 9.

13. Ibid., 7.

14. Ibid., 64.

15. Ibid., 75, where he specifically connects the temple to the social and political system of ancient Judaism.

16. Ibid., 66.

17. Ibid., 69.

18. Ibid., 73.

19. Ibid., 69.

20. Ibid., 69–70.

21. Ibid., 71.

22. Ibid., 72.

23. Ibid., 73.

24. Ibid., 74.

25. Ibid., 75.

26. John Killinger, "Jesus and the Temple Religion," *Pulpit Digest* 68 (1988): 105–8. Based on Mark 14:55–59 and John 21:1–14.

27. Ibid., 105.

28. Ibid., 107.

29. Ibid., 105–6, 107.

30. Eduard Schweizer, *The Good News according to Mark,* trans. Donald H. Madvig (Atlanta: John Knox Press, 1970) 325.

31. Killinger, "Jesus and Temple Religion," 106.

## 11. Beyond Interpretative Boundaries

1. This micro-interpersonal interpretative process is at work in a powerful way in several other communicative contexts, which we cannot investigate at length here. For example, in Hispanic theology in the United States the image of the "alien" is crucial to the interpretative move. Using the Old Testament imagery of the Hebrew as a wanderer in a strange land, Hispanic-American theology applies sociopolitical as well as religious emphases to text analyses. Cf. Virgilio Elizondo, *Galilean Journey: The Mexican American Promise* (Maryknoll, N.Y.: Orbis Books, 1983). Elizondo writes of Jesus the marginal who goes to Jerusalem as Hispanics travel as aliens in the United States. Cf. Javier Quinónes-Ortiz, "The Mestizo Journey: Challenges for Hispanic Theology," *Apuntes* 11, no. 3 (1991): 63–72. Describing *mestizo* as Spanish for a racially "mixed" or "hybrid" person, Quinónes-Ortiz picks up on Elizondo's dismissal of the term's derogatory sense, and uses it with Elizondo so that "both the suffering and the positive potential symbolized in this concept are redeemed" (p. 62). Quinónes-Ortiz's view of Hispanic-American theology is one that reflects through theological interpretation this *mestizo* reality in the United States. Cf. also Justo González, *Mañana: Christian Theology from a Hispanic Perspective* (Nashville: Abingdon Press, 1990). A similar process is also taking place in Haitian theology and theological interpretation originating in Peru. In each case the biblical material is refracted through the sociopolitical lens that forms the context of existence for the community in question.

Feminism and, to a lesser extent, womanism provide more long-standing examples. From the feminist perspective, the androcentric perspective on and in the biblical texts forms the "center" about which Enrique Dussel was so concerned. Interpretations are made in light of that "center" and any interpretations that are not in sympathy with the exegetical procedures and overall understandings of the center are thereby considered academically suspect. Maleness becomes the normative way of comprehending reality. The impact is considerable. As Rosemary Radford Ruether argues, "One is not even able to remark upon or notice women's absence, since women's silence and absence is the norm." ("Feminist Interpretation: A Method of Correlation," in *Feminist Interpretation of the Bible,* ed. Letty M. Russell [Philadelphia: The Westminster Press, 1985] 113.)

The response that has been brought to bear on this androcentrism in biblical interpretation is feminism as a prophetic voice. Katherine Doob Sakenfeld describes it this way: "Feminism may be viewed as a contemporary prophetic movement that announces judgment on the patriarchy of contemporary culture and calls for repentance and change." (Katherine Doob Sakenfeld, "Feminist Uses of Biblical Materials," in Russell, ed., *Feminist Interpretation of the Bible,* 55.) As did the Hebrew prophets, who highlighted the often forgotten traditions of Israel, reinterpreted misunderstood traditions, or rejected time-honored ones that were false, the Christian feminist sees her or his role as "address[ing] themselves to the authority of the Bible in the life of their community of faith. They must seek faithful ways of recovering, reinterpreting, and discerning God's way in the tradition handed on in the Bible" (ibid.). This particular case of biblical hermeneutics suggests that the role of the feminist prophet is one of reinterpreting a biblical text and tradition that has historically ignored women and their experiences.

At the level of the macro-interpersonal life relation Christian feminist interpreters want to demonstrate a clear and viable exegetical and hermeneutical program whose validity is as solid as that of "normative," androcentric text interpretation. A feminist critical hermeneutics is posited. In her book *In Memory of Her,* Elisabeth Schüssler Fiorenza argues that such a hermeneutics would move from analyzing the androcentric texts themselves to the social-historical contexts that produced them. It is therefore prophetic on two levels, challenging androcentrism both at the level of text interpretation and at the original level of text production. "It not only has to claim the contemporary community of women struggling for liberation as its locus of revelation, it also must reclaim its foresisters as victims *and* subjects participating in patriarchal structure." (*In Memory of Her: A Feminist Theological Reconstruction of Christian Origins* [New York: Crossroad: New York, 1986], 9.)

The first principle of such a hermeneutic is a position of radical suspicion much like, in principle at any rate, that which I argued was exhibited by the Negro slave singing the spirituals. Just as the slaves took a religion that was given to them as an opiate and critically appraised the way in which it was interpreted to them, turning it instead into a liberating force, so also Christian feminists believe that androcentrically produced and interpreted texts can be appraised in a way that is liberating and affirming for women. Schüssler Fiorenza notes that here suspicion rather than acceptance of biblical authority becomes the rule. While some feminists believe that the hermeneutics of suspicion should be applied only to the way in which male scholarship has *interpreted* the texts, Schüssler Fiorenza proposes that one carry this suspicious nature even to the actual texts themselves, because the texts were authored by men caught up in an androcentric worldview. The hermeneutics of suspicion is used therefore to detect the antipatriarchal elements and functions of the biblical text that are almost always obscured *by* and therefore hidden beneath the surface *of* the androcentric language.

The design then is to operate according to historical and critical principles when approaching the texts, but to do so in a context of hermeneutical suspicion. Functioning in this manner, several operational options present themselves on this macro-interpersonal level of the life relation. The preunderstanding behind each of these options is that the Bible, though a patriarchal document, has within it liberating elements, designs, and patterns. It would otherwise need to be rejected out of hand. A hermeneutics of suspicion is to look through and beyond the androcentric surface to find the liberating elements beneath.

Another option, which Ruether calls *correlation,* sees a correlation between biblical and feminist critical principles. Correlation presupposes that the biblical texts themselves speak out prophetically against the very kind of androcentric bias that so deeply pervades its writers and readers: "It can be seen that there is a correlation between the feminist critical principle and the critical principle by which biblical thought critiques itself and renews itself as the authentic Word of God over against corrupting and sinful deformations" (Ruether, "Feminist Interpretation," 117).

Schüssler Fiorenza, however, challenges this option of correlation with one of critical evaluation. The idea here is to "sort through particular biblical texts and test out in a process of critical analysis and evaluation how much their content and function perpetuates and legitimates patriarchal structures, not only in their original historical contexts but also in contemporary situations" (*In Memory of Her*, 131). This option prefers to challenge the texts directly rather than look for points of agreement between the text and feminist hermeneutics.

While those two examples do not by any means exhaust the kinds of strategies employed by Christian feminists, they do amply illustrate how their hermeneutics of suspicion would operate at the macro-interpersonal level of biblical hermeneutics. In any case, whatever the parameters of the particular option, I think Schüssler Fiorenza is correct when she notes that the method must creatively challenge the "blueprints of androcentric design" in a way that instead assumes a feminist pattern that can place women as well as men at the center of history (*In Memory Of Her*, 41). The idea is to enter an old text from a new critical position: "Such a feminist critical method could be likened to the work of a detective insofar as it does not rely solely on historical 'facts' nor invents its evidence, but is engaged in an imaginative reconstruction of historical reality" (ibid.).

Such a statement clarifies the preunderstanding that drives this feminist hermeneutic of suspicion along. The macro-interpersonal preunderstanding is that in the biblical texts and biblical history itself there are liberating and affirming messages for women that have been hidden or diluted by centuries of androcentric interpretation. Early Christian texts were formulated and conditioned by patriarchal history and an androcentric milieu of ideas. The feminist hermeneutic must therefore become conscious of the interrelationship between this patriarchal perspective and the theological texts and traditions behind them. This endeavor is driven by a specific preunderstanding that the locus of God's revelation is *not* in the androcentric texts and traditions but in the life and ministry of Jesus and the movement of men and women called forth by him (Schüssler Fiorenza, *In Memory of Her*, 131). In that life and ministry of Jesus is the affirmation of women and women's experience. The task of a feminist hermeneutic driven by such a preunderstanding is to search out the biblical message that has been silenced on the surface. "Rather than reject the argument from silence as a valid historical argument, we must learn to read the silences of androcentric texts in such a way that they can provide 'clues' to the egalitarian reality of the early Christian movement" (ibid.).

This, of course, brings us directly to the micro-interpersonal life relation in which feminists find that an androcentric world view still denies the value of women's experience as a source for biblical knowledge and interpretation. Ruether is very helpful in defining this life relation. She recognizes what we have been saying all along, that "human experience is both the starting point and ending point of the circle of interpretation" (Ruether, "Feminist Interpretation," 111.) The problem is that not all of human experience, particularly women's experience in this case, is equally valued in this interpretative process. She notes first that women have been excluded from using their experience to interpret the text as preachers and teachers, and, second, tradition has been interpreted against women's experience.

Helpfully, she also describes what women's experience is. She sees it as, first, a recognition that biological differences are not irrelevant. Women have some distinctive experiences of the world that men do not have, and therefore devalue. She speaks of menstruation and childbearing as examples of unique experiences that have been devalued by androcentrism as pollution. We will note that in the ancient Jewish context of the Bible both of these situations were codified impurities that disallowed a woman's full participation in the cult. Women's experience, then, is the recognition of these differences in worldview, and the recognition that a male's devaluing of them is inappropriate. So, when we talk of women's experience as a micro-interpersonal life relation, "we mean precisely that experience which arises when women become critically aware of these falsifying and alienating experiences imposed upon them as women by a male dominated culture. . . . It is this process of the critical naming of women's experience of androcentric culture that we refer to when we say that women's experience is an interpretive key for feminist theology" (Ruether, "Feminist Interpretation," 144).

The micro-interpersonal preunderstanding that results is a critical rejection of sexism and an affirmation of the full humanity of women. It is this preunderstanding that drives the feminist approach to the biblical texts, and has direct implications for the interpretation of the biblical material: "Theologically speaking, this means that whatever diminishes or denies the full humanity of women must be presumed not to reflect the divine or authentic relation to the divine, or to reflect the authentic nature of things, or to be the message or work of an authentic redeemer or a community of redemption. This negative principle also implies the positive principle: What does promote the full humanity of women is of the Holy, does reflect true relation to the divine, is the true nature of things, is the authentic message of redemption and the mission of redemptive community" (ibid.).

The feminist critique is helpful because it uncovers the androcentrism that masquerades as objective biblical analysis and exposes it for what it is, an orientation to a text derived by men in a patriarchal world whose primary images of God and God's revelation of Godself are male. The problem, though, is that in uncovering this male preunderstanding of both biblical writers and interpreters feminists can exchange one oppressive center for another. As a challenge to the worldview of white men, they have, many black women scholars note, established the efficacy of a worldview of white women. By implying that the micro-interpersonal experience of white women is the experience of all women, feminists have therefore created as oppressive an interpretive instrument as did white males before them. It is only when feminism recognizes that it does not speak for all women, that is, when it recognizes that it accesses only a portion of the "meaning potential" significant for women, that it honestly encourages the kind of inclusivity it professes.

Knowing that feminists want correctly to interpret Scripture out of the experiences of women, Jacquelyn Grant nonetheless charges that the sources they use for those "experiences" are predominately the life situations of white women: "What is often unmentioned is that feminist theologians' sources for women's experience refer almost exclusively to white women's experience" (Jacquelyn Grant, *White Women's*

*Christ and Black Women's Jesus: Feminist Christology and Womanist Response* [Atlanta: Scholars Press, 1989], 195). This white orientation is labelled "racist" because it assumes a position of interpretative power. The experiences of women of color are marginalized. "To misname themselves as 'feminists' who appeal to 'women's experience' is to do what oppressors always do; it is to define the rules and then solicit others to play the game" (ibid., 200).

One gets the sense from reading Grant, Katie G. Cannon, Renita J. Weems, and others that at the macro-interpersonal level a great deal of agreement exists between feminists and black women interpreters. Both groups desire to analyze the text critically and have the preunderstanding that challenges the androcentrism in the text and androcentric interpretations of it. But the new micro-interpersonal life relation guarantees that the manner in which those macro-interpersonal variables are played out will be radically different. The new micro-interpersonal life relation is, of course, the experience of the black woman in the United States. Grant argues that because of slavery and segregation the realities of black and white women are radically distinct, so much so that while feminists tend to talk about issues of fulfillment in the Scriptures, black women tend towards issues of survival. There was, she says, in fact a direct sense of oppressive injustice in the life of the black woman that came from the harshness of white women. As Katie Cannon puts it, "The Black woman was defined as 'brood sow' and 'work ox'" (Katie Geneva Cannon, "The Emergence of Black Feminist Consciousness," in Russell, ed., *Feminist Interpretation of the Bible*, 31.) Grant argues that therefore no sisterhood between black and white women exists as regards the time of and after slavery. Since that Victorian concept of ladyhood was never applied to black women, they were never awarded the protection of patriarchy. Indeed, they were, like their black male counterparts, considered part of the animal species. Cannon points out that with the state law of *partus sequitur ventrem*, where the child follows the condition of the mother, regardless of the race of her mate, the black woman became the hereditary bearer of the slave tradition. Masters and masters' sons could have unlimited access to the bodies of black women with comfortable assurance that any mixed offspring would have none of the privileges of the father's lineage (Cannon, "The Emergence," 32). "Brutality was administered not only by masters and foremen but also by mistresses, reflecting the fact that White women were just as much participants in this system of slavery as were White men" (Grant, *White Women's Christ*, 197). Grant goes on to say that the white women who were the immediate supervisors of black women during and after slavery, supervisors who treated them with open contempt, were equally or even more dehumanizing than white men. Such radical differences of life situation guarantee that when one speaks of "women's experience" it will historically not be the same for white and black women.

One then needs to define exactly what the micro-interpersonal life relation of the black woman is. Grant calls it a tridimensional reality of racism/sexism/classism. Because of this tridimensionality the black woman has a universal connection to all oppressed persons. She knows the degradation of being oppressed because of one's different racial or ethnic origin. In this she shares with black men and all other peoples who are discriminated against because of ethnicity or nationality. She can also appreciate with all women the reality of being oppressed on the basis of gender.

She has known unequal, unfair, and violent treatment at the hands of both black and white men. Particularly unsettling is the fact that as black male churchmen, theologians, and leaders fought for civil rights and human equality, they did so in a way that often eliminated the input and debased the value of the black female. Finally, because black women have tended to populate those groups living at the lowest rungs of the economic ladder, they can identify with those in the lower and underclasses of society who are economically oppressed. It is because of this tridimensional character that the black woman has a unique connection not only with all oppressed peoples but with Jesus as well. "To speak of Black women's tridimensional reality, therefore, is not to speak of Black women exclusively, for there is an implied universality which connects them with others. . . . Likewise, with Jesus Christ, there was an implied universality which made him identify with others—the poor, the woman, the stranger" (ibid., 217).

Katie Cannon is even more helpful because she traces this tridimensional reality of black woman's experience through some key historical moments in the United States. From her analysis one can determine how each new life relation bears a consistent element, that of suffering and oppression. The preunderstanding that results is just as consistent. "By tracking down the central and formative facts in the Black woman's social world, one can identify the determinant and determining structures of oppression that have shaped the context in which Black women discriminately and critically interpret scripture, in order to apprehend the divine Word from the perspective of their own situation" (Cannon, "The Emergence," 30.)

She starts with the life relation of the black woman as slave, utilizing West African religious concepts syncretistically with colonial Christianity. Two divergent understandings developed from this mixture of African faith, Christianity, and slave situation: accommodation to the status quo, or challenge of the status quo. Cannon argues that most often, like the slave church of which she was a part, the black woman opted for the latter perspective in her understanding of the biblical story. After the war the disenfranchisement and social segregation of the Jim Crow laws assured the maintenance of an oppressive system arrayed against black women. The resulting preunderstanding developed out of Scripture lessons that focused most on a need to help the social order come into harmony with God's divine plan (ibid., 34).

Alice Walker names this preunderstanding "womanist," a name affirmed by black women scholars in religion. A black woman with a womanist preunderstanding is one who interprets the Scriptures directly out of this oppressive tridimensional reality. This translates into a direct attempt to read the text with an attempt to hear the voices of the oppressed and to interpret the situation of black women through their own situation. This also means that where the Bible presents a picture that is oppressive to women or antagonistic to the black woman's sense of liberty and dignity, it must be resisted. It is not only a matter of interpreting the text, therefore, it is also a matter of judging it. This micro-interpersonal life relation and preunderstanding leads the womanist interpreter towards a particular kind of interpretative strategy when approaching biblical texts. As Cannon remarks, "Black womanists search the scriptures to learn how to dispel the threat of death in order to seize the present life" (ibid., 40).

An interplay between Scripture and experience is envisioned. As Grant notes, the Bible is considered to be a source for religious validation in their lives. This means, of course, that once again we are brought before an interpretative strategy that places life first. God's direct revelation to black women takes precedence over the revelation as it is witnessed in the Bible and understood in the context of their experience (Grant, *White Women's Christ,* 211). And when one begins with the experience of black women, the interpretation of the Bible becomes an enterprise in a whole new light. Jesus, for example, becomes the divine co-sufferer with black women. Jesus becomes a political messiah who means freedom from the kinds of oppression that beset the world of black women, that tridimensional world that connects black women with the oppressed everywhere. Jesus, in this sense, becomes black. "The condition of Black people today reflects the cross of Jesus. Yet the resurrection brings the hope that liberation from oppression is immanent. The resurrected Black Christ signifies this hope" (ibid., 216). This does not mean that Jesus is black in the terms of physical characteristics. He is black in terms of the oppression he shares with black people, and black in terms of the struggle he bears to overcome this oppression. Jesus shares with those who are the weakest in society, he becomes them in their struggle for dignity and liberation. If this is the case, then, in U.S. society, Jesus must become black. In fact, in a very powerful way he becomes a black female. Such an interpretative preunderstanding obviously raises havoc with traditional interpretative strategies.

2. Johann Philipp Gabler, "An Oration on the Proper Distinction between Biblical and Dogmatic Theology and the Specific Objectives of Each," in John Sandys-Wunsch and Laurence Eldredge, "J. P. Gabler and the Distinction Between Biblical and Dogmatic Theology: Translation, Commentary, and Discussion of His Originality," *Scottish Journal of Theology* 33:136.

In terms of our methodology Gabler wanted to prevent micro-interpersonal factors, external as well as internal, from distorting the interpretation of the biblical texts. Like most of the traditional scholarship we reviewed, he was concerned with the textual, ideational, and macro-interpersonal features of the language of the biblical texts. He hoped that an emphasis on what were in his time the new techniques of philology and historical-critical exegesis would alleviate some of the confusion surrounding a text's meaning.

It was at the point of what Gabler referred to as the broad or true and narrow or pure forms of biblical theology that his ideational and macro-interpersonal interests found their primary points of expression. By the use of broad meanings Gabler intended to establish a true biblical theology that would provide a systematic description of biblical religion that attended to all concepts equally, even those that were historically contingent. In other words, at the level of true biblical theology Gabler hoped to provide a macro-interpersonal reconstruction of the primitive, historically contingent biblical religion as it is described in the New Testament materials. Its task was to present a true picture of biblical religion. Gabler's concern for the narrow meanings brings us to the ideational level he called pure biblical theology. Operating from the base information ascertained at the phase of true biblical theology, pure biblical theology attempts to universalize the findings. Pure biblical theology attempts to identify the contingent concepts and eliminate them from further consideration.

This effort will theoretically leave in place only those universal, unchanging divine concepts that were presented to the biblical authors through inspiration. This unchanging, divine information becomes the basis on which dogmatic theology may appropriately be founded.

Gabler's plan was based on the notion that this textual, ideational, and macro-interpersonal procedure of separating pure from true biblical theology was free from micro-interpersonal determinations. The true biblical theology was intended to be a macro-interpersonal reconstruction of the earliest biblical period and its religion, free of modern micro-interpersonal influences. Pure biblical theology in this way was not only purified of modern interpretative contingencies, but of historical, first-century ones as well; it was a macro-interpersonal reconstruction of the universal biblical religion that was free of both ancient and modern micro-interpersonal determinations.

The problem with Gabler's approach and the traditional historical-critical approaches that followed him is that micro-interpersonal influences cannot be eliminated in this way from the initial phases of the interpretative process. Our review of traditional research on the trial scenes demonstrated that researchers were not able to avoid the effect of micro-interpersonal factors at the macro-interpersonal phase of investigation that Gabler called true biblical theology. Every attempt at a reconstruction of the historical circumstances that formed the sociolinguistic background of the authors and original readers was shown to be micro-interpersonally determined by the interpreter's own academic and/or personal circumstances. Gabler's intention of establishing a neutral, true biblical theology that recreates an unbiased picture of the historically contingent first-century Palestinian situation has proved to be an impossible ideal. Furthermore, Gabler's pure biblical theology could not secure itself against micro-interpersonal influences. Since pure biblical theology is based on the findings of a true biblical theology that cannot escape micro-interpersonal influences, there can be no such thing as a theological interpretation free from micro-interpersonal influences.

# Bibliography

## Black Preaching: Theory

DAVIS, Gerald L. *I Got The Word In Me And I Can Sing It, You Know: A Study of the Performed African-American Sermon.* Philadelphia: University of Pennsylvania Press, 1985.

FELDER, Cain Hope, editor. *Stony The Road We Trod: African American Biblical Interpretation.* Minneapolis: Fortress Press, 1991.

HAMILTON, Charles V. *The Black Preacher in America.* New York: William Morrow and Company, 1972.

MITCHELL, Henry H. "Black Preaching." *Black Church Life-Styles.* Emmanuel L. McCall, editor. Nashville: Broadman Press, 1986.

————. *Black Preaching: The Recovery of a Powerful Art.* Nashville: Abingdon Press, 1990.

REID, Stephen Breck. *Experience and Tradition: A Primer in Black Biblical Hermeneutics.* Nashville: Abingdon Press, 1990.

SHANNON, David T. "An Ante-Bellum Sermon: A Resource for an African American Hermeneutic." In *Stony The Road We Trod: African American Biblical Interpretation.* Cain Hope Felder, editor. Minneapolis: Fortress Press, 1991.

STEWART, Warren H. *Interpreting God's Word in Black Preaching*. Valley Forge, Pa.: Judson Press, 1984.

TRULEAR, Harold Dean. "The Lord Will Make A Way Somehow: Black Worship and the Afro-American Story." *Journal of the Interdenominational Theological Center* 13, no. 1 (Fall 1985): 87–104.

WARREN, Mervyn A. *Black Preaching: Truth and Soul*. Washington, D.C.: University Press of America, 1977.

WIMBUSH, Vincent. "Biblical-Historical Study as Liberation: Toward An Afro-Christian Hermeneutic." *The Journal of Religious Thought* 42, no. 2 (1985–86): 9–21.

### Black Preaching: Sermons

BENN, J. Solomon III, editor. *Preaching in Ebony*. Grand Rapids, Mich.: Baker Book House, 1981.

HOARD, Walter B., editor. *Outstanding Black Sermons*. Volume 2. Valley Forge, Pa.: Judson Press, 1979.

MITCHELL, Ella Pearson, editor. *Those Preachin' Women: Sermons by Black Women Preachers*. Valley Forge, Pa.: Judson Press, 1985.

————. *Those Preaching Women: More Sermons by Black Women Preachers*. Valley Forge, Pa.: Judson Press, 1986.

PHILPOT, William M., editor. *Best Black Sermons*. Valley Forge, Pa.: Judson Press, 1972.

SMITH, J. Alfred, Sr. *Outstanding Black Sermons*. Valley Forge, Pa.: Judson Press, 1976.

YOUNG, Henry J., editor. *Preaching the Gospel*. Philadelphia: Fortress Press, 1976.

### Feminist and Womanist Theology

GRANT, Jacquelyn. *White Women's Christ and Black Women's Jesus: Feminist Christology and Womanist Response*. Atlanta: Scholars Press, 1989.

NEWSOM, Carol and Sharon Ringe, editors. *The Women's Bible Commentary*. Louisville: Westminster/John Knox, 1992.

RUSSELL, Letty M., editor. *Feminist Interpretation of the Bible*. Philadelphia: The Westminster Press, 1985.

SCHÜSSLER FIORENZA, Elisabeth. *But She Said: Feminist Practices of Biblical Interpretation*. Boston: Beacon Press, 1992.

————. *In Memory Of Her: A Feminist Theological Reconstruction of Christian Origins*. New York: Crossroad, 1986.

TOLBERT, Mary Ann, editor. *The Bible and Feminist Hermeneutics*. Chico, Calif.: Scholars Press, 1983.

WEEMS, Renita. "Reading *Her* Way Through The Struggle: African American Women and The Bible." In *Stony The Road We Trod: African American Biblical Interpretation*. Cain Hope Felder, editor. Minneapolis: Fortress Press, 1991.

WILLIAMS, Delores S. *Sisters in the Wilderness: The Challenge of Womanist God Talk*. Maryknoll, N.Y.: Orbis Books, 1993.

## Hispanic Theology

ELIZONDO, Virgilio. *Galilean Journey: The Mexican-American Promise*. Maryknoll, N.Y.: Orbis Books, 1991.

GONZALEZ, Justo L. *Mañana: Christian Theology From A Hispanic Perspective*. Nashville: Abingdon Press, 1990.

GOIZUETA, Roberto S., editor. *We Are A People! Initiatives in Hispanic American Theology*. Minneapolis: Fortress Press, 1992.

QUINÔNES-ORTIZ, Javier. "The Mestizo Journey: Challenges For Hispanic Theology." *Apuntes* 11, no. 3 (1991): 63–72.

## Latin American Liberation Theology

BOFF, Clodovis. *Theology and Praxis: Epistemological Foundations*. Translated by Robert R. Barr. Maryknoll, N.Y.: Orbis Books, 1987.

DUSSEL, Enrique. *Ethics and Community*. Translated by Robert R. Barr. Maryknoll, N.Y.: Orbis Books, 1988.

———. *History and the Theology of Liberation: A Latin American Perspective*. Maryknoll, N.Y.: Orbis Books, 1976.

———. *Philosophy of Liberation*. Translated by Aquilina Martinez and Christine Morkovsky. Maryknoll, N.Y.: Orbis Books, 1985.

GUTIÈRREZ, Gustavo. *A Theology of Liberation: History, Politics, and Salvation*. Maryknoll, N.Y.: Orbis Books, 1973, reprint, 1988.

ROWLAND, Christopher and Mark Corner. *Liberating Exegesis: The Challenge of Liberation Theology to Biblical Studies*. Louisville: Westminster/John Knox Press, 1989.

## Sociolinguistics

DITTMAR, Norbert. *Sociolinguistics: A Critical Survey of Theory and Application*. London: Edward Arnold, 1976.

EDWARDS, John. *Language, Society and Identity*. Oxford: Basil Blackwell, 1985.

FAIRCLOUGH, Norman. *Language and Power.* New York: Longman, 1989.

FASOLD, Ralph. *The Sociolinguistics of Language.* Cambridge, Mass.: Basil Blackwell, 1990.

GRIMSHAW, Allen D. *Language as Social Resource.* Stanford: Stanford University Press, 1981.

GUMPERZ, John J., and Dell Hymes, editors. *Directions in Sociolinguistics: The Ethnography of Communication.* New York: Holt, Rinehart and Winston, 1972.

HALLIDAY, M. A. K. *An Introduction to Functional Grammar.* London: Edward Arnold, 1985.

————. *Explorations in the Functions of Language.* London: Edward Arnold, 1973.

————. *Language as Social Semiotic: The Social Interpretation of Language and Meaning.* London: Edward Arnold, 1978.

————. *Learning How To Mean: Explorations in the Development of Language.* London: Edward Arnold, 1975.

HODGE, Robert and Gunther Kress. *Social Semiotics.* Ithaca: Cornell University Press, 1988.

HUDSON, R. A. *Sociolinguistics.* Cambridge: Cambridge University Press, 1980.

## Negro Spirituals: List

FISHER, William Arms. *Seventy Negro Spirituals.* Boston: Oliver Ditson Company, 1926.

JOHNSON, James Weldon and J. Rosamond Johnson. *The Books of American Negro Spirituals.* New York: Da Capo Press, Inc., 1977. First printed in separate editions by Viking Press as *The Book of American Negro Spirituals* (1925), and *The Second Book of Negro Spirituals* (1926).

## Negro Spirituals: Theory

BERGESEN, Albert. "Spirituals, Jazz, Blues, and Soul Music: Role of Elaborated and Restricted Codes in the Maintenance of Social Solidarity." In *The Religious Dimension: New Directions in Quantative Research,* 333–50. Robert Wuthnow, editor. New York: Academic Press, 1979.

BRAWLEY, Benjamin. "The Singing of Spirituals." *Journal of Black Sacred Music* 1, no. 2 (Fall 1987): 29–32.

CONE, James. "Black Spirituals: A Theological Interpretation." In *Music and the Experience of God.* Mary Collins, David Power, and Mellonee Burnin, editors. Edinburgh: T & T Clark, 1989.

————. "The Meaning of God in the Black Spirituals." In *God as Father,* 57–60. Johannes-Baptist Metz, editor. New York: Seabury Press, 1981.

————. "The Meaning of Heaven in the Black Spirituals." In *Heaven,* 60–71. Edited by Bas Van Iersel and Edward Schillebeeckx. New York: Seabury Press, 1979.

————. *The Spirituals and the Blues: An Interpretation.* New York: The Seabury Press, 1972.

DIXON, C. R. *Negro Spirituals: From Bible to Folksong.* Philadelphia: Fortress Press, 1976.

KATZ, Bernard, editor. *The Social Implications of Early Negro Music in the United States.* New York: Arno Press and the New York Times, 1969.

PROCTOR, Henry Hugh. "The Theology of the Songs of the Southern Slave." *Journal of Black Sacred Music* 2, no. 1 (1988): 51–64.

## The Trial Scenes In Mark

BAMMEL, Ernst. *The Trial of Jesus.* Naperville, Ill.: Alec R. Allison, 1970.

CATCHPOLE, David. *The Trial of Jesus: A Study in the Gospels and Jewish Historiography from 1770 to the Present Day.* Studia Post-Biblica 18. Leiden: Brill, 1971.

COHN, Haim. *The Trial and Death of Jesus.* New York: KTAV Publishing House, 1977.

DONAHUE, John R. *Are You The Christ? The Trial Narrative in the Gospel of Mark.* Missoula, Mont.: Society of Biblical Literature, 1973.

GREEN, Joel B. *The Death of Jesus: Tradition and Interpretation in the Passion Narrative.* Tübingen: J. C. B. Mohr, 1988.

JUEL, Donald. *Messiah and Temple: The Trial of Jesus in the Gospel of Mark.* Missoula, Mont.: Society of Biblical Literature, 1977.

KELBER, Werner, editor. *The Passion in Mark: Studies on Mark 14–16.* Philadelphia: Fortress Press, 1976.

MARCUS, Joel. "Mark 14:61: Are You the Messiah-Son-of-God?" *Novum Testamentum* 31 (April 1989): 125–41.

PERRIN, Norman. "Mark XIV. 62: The End Product of a Christian Pesher Tradition." *New Testament Studies* 12 (1965–66): 150–55.

# Indexes

## Subjects

## Authors

Printed in the United States
66261LVS00002B/253-282